American Home Landscapes

A DESIGN GUIDE TO CREATING PERIOD GARDEN STYLES

American Home Landscapes

A DESIGN GUIDE TO CREATING PERIOD GARDEN STYLES

DENISE WILES ADAMS and LAURA L. S. BURCHFIELD

Timber Press
Portland · London

Published in 2013 by Timber Press, Inc.

The Haseltine Building
133 S.W. Second Avenue, Suite 450
Portland, Oregon 97204-3527
timberpress.com

2 The Quadrant
135 Salusbury Road
London NW6 6RJ
timberpress.co.uk

Printed in China
Book design by Breanna Goodrow

Adams, Denise W.
  American home landscapes : a design guide to creating
period garden styles / Denise Wiles
Adams, Laura L. S. Burchfield. – 1st ed.
      p. cm.
  Includes bibliographical references and index.
  ISBN 978-1-60469-040-8
  1. Landscape design–United States–History. 2. Gardens,
American–Design–History. I. Burchfield,
Laura L. S. II. Title.
  SB473.A247 2013
  712–dc23
                    2012020999

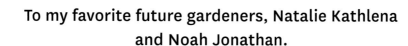

To my favorite future gardeners, Natalie Kathlena
and Noah Jonathan.

—DWA

To my mother, who inspired my love of gardens.

—LLSB

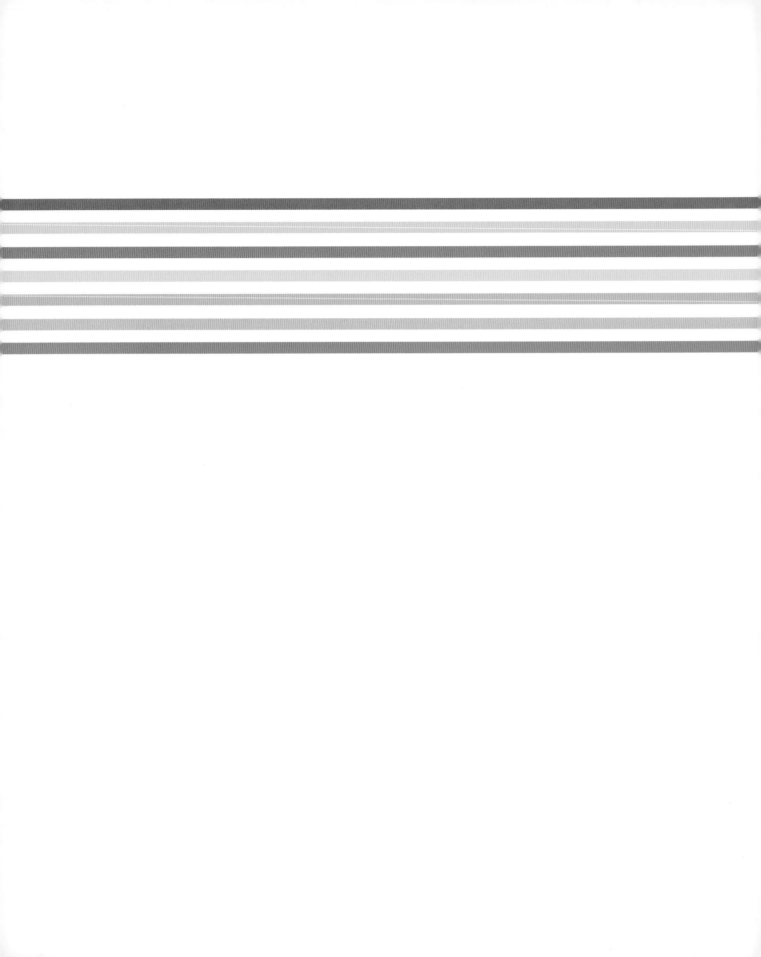

CONTENTS

ACKNOWLEDGMENTS

From Denise: Working on a book of this magnitude would be impossible if not for the love and support of family and friends. My dear family members—Heather, Jens, Jonathan, and Melanie—have always "been there" for me and kept track of my progress over the many months. Tracy DiSabato-Aust was my mentor in garden writing, and I thank her for her sound advice and unfailing support. Debra and Tony Knapke and Sherry Hawley were true friends, ever ready to offer support when my morale was flagging and good horticultural information as needed. Finally, Moti Kopilovitch was my devoted confidant, always patient, always encouraging, as I struggled with research, writing, travel, and deadlines.

From Laura: First and foremost I would like to thank my husband, Jim Burchfield, whose continuing love, support, and encouragement have only been magnified during the process of working on this book; and my children, James and Ruby, whose love and support are also ever present. I am thankful for Dan Struve, Peg McMahon, and Denise Johnson, dear friends and colleagues who offered encouragement and advice when most needed as I tried to balance work and "book" work. Andrew Muntz has my gratitude for acting as a sounding board, as needed, and keeping up my garden when I was too busy. And special thanks to my mother, for generously sharing her garden books from the 1960s and '70s; my wonderful friends, Andrea Martin, Kelly Koren, and Tina Semon, for willingly poring through old family photo albums in search of needed images; and my students, for inspiration and for understanding my occasional distraction over the past year.

We both wish to acknowledge our appreciation for assistance from the staff at the New Orleans Notarial Archives and the New York Public Library. Also, roses to all the homeowners who joined us in presenting our properties for historical analysis, including John and Jan Maggs, David and Lynn Adams, Susan Hitchcock and Jim Garner, Carlon Dawson and Michael Kehlmeier, Charm Logan and Jim Crandall, and Emmy Regnier and Kent Harrison. This book would have been impossible without your gracious cooperation and lovely landscapes! Finally, we are grateful to Tom Fischer, Franni Farrell, and Mike Dempsey, whose patience and excellent editing skills enhanced the development of this book and made it all possible.

INTRODUCTION

This book is primarily a resource to assist the landscape designer or homeowner in planning an authentic landscape for a house of any age. Our objective is to provide a sound basis for landscape design, along with the details to create designs for historic periods that are appropriate and individualized to your specific needs. You may wish to design an appropriate period landscape to match the era of your antique residence. Or your goal might be to feature period plants or garden accessories that would complement certain aspects of your heirloom home. Maybe you are charged with conveying the history of an old house and its landscape, but synchronizing period elements with contemporary function is your challenge. Perhaps you are simply an avid reader, interested in details of residential fashion and gardening from generations past to the present time, and the practical application might not be so important to you. Whatever your goals, you will find valuable, historic information about American gardens and landscapes within these pages.

Chapter 1 discusses the resources available to a landscape researcher and how to approach the challenge of creating a beautiful and functional design for an heirloom house. We explain the design process and suggest resources that will help you to accumulate information about the era for which you are making a landscape design. Each succeeding chapter discusses and describes the landscape and garden styles of a particular era, based mainly on the published writings of the time. Each era is identified not only by a period of years but also by the house architectural types that were common or fashionable during those years in the United States. We supply photos and illustrations wherever possible.

Linking a landscape to the architecture of the building it surrounds is not a foolproof method. Architectural styles differ across America, and few "pure" types exist. In addition to each region having its own vernacular architecture based on local materials and traditions, many houses that started "life" as a high-style building have been changed, added to, or remodeled along the way. We hope that it will be helpful to see what the prevailing fashions were in both architecture and landscape publications for identifiable eras in American history. Then you can determine how this information fits with the goals for your unique residential landscape.

Each chapter is divided into five basic sections: architecture styles, landscape design, landscape features, case studies (two of them featuring our own homes), and plant lists. Each chapter begins with a horticultural timeline to put the chapter's information into a chronological context—imagine gardening at a time before Japanese beetles plagued the land! Also at the beginning of each chapter we identify a person or persons who, in our opinion, influenced the elements of design for which the era is noted. These are people who wrote about gardens and/or actually designed landscapes for the period; for additional information—and opinions!—about practicing designers, we recommend two books: *Pioneers of American Landscape Design* (Birnbaum and Karson 2000) and *Shaping the American Landscape* (Birnbaum and Foell 2009). Every chapter also features one or more "Essential Elements" bulleted lists. These include features of landscape design that we found mentioned over and over again in contemporary publications; they will give you an instant vision of important details for each period landscape.

Regions

New England
Connecticut, Maine, Massachusetts, New Hampshire,
Rhode Island, Vermont

Middle Atlantic
Delaware, Maryland, New Jersey, New York, Pennsylvania

Southern
Alabama, Arkansas, Florida, Georgia, Kentucky, Louisiana, Mississippi, North Carolina,
South Carolina, Tennessee, Texas, Virginia, West Virginia

Great Lakes
Illinois, Indiana, Michigan, Minnesota, Ohio, Wisconsin

Central States and Great Plains
Iowa, Kansas, Missouri, Nebraska, North Dakota, Oklahoma, South Dakota

Far West and Mountain States
Arizona, California, Colorado, Idaho, Montana, Nevada, New Mexico, Oregon,
Utah, Washington, Wyoming

The plant lists, which are offered first by region and then by plant type, are based primarily on the nursery offerings of the time and place. We also used other sources, including descriptions from period gardeners as to what they were growing or from travelers who described the gardens they visited. Once a plant has been introduced to American gardens, chances are good that it will remain somewhere in the landscape; in this sense, all plant lists, technically, are cumulative with lists from preceding periods.

The regions are quite large (see opposite), and, obviously, conditions will vary within each region as far as heat and cold, rainfall, soil conditions, and other variables that affect the ability of a plant to thrive. Especially for the Far West and Mountain States, the plant lists were assembled from nurseries in diverse environments; the reader will have to adapt each list to his or her specific growing conditions. As we approached the present time, we also took into consideration that it was not so likely that people would limit themselves to the nursery or seed offerings of firms in their vicinity. Thus, the lists become more consolidated.

Each individual plant list represents those plants that appeared *most frequently* in the nursery catalogs of that particular era in that region. You will see that many ornamental plants remained popular over many years in this country. Often, cultivars ("cultivated varieties") can be linked to a certain era; wherever possible, we have traced the introduction of cultivars (especially among *Narcissus* and other bulbs, roses, and peonies) and provided the name of a period cultivar or two that are still commercially available. Heirloom varieties are increasingly available to twenty-first-century gardeners, thanks to the efforts of people like Scott Kunst, Brent and Becky Heath, Roy Klehm, Rachel Kane, the folks at Select Seeds, and "old rose rustlers" and historic iris fans.

Plants that might be too vigorous or possibly invasive to the landscape are indicated with an asterisk (*). We edited the lists to remove entirely some major offenders like Japanese honeysuckle and Norway maple—both plants that enjoyed extreme popularity in previous times. Before adding any plant to your landscape, you should *always* check the invasive species lists for your state and locality! A good Internet resource is invasive.org.

Finally, you will find a bibliography, arranged by chapter, for easy access to references cited in text or that pertain to your era of interest or the specific focus of your design. Our glossary will define any terms that might be unfamiliar to you.

One additional consideration, not to put a damper on your enthusiasm to recreate a historic garden, is to realize that many dwellings in former times did not have extensive gardens or well-developed cultivated landscapes, and photos and records that you find may convey this. Sometimes the ornamental plantings consisted entirely of a morning glory twining up a string and a red maple in the front yard—not so different in details from what we observe when driving through an average suburban neighborhood today. Many homes did and do not have elaborate landscapes; simplicity has merit, too.

Now is the time to get out a piece of paper and start taking notes . . . notes about the details of your dream heirloom landscape. We hope the process of learning about your landscape and choosing details that work best for you will be as pleasurable as sitting back and enjoying the finished product!

1

So You Want to Design a Historic Landscape

ny landscape project requires a process, a series of steps to reach the end goal, your desired landscape. The difference in designing a historic landscape is in the details. And those details are important. You must first decide what it is you want to achieve with your landscape. What is the purpose? How do you see yourself using your outdoor space? Do you have outdoor activities that you and other members of your household like to pursue? What types of areas, features, and equipment are required for those activities? Do you entertain friends and family? How many people will be using the outdoor spaces at any given time? It can be helpful at this point to make a list of the desired uses and amenities you would like for your landscape.

Lifestyles may have changed a great deal from the time your property was built. How we use and what we expect from our landscapes also has changed. The challenge is how to blend the historic landscape style with modern life. Consider the level of historic accuracy you hope to achieve. Designing a historic landscape for a museum property would be very different from designing a historic landscape for a family home. What compromises are you willing to make to combine historic accuracy with modern living?

You will need to determine your historic intent from the beginning. If you are designing a museum property, or are in a historic district, or are just passionate about historic preservation, you may want to create a very accurate landscape for your period house. Or you may want your landscape to have a style that fits the period but leaves room for modern conveniences. Many earlier landscapes were less ornamental and more functional, with space allocated to necessities no longer needed with the advent of indoor plumbing, supermarkets, and front load dryers.

The *Guidelines for the Treatment of Cultural Landscapes* developed by the National Park Service describe four approaches to historic landscapes that can help you to determine your personal approach.

• **Preservation** is the act or process of applying measures necessary to sustain the existing form, integrity, and materials of a historic property. Work, including preliminary measures to protect and stabilize the property, generally focuses upon the ongoing maintenance and repair of historic materials and features, rather than extensive replacement and new construction. New additions are not within the scope of this treatment; however, the limited and sensitive upgrading of mechanical, electrical, and plumbing systems and other code-required work to make properties functional is appropriate within a preservation project.

• **Rehabilitation** is the act or process of making possible a compatible use for a property through repair, alterations, and additions while preserving those portions or features that convey its historical or cultural values.

• **Restoration** is the act or process of accurately depicting the form, features, and character of a property as it appeared at a particular period of time by means of the removal of features from other periods in its history and reconstruction of missing features from the period of significance.

• **Reconstruction** is the act or process of depicting, by means of new construction, the form, features, and detailing of a non-surviving site, landscape, building, structure, or object for the purpose of replicating its appearance at a specific period of time and in its historic location.

The first step is to determine a "period of significance." This is the time period for which you will connect the landscape to the building. Sometimes (particularly in the case of a museum) the years when a particular person resided in a residence are significant, but most often this period is related to the architectural style of the house or the year or era in which it was built. Such dates are not always easy to determine, since many old houses have been renovated or additions have been made that change the façade and interiors. Real estate records in your county offices often provide a year of construction or, by indicating an increase in tax value for the property, will reveal when a residence was initially built. The main question is, what era do *you* wish to represent?

Another situation that affects the period of significance is the original function of the building. For example, a certain property in Gravel Hill, Virginia, began life as a store and post office in the late eighteenth century, with a tavern (now the house) added in 1843. Taverns in nineteenth-century Virginia did not typically display ornamental landscapes, although they might have had a kitchen garden or orchard; but a woman from New Orleans owned this central Virginia property during the 1950s and '60s. She installed a New Orleans–style landscape with courtyards, fountains, and winding paths. There was a boxwood parterre and few herbaceous plants. It is our view that those years could comprise a second period of significance for this landscape. It's important to remember that landscapes continue to evolve both naturally and under the influence of generations of land stewards.

The architecture of the house not only helps to define a period of significance but also provides guidance as to the shape and extent of the accompanying landscape. Whether a building is high style or of vernacular design conveys the economic status of the owner—indicating how much time and money might have been invested in the landscape. A Greek Revival antebellum mansion in South Carolina implies a more formal landscape than an Iowa farmhouse. An excellent general reference for architectural style across the United States is Virginia and Lee McAlester's *A Field Guide to American Houses* (1984).

Settling upon your historical approach is only the beginning. Landscape design is a series of steps that allow you to create a beautiful, functional landscape in an organized fashion for all historical perspectives.

Research and Site Inventory

We begin with the research and inventory of the site. Both may start at the same time, as some information may overlap. The extent of the historic research will be directed by the approach you have chosen. In addition to researching the history of your site, you must take into account its existing physical conditions. An understanding of your site's potentials and limitations is key to good design.

The site inventory is the identification and recording of important characteristics of the property and the gathering of all relevant facts about the site's physical condi-

The c. 1955 New Orleans–style landscape at the rear of this central Virginia property speaks of a second period of significance.

West's tavern (1843) and store and post office (1799), Gravel Hill, Virginia.

tions. A thorough site inventory begins with determining the boundaries for the landscape design. In most cases this is the property line, but it may be limited to an area around the structures, if it is a large property, or a selected area of the site, such as the front yard or entry area, if you want to limit the historical landscape to a specific section of the property.

It is best to create a base map of the area you are designing. This is a drawing or sketch of the site that shows all existing features of the property. Do not worry if you cannot draw well; it just needs to be something you can understand. You may want to use a drawing program on your computer; most have simple programs for drawing that can work well for creating a base map.

It is important to accurately determine where the property lines are for your site. This information may be available to you from your deed records, or the property records from your county auditor or recorder, depending on where you live. You may need to hire a surveyor to determine where the property lines are, if this information is not available to you. If your property has steep or complicated grade changes you may also want to have a professional topographic base map prepared.

A scale drawing is a drawing that represents a real object. The scales commonly used when drawing up a base map are the architect's scale (1 inch = 8 feet) or the engineer's scale (1 inch = 10 feet). Choose whatever scale you are most comfortable using. Measuring scales can be found in most office supply stores. You may also use graph paper, which most commonly comes in four or five squares per inch. The squares represent two feet each for 8 or 10 scale, respectively.

Once you have the property map, you can begin to locate the existing structures. You will need a tape measure, a copy of the property map (if available), something to write with, and ideally someone to assist you with measuring. If you have access to laser measuring equipment you may use that, of course. If you have a very large property, it may be easier to do your base map in sections. To get the most accurate base map, start outside and sketch in a rough map. Once your rough map is finished, sit down and refine it so that you have an accurately scaled base map.

Begin by locating the house; draw this on your map using a scale or showing the dimensions. Use the house as a starting point before drawing in the other features of your property. Measure off the corners of the house, so that you have accurate reference points; it is best to work in an organized way moving around the property in one direction so you do not miss anything. There are three methods of measuring:

• **Direct measuring** determines the distance between two fixed points. Running measurements are used for a series of measurements along a surface or wall. Stretching one tape along the edge of a wall or fence eliminates the need to continually move the tape and reduces error in measurements.

• **Baseline measuring** is a method that aligns the tape measure along a known line, referred to as a baseline, and locates other points or edges along that baseline. This is good for locating offset objects and curves of walkways and beds.

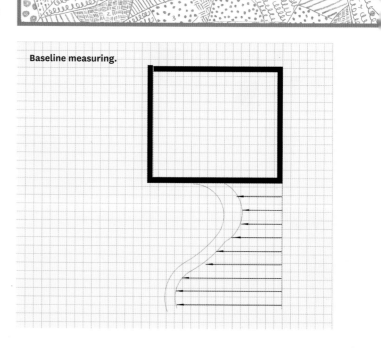

Baseline measuring.

going to be more comfortable with some shade on summer afternoons. The movement of the prevailing winds should also be noted. Are there places where the wind is funneled? You may want to block or redirect it if it will be an area in which people will be gathering.

Historic Landscape Research

For your approach to the historical background of your property, imagine that you have an enormous jigsaw puzzle to complete. Some of the puzzle pieces are obvious, showing details of the residential architectural style, for example, or details gleaned from the site inventory like the position of the driveway or the location of an old apple tree. They fit together very nicely. Details of other pieces must be determined from period books and magazines, photographs, diaries, oral histories, maps, etc. Coordinating all the pieces into an accurate-as-possible and comprehensive picture and plan is the garden researcher's challenge.

You may be fortunate to have a diary, letter, or other written record describing your home landscape in an earlier time. Perhaps people who still live in the neighborhood can describe its features from their own memories or from the stories of their grandparents. For many, however, historic landscape decisions will be made on the basis of documentary evidence from parallel sites—that is, evidence from similar landscapes in the same region and time period, of the same architectural style and economic class. This is where informed interpretation will guide your design process.

Primary sources for historic landscape research include firsthand testimony about the event or scene being described. Such evidence is always considered the most reliable evidence; although, depending on the biases of the writer, a primary source may or may not be completely accurate. A classic example is to consider two accounts of a Civil War battle, both from soldiers who participated, but one is a Union soldier and the other a Confederate. Obviously the details of the skirmish will be very different, depending on the point of view of the writer. Some examples of primary sources follow.

- Site inventory
- Government documents: deeds, tax files, wills, probate records, census data
- Visual documents: photographs, drawings, paintings, postcards
- Letters or other personal papers
- Landscape designs, garden plans
- Diaries, autobiographies
- Journals, travel accounts
- Floras, herbaria
- Interviews, oral histories
- Books, periodicals
- Newspapers
- Nursery catalogs
- Maps

Secondary sources—reference books, textbooks, contemporary journals, websites—may compile and interpret information from primary sources about a site or an event. A secondary source also might synthesize or evaluate information from other contemporary writers. Often the value of secondary sources lies in their bibliographies, which can direct you to more primary information.

The following items should be considered first as possible site-specific resources and secondly (if no such resource exists) as parallel-site models for making design decisions.

Wills and probate materials

Details of property and possessions may be found in wills and probate records of early property owners. Alice Lockwood (1931) provides a very early example of this type of evidence, quoting from the will of John Endecott of Massachusetts Bay, dated May 1659:

> Imprimis I give to my . . . Wiefe Elizabeth Endecott all my ffarme called orchard lying within the bound of Salem together with the Dwelling House, Outhowses,

2

1. Tough roadside survivors: yucca and orange daylily, aka ditch lily (*Hemerocallis fulva*).

2. And the rest, as they say, is history . . . (*Garden Magazine* 1920).

3. Lilac (*Syringa vulgaris*) has been loved for generations for its lovely flowers and fragrance.

3

Plan to record all existing plants over several seasons, if possible. It is surprising what is obvious in the early spring as compared with late summer. Daffodils or other bulbs that have endured through many generations might emerge. Peonies, daylilies, yucca, and roses often survive many decades in a garden. If possible, *nothing should be removed* until this inventory has been completed. It might be difficult to wait, but don't clean up until everything is recorded. Stroll around in the neighborhood to observe plantings in local gardens. See what is growing in roadside culverts or what has naturalized in other nearby places. In the Midwest, the upper South, and even in the Pacific Northwest, we have observed everlasting peas, yucca, orange daylilies, honesty, bearded irises, and daffodils—all growing along roadsides, all escapees from past gardens.

Woody plants can represent the evolution of a garden better than any other vegetative feature. The size and maturity of original trees and shrubs will help determine the age of a garden. Of course, trees and shrubs may be original plantings or they might be exotic intruders that have taken over the garden—species like Norway maple (*Acer platanoides*) and multiflora rose (*Rosa multiflora*) in the Northeast, Japanese honeysuckle (*Lonicera japonica*) in the Middle Atlantic states, kudzu (*Pueraria lobata*) in the South, buckthorn (*Rhamnus cathartica*) in the Midwest, and multiple species of *Tamarix* and *Ipomoea* (morning glory) in the West. The irony is that many of these plants were originally planted as garden ornamentals—but they became thugs. Often these trees and woody vines must be cleared before original plantings can be identified. Just remember to do any such clearing cautiously.

Perhaps you found an old lilac by the door, a lilac that is tall and spindly, and in declining health caused by age and neglect. You will eventually need to make a design decision: either to renew such a historical plant, to remove it while possibly obtaining a cutting, or to replace it with the same or similar species and cultivar. In the case of the iconic lilac, the main reason for decline is often worn out and depleted soil. Disease, pollution, and borers may also have adversely affected it. Improving your soil is the first step to a healthy lilac and other significant shrubs. Selective or rehabilitative pruning might be warranted. Similar treatment may be necessary for other woody plant specimens on the property. A certified arborist may be con-

tacted to get a professional opinion on maintaining your surviving trees and shrubs.

Once you have a base map, make several copies so you can make additional notes about the site. Are there good views that you want to keep or enhance, or unsightly views you want to hide? Make sure you consider views looking out from the site and looking on to the site as you approach or pass by. It is helpful to document these view areas with photographs so you can refer to them when you are designing. In addition to these, any general photographs that illustrate conditions of your site would be useful when you begin to design, providing the "before" images to compare to the "after" when your design is completed. Numbering each photo and referencing that number to the base map is a good way to keep track of the information. We also like to think of photographs as providing the future historic record for those who come after us.

What are the physical conditions of the site? You should determine soil type by doing a soil test. Check with your local county extension service for resources including local labs that will test soil samples that you submit to them. Knowing soil type and pH will help you to select plants that can thrive in your landscape.

Water is another major physical condition that must be understood. Make notes or sketches of how water moves across your property, where it stands and for how long. Know what happens to the water when it leaves the roof and gutters. Are there areas of erosion? Are there areas that are particularly dry? Note this information on a copy of your base map.

What are the sun and shade patterns? This is best observed at different times of the day as well as different times of the year, if at all possible. A general guideline is that the sun intensity around a building differs based on direction and movement of the sun. North usually has the most shade, followed by east, which receives morning light. South is sunny and warm; west gets the stronger afternoon sun. The aspect or angle of slopes will change the sun patterns. A south-facing slope will stay sunnier longer and warm up faster than a north-facing slope. Other factors such as buildings, fences, walls, trees, and shrubs can affect the sun and shade conditions of a landscape. This is important to know for both plants and people. Plants have specific sun and shade requirements. People are generally

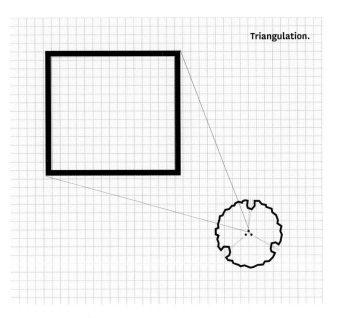

Triangulation.

• **Triangulation** is measuring from a known point or corner to the center of an object, and then from the center of the object to a second known point or corner. This is used for locating trees, utilities, and irregular corners.

Show the locations and widths of the ground floor windows and doors. You may want to indicate sill and doorstep heights and any steps or changes in grade. Indicate the locations of utility lines, both overhead and underground. Include all additionally built structures, such as walls, fences, patios, and walkways.

In addition to providing the framework for your design, the site inventory is a major research step to determine the characteristics of a historic landscape. Evidence from the past is often right beneath your feet. This inventory involves looking for all artifacts of past landscape design or function, including hardscape such as paths, driveways, fences, outbuildings, etc., as well as any surviving plants.

Buildings—garages, barns, privies, sheds, summerhouses, gazebos—help to tell the story of earlier land use. Structures may be intact and usable, or you might find a remnant of a post or stones from a foundation. In the past, service areas were more clearly delineated from ornamental areas, and there was not as much emphasis on "living"

in the landscape, as we now do; until the mid-twentieth century, one did not often find outdoor cooking facilities, for example, but you might find an old clothesline pole.

The circulation pattern between the main structure and any existing dependencies will reveal details about the landscape. Look for remnants of roads, paths, walkways, and steps. Often layers of soil and wear obscure such permanent features. At a c. 1845 house in Ohio, a row of 'Festiva Maxima' peonies (introduced in 1851) lined the path between the house and the outhouse, long since razed, testifying both to a path and also to the existence of the early functional structure. At an 1806 Federal-style residence nearby, locating an early well helped to uncover a brick pathway, buried about ten inches deep. Anyone who has edged grass away from a sidewalk will understand how quickly grass will encroach on the paved surface. At a 1914 Arts and Crafts–style residence in New York, the existence of two disembodied steps by the road testifies to the previous existence of a walkway made of concrete embedded with very small pieces of gravel.

Decorative garden features may still be obvious or be camouflaged or hidden under debris. The brick outline of a long-ago garden is apparent to visitors at the Oxford, Mississippi, home of author William Faulkner. At a garden in Newark, Ohio, an early twentieth-century fountain and pool were buried under trash at the rear of the property; even the concrete waterlily boxes remained. At this same property, modern rose beds occupy the space formerly marking the pathways in the garden. At the Dayton, Ohio, residence of poet Paul Dunbar, now a museum, remnants of an old arbor, a bed of lily-of-the-valley (*Convallaria majalis*), and pieces of a wire fence were noted at the time of its inventory. So look carefully—you never know what you may find!

The next step is to locate and add to your drawing any major plants you plan to keep as part of your design. Triangulation is usually the best method for locating trees and shrubs. Plant inventory is often limited to trees and shrubs, but you should include herbaceous plants that may be original to the landscape or that you plan to keep in your new design. You may also want to indicate existing bed lines, which may be original to the landscape. Make notes on the species, age, and condition of the plants. You may want to document this information with photographs in addition to adding them to your base map.

Barnes, stables, Cowhowses[, and] all the Orchards nurseries of fruit trees, gardens, fences, meadow and salt marsh thereunto appertaining.

U.S. census records

The National Archives (archives.gov) has census records available on microfilm for the years 1790–1930; most of the 1890 census was lost in a fire at the Department of Commerce. Records are confidential until seventy-two years have passed; thus, in 2012 the 1940 census was released. These records can provide details concerning the family composition and social and economic status of a previous owner of your residence.

Diaries, letters, personal papers

If you have a detailed journal or diary from the original owner of your house, you would need little else to support your decisions for the historic landscape. But, just as we suspect that you are not writing a detailed garden journal yourself, so also in the past it was not a typical activity. Published diaries and journals do exist for some historic properties. You may be familiar with the "Garden Book" Thomas Jefferson kept at Monticello, or the published letters of early gardeners such as John Custis of Williamsburg and John Bartram of Philadelphia.

Letters, journals, and memoirs of past gardeners for various regions may sometimes be available. One such book is *Life on a Liberty County Plantation, The Journal of Cornelia Jones Pond*, privately printed in Darien, Georgia, in 1974. Cornelia's memories are vivid and invaluable:

> My earliest recollection of our plantation house is a house of two stories. . . . There was a wide front piazza fronting on a pretty flower garden in the form of a semi-circle. The house was situated in a large grove filled with beautiful trees of native growth. . . . Two beautiful large magnolia grandiflora trees were to the right of the house on the side as you drive up. . . . Four large live oaks were in the backyard. They were planted by my father before I was born [in 1834]. In the flower garden was the magnolia fuscata, "banana shrub," having been bought by my father from a florist in New Haven, Conn. There were also camellias, roses, violets, hyacinths, narcissus, and many others.

Tres-colores or Joseph's coat (*Amaranthus tricolor*).

Landscape designs and garden plans

The ultimate treasure would be to locate an original garden plan for your site—complete with plant list. Usually we must rely on plans that have been reproduced in books of a later period—some based on actual remnants of a garden and others based on memoirs and records—that tell us about fashionable styles and plantings of the period. Books written by garden clubs in the 1930s about gardens in their states, including Georgia, Virginia, North Carolina, Kentucky, and Tennessee, are good resources.

Travelers' accounts

Travelers' descriptive accounts of the landscape and gardens of a region or town can be very rich and detailed. Clark's *Travels in the Old South* (1956) is a multiple-volume bibliography of travel records dealing with the South during earlier years that might be a starting place for designers of old southern landscapes. A very early example comes from John Lawson in his *A New Voyage to Carolina* (1709):

> We have also the Wood-bind, much the same as in *England*; Princes-feather, very large and beautiful in the Garden; *Tres-Colores*, branch'd Sun-flower, Double Poppies, Lupines, of several pretty sorts, spontaneous; and the *Sensible* Plant is said to be near the Mountains, which I have not yet seen.

From this we can see several plants that were cultivated in the Carolina region during the early years of settlement. Common names for plants can be ambiguous, however. "Princes-feather" could be either *Amaranthus* or *Polygonum* by current nomenclature. The fact that Lawson adds "very large and beautiful" makes one think that he was referring to *Amaranthus hypochondriacus*, which is a dramatic-looking plant, as opposed to *Polygonum orientale*, which also grows tall but has a sparser habit. Tres-colores may have been *Amaranthus tricolor*, also known as Joseph's coat.

It is possible that a traveler's account might contradict the observations of a contemporary. Basil Hall, traveling in North America in the 1820s, wrote, "In all the streets and squares of Savannah, most of which are very tastefully laid out, numerous rows of Pride-of-India trees have been planted, which serve to shade the walks and add a tropical air to the scene." Hall explains elsewhere that he believes this tree to be *Melia azedarach* (chinaberry). In his *Encyclopedia of Gardening* (1838), by contrast, John Loudon wrote:

> The village of Riceborough is very picturesque. Most of the houses have verandas; and it is observed by Captain Hall, and by Mr. Stuart, that the pride of India, the Lagerstroemia indica, is planted along the streets, as well as those in most of the southern towns, particularly Charleston and Savannah.

Lagerstroemia indica is the botanical name for crepe myrtle.

Another firsthand account comes from Harriet Martineau, who traveled through the South in 1837:

> In the neighborhood of Mobile, my relative, who has a true English love of gardening, had introduced the practice; there I saw villages and cottages surrounded with a luxuriant growth of Cherokee roses, honeysuckles, and myrtles, while groves of orange-trees appeared in the background.

Books and periodicals

We all rely on books when doing historic research. But, as discussed earlier, the first consideration in choosing references is whether it is a primary or a secondary source. Primary sources, as you know, are of the period and written from personal experience and observation. Secondary sources are usually compilations and synthesis of primary sources—or other secondary sources. The first thing we do when looking at a book relating to garden history is to check out the bibliography. We frequently purchase books only for the bibliography!

Even if a book is considered "primary," it can be a challenge to determine what was *real* and what was the *ideal*. Both types of information can help to direct your garden design and plant selection. For the most accurate information, we look for first-person narratives: descriptions of landscapes that the writer has either seen or cultivated him- or herself.

In determining the veracity of a book, you also must ask, "Does the author hope to gain any advantage from writing this book?" Is he a nursery owner? Is this book an advertisement for his products? For example, Joseph Breck (1858) was the owner of a prominent nursery in Boston; and the plants listed in *The Flower-Garden* presumably are the ones he had for sale. This does not diminish the importance or reliability of the book but places it in a marketing context.

The writer may offer his own observations or may make suggestions for fashionable garden making and plant use. When looking at recommendations, it is useful to study several references from the period to see if the information, or something like it, is replicated. For example, Robert Copeland (1867) suggested that those with "small and unpretending" houses should coordinate with their neighbors, each property featuring a different genus or type of flower, so that the street is a series of complementary flower gardens; this notion, while having its merits, does not appear in other resources of the period. The conclusion? Most likely harmonizing the landscapes in a neighborhood was not a common practice. On the other hand, suggestions for the placement of a circular flower garden in the landscape where it can be viewed from a window in the house are found in many references of the period.

Another aspect to consider when perusing an old garden book is the provenance of its information. Bernard M'Mahon's *The American Gardener's Calendar* (1806) was the first garden book published in America. What many people do not realize is that scholars have determined that much of this book was "borrowed" from earlier English books, in particular John Abercrombie and Thomas Mawe's *Every Man His Own Gardener*, published in England in 1767; and that after M'Mahon wrote his book (which was published in eleven editions), someone who called himself "An Old Gardener" brought out *The Practical American Gardener* (1822), which borrowed heavily from M'Mahon's. Researchers have called such books more "adopted" than "adapted" for American use.

We have found that early horticultural periodicals are of particular merit in determining plants and garden design. In their pages you will find recommendations and observations, travelers' accounts, illustrations, garden design, and new introductions. Some of the best observations for vernacular gardens can be found in letters to the editor, such as this one written by a Texas gardener to the editor of *Vick's Monthly Magazine* in 1878:

> I wish you could look down here, and see my brush summer-house covered with Morning Glories; my huge Cypress cones, and arches (made of hickory poles and barrel hoops); my splendid double rose Balsams, my mounds, blazing with double Portulaca, Verbenas, Petu-nias and Phlox. By every tree I have a climber–Clematis, Jasmine and Honeysuckle. I have not said anything about my magnificent Zinnias, nor my comical Pansies.

The editors of such periodicals were knowledgeable about garden fashion and design and the availability of plants. They communicated with their counterparts in Europe and published their findings as well. Articles in gardening periodicals included both ideas for "the ideal" as well as observations of "the real." Over time you will find that the focus of the general gardening magazines shifted from an emphasis on fruits and glasshouse gardening to more conventional (as we know it) ornamental gardening.

Maps

When you begin to research your landscape site, a good place to start is with maps of the area. Early local maps are available at many historical societies and can provide varying levels of detail, even to new buildings and streets.

The National Archives in Washington, D.C., holds a collection of more than 15 million items, including maps, charts, aerial photographs, and architectural drawings.

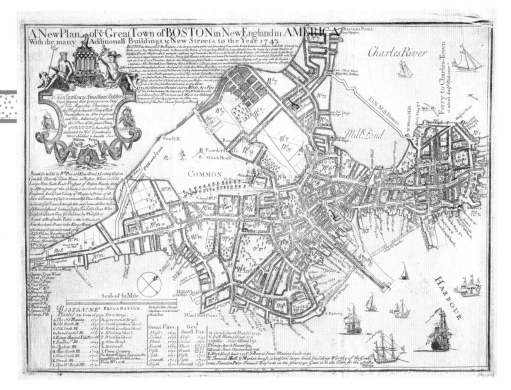

This 1743 map delineates the outline of the "great town" of Boston. I. N. Phelps Stokes Collection, Miriam and Ira D. Wallach Division of Art, Prints and Photographs, The New York Public Library, Astor, Lenox and Tilden Foundations.

Maps are not available online, but regional offices may be contacted for assistance. See the website at archives.gov/research/start/by-format.html for specific information for your state or region.

The Sanborn Fire Insurance Maps for more than twelve thousand American towns and cities provide information for years from 1867 to 1970. These maps document buildings, construction details of those buildings, street and sidewalk widths, property boundaries, and building use, among other details, for each municipality. Maps are available to libraries for a subscription fee. See sanborn.umi.com/HelpFiles/about.html for more information.

County atlases illustrate landscape form and functionality. These books of maps were published mainly in the 1870s and 1880s, when mapmakers would allow property owners to have their residence and landscape included in the official county atlas, for a fee. They contain considerable details of counties, cities, and townships as well as single-family residences. Artists may have exercised a certain amount of license in their renderings, so we cannot be certain that all the details in a particular landscape actually existed; however, we can assume that all the garden details indicate fashionable trends of the era for that region. County atlases are usually available at state or local/county libraries. Libraries, including the New York Public Library, have digitized some county atlases for easier access to the researcher. Reprints published to honor centennials and other historical milestones are also available.

Newspapers

Newspapers have always been invaluable sources for information of all types. Reports on gardens and horticultural practices as well as advertisements for plants, gardeners, and horticultural implements are among the historic research riches to be found in their pages. For example, the *Boston Gazette* featured seeds in the first known published advertisement, in 1719. Eighteenth-century Charleston newspapers yield information concerning plant imports from those years, including boxwood and bulbs. Many local and state historical societies hold archives of newspapers, usually on microfilm or microfiche.

Residence of Thomas Fallon, Esq., corner of San Pedro and San Augustine Streets, San Jose (*New Historical Atlas of Santa-Clara Co. California* 1876).

1. Brick house covered in vines, Albany, New York, 1890.

2. The same brick house in 2011.

Paintings

Historical paintings from a particular period and region can offer many clues as to plants in cultivation and fashion garden design, and a visit to most any major art museum will reveal painterly renderings of American gardens. Sometimes art books written for a different focus or audience can be helpful to the garden history researcher. *The Planter's Prospect* by John Michael Vlach (Chapel Hill: University of North Carolina Press, 2002) features southern landscape painters and their works—people like Charles Fraser (Charleston and Low Country), Adrien Persac (Louisiana), and Francis Guy (Maryland). Vlach wrote his book to illustrate details of the slave economy, but the paintings illustrate details that are equally useful to the garden historian. Art historian May Brawley Hill (1995) based many descriptions of features in the old-fashioned gardens that were popular at the turn of the twentieth century on details she observed in paintings from that era. Another compilation of paintings that depicts gardens is Betsy G. Fryberger's *The Changing Garden: Four Centuries of European and American Art* (Berkeley: University of California Press, 2003).

Photographs

Photography was invented in the late 1830s, the technology improved over the ensuing years, and it was a relatively common procedure by the last quarter of the nineteenth century. Often people would have their pictures taken in their gardens or in front of their houses, and it is in these images that we can find landscape details.

Some historians have raised the question as to whether or not photographs are actually "accurate" historic documents. Of course, cameras have the potential to record every detail, but the photographer can also isolate, alter, or change the focus and perspective of a scene—even in the days before Photoshop! Photographs have the greatest value, of course, when they include proper documentation: date, place, and name of photographer. If you are so fortunate as to have an early photograph of your property, then you can confirm early details with accuracy.

Photo types that you may encounter in your research include daguerreotypes (1837), cyanotypes (1842), ambrotypes (c. 1853), tintypes (1856), cabinet photos (c. 1866), and aerial photos (first time in 1858 from a balloon!).

1

Stereographs (c. 1840) are a subcategory of photographs. The stereoscopic view is a double image, which was developed to add the sense of what we now call "depth of field" to a photograph. The two photos were rarely exactly alike. It made the scene multidimensional when viewed through a special handheld projector called a stereoscope. Many early stereographs were taken of public landscapes, both cultivated and wild. Additionally we find those of private residences, which can show us details of the garden and plantings. The stereograph was invented about the same time as the daguerreotype; it enjoyed some popularity in the 1850s and then again, throughout the late nineteenth century to the 1930s.

There are three important collections of American landscape photographs:

• Archives of American Gardens at the Smithsonian Institution in Washington, D.C. "The Archives of American Gardens, housed in the Smithsonian Gardens, includes a collection of approximately sixty thousand photographic images and records that document historic and contemporary gardens throughout the United States. The images, which show views from colonial times to the present, include a considerable range of garden features such as furniture and ornamentation, as well as all manner of design styles." Visit sirismm.si.edu/siris/collectionaag1.htm

• American Memory Archives, Library of Congress. "American Memory provides free and open access through the Internet to written and spoken words, sound recordings, still and moving images, prints, maps, and sheet music that document the American experience. It is a digital record of American history and creativity. These materials, from the collections of the Library of Congress

2

1. Cyanotype.

2. Cabinet photo.

▶ NEXT SPREAD Stereograph.

and other institutions, chronicle historical events, people, places, and ideas that continue to shape America, serving the public as a resource for education and lifelong learning." Contained within the archives is the Historic American Landscape Survey (HALS), which documents "achievements in landscape design" from 1933 to the present. Visit memory.loc.gov/ ammem/index.html and memory.loc.gov/ ammem/collections/habs_haer/index. html

• **National Park Service.** The National Park Service administers the documentation for U.S. landscape history through its Heritage Documentation Programs. For more information, go to nps.gov/history/hdp/.

Postcards

Postcards are yet another means to publish images, and the personal photographic postcard is an invaluable resource for looking at landscapes of the past. Eastman Kodak Co. first issued postcard-size photographic paper in 1902. Within a few years, a postcard fad motivated people to have personal photos, town photos, and photos of their homes all reproduced for mailing to friends and neighbors. Some cards are obviously vernacular and others capture elaborate formal landscapes. If the postcard was actually posted, then you have the additional information of place and date in the postmark. If not posted, then it is possible to date postcards by the type of paper used and the symbols on the address side. More information on postcard dating can be found in *Prairie Fires and Paper Moons: The American Photographic Postcard: 1900–1920* by Hal Morgan and Andreas Brown (Boston: David R. Godine, 1981).

Herbaria and local flora

Herbaria are collections of dried and pressed plants that document cultivated or indigenous plants observed in earlier times. Often schoolgirls and -boys prepared these collections, as it was a frequent practice in the late nineteenth century. Many herbaria still survive. A very good example resides in the David McKell Library of the Ross County Historical Society in Chillicothe, Ohio: the herbarium collection of Mary Clark offers documentation of the plants cultivated there in 1835. Their identification may or may not be correct (her sweet William looks less like *Dianthus barbatus* and more like the wild sweet William of *Phlox*), but with dried specimens to work with, verification is an easier task than with some other types of documentation.

"Real-Life" postcards, as they are called, gave homeowners a chance to show off their property, c. 1910.

Nursery and seed catalogs

William Prince, of Flushing, New York, issued the earliest extant American nursery catalog, in 1771. Other extant eighteenth-century catalogs include those from John Bartram of Philadelphia and Goldthwaite and Moore of Baltimore. Production and distribution of nursery catalogs began to accelerate by the 1820s, and by the mid-nineteenth century they were a common feature of horticultural life in the United States. Catalogs began as simple plant lists, with or without prices, and evolved into compendiums of information about plants, their culture, and the art of beautifying the home landscape.

Using antique seed catalogs for research has its difficulties; several biases must be confronted right from the start. Catalogs typically represent only those nurseries or seed houses that were prosperous enough to issue them for distribution. For example, in the main national collections of catalogs, only thirty-six of the more than a thousand firms known to have existed in nineteenth-century Ohio are represented; obviously data based on just those catalogs is skewed. Moreover, catalogs had to be of sufficient quality to survive for more than a century in less-than-optimal conditions. And someone, somewhere, had to be motivated to save his or her catalogs for future generations.

Vick's Floral Guide reported that it issued some 200,000 copies annually. Only a handful of these have survived. It is no wonder that modern book dealers refer to this type of document as "ephemera." We usually do not have sales records, so it is impossible to tell if the nursery actually sold a particular plant featured in the catalog; furthermore, plants could have been misidentified to begin with, or the nursery might have had a crop failure and could not supply the plants or seeds. Despite all these unknowns, catalogs remain one of the soundest means for studying horticultural tastes of a previous era.

It is difficult to chronicle actual plant introductions in the catalogs, but you can certainly get an idea of how early something became commercially available. Typically it takes a few years between actual introduction into cultivation and widespread production. *Lilium auratum*, for instance, was introduced in the early 1860s via Parsons Nursery in New York and Parkman's in Boston; by that decade's close, it appeared in several catalogs, and by the

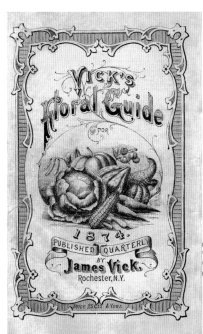

The cover of *Vick's Floral Guide*, 1874.

Lilium auratum (B. K. Bliss' Descriptive Seed Catalogue 1869).

end of the century, in a majority of nursery lists featuring any bulbs.

The price of seeds and plants did not vary much over the course of the nineteenth century; still, small changes in pricing can imply who might have purchased a certain plant. Prince's 1844 catalog offered perennials for prices ranging from eighteen to fifty cents. At this time, agricultural laborers received eight to twelve dollars a month plus board, while craftsmen received twelve to eighteen dollars. Obviously you had to be somewhat affluent to buy plants. Forty years later, in the 1880s, James Vick of Rochester, New York, offered perennial plants for twenty-five to thirty cents apiece; fifty cents purchased certain hostas and other "rarer" plants. Novelties, including unusual *Lilium* bulbs or cultivars of *Paeonia*, were priced at anywhere from fifty cents to ten dollars. By this time, although farm wages remained about twelve dollars a month, craftsmen were earning up to fifty dollars a month: as the buying power of the newly evolving "middle class" increased, so too do our assumptions about the extent of their plant purchases.

Plant names themselves are a challenge, in any written record. Many have changed over the years, sometimes multiple times, so determining correct nomenclature is important. Take *Hosta*: in nineteenth-century nursery and seed catalogs *H. plantaginea* was also known as *Funkia alba*, *F. subcordata*, *F. liliiflora*, and *F. japonica*; and *Hemerocallis japonica* and *H. subcordata*. Common names, which are always trouble, were similarly varied: funkia, hosta, white daylily, Japan daylily, plantain lily. Be ready to keep digging, tracing a plant to its currently accepted scientific name, if you hope to find the plant you're truly after in your local nursery or online.

Analysis and Developing a Program

Once the site has been inventoried and you have completed the historical research, it is time to synthesize the information you have gathered and to think about how you will use it to create your landscape. Although your primary goal is to demonstrate and preserve the historic character of the site, this is the time to look at everything from a practical perspective and determine how your landscape

will actually work for you in the twenty-first century. Now is also the time to consider how you want to use your landscape and what your desires are for the various areas. List the activities you see happening in your landscape. Your list may include a welcoming entry, with individual details such as large urns or a water feature, or a children's play area.

Don't be afraid to think big! Idealize your vision of your landscape. You can always pare back if budget constraints require it. And remember: you can accomplish the changes you want to make to your landscape in phases, over time; so at this point, try to think of every possibility you can for your eventual, ideal landscape. Once you have the list of desired amenities and spaces, you should prioritize them. What is most important to you? What do you want to see first?

The list of desired elements for your landscape, or design program, is a road map of how to proceed and what to include. It will guide the design so that your finished landscape will fulfill all your goals: practical, aesthetic, and historical.

Considering function

Your landscape's functions should suit your needs and intended uses. You will need to consider the sizes of areas, to assure they will work for their purpose, and to site them in such a way that they are convenient. For example, an outside dining area should ideally be situated near the food preparation area of the house; a children's play area should be in a place where adults may comfortably supervise it.

Typical outdoor spaces include areas for entertaining and dining, pedestrian and vehicular entry and arrival areas, utility and storage areas, recreation areas, gardening areas (whether for ornamentation or culinary purposes—or both), a sanctuary for retreat or relaxation, and children's areas. The sizes of these areas will vary, depending on the number of users, the type of activity, and the available space. You will want to think about what will work best for your individual circumstances. There are reference books with guidelines to help determine the minimum area needed for various activities.

Once you have determined the types of areas you need and the amount of space for each, you should think about the placement of these areas within the landscape. It can

Classic Victorian details of an iron fence and cast iron urn filled
with bright flowers adorn this Columbus, Ohio, residence.

be helpful to try several different arrangements to develop the best one. This can be done by making a few sketches of the alternatives, or you can cut out shapes of the various areas and move them around on your base map to determine which layout you think will work best. Remember: whichever method you use, the discrete areas need to be to the scale you are using.

Once you have decided upon the layout of spaces, it is time to consider the circulation, or how you will move between, around, and through the areas. This will determine where walkways and paths will be, if you have decided not to use existing pathways. The form they take will depend on the period and style of your landscape and will be determined, along with materials, as you move into the design phase. Consider the widths needed for circulation at this time. Although width recommendations will vary depending on the scale of the property and the period of significance, modern standards for comfort and practicality may also be considered. Two people walking side by side need at least four feet of width. Minor paths can be narrower. An automobile needs a minimum ten-foot width, more when there are walls or landscape beds alongside, or if turns are required.

Design and design documentation

After you have accomplished all the background work for your historic landscape, then it is time to begin the design. Every planned landscape is created through the use of the elements and principles of design; the goal is to arrange the landscape in a visually pleasing manner. Your historic landscape design will be influenced by the prevailing trends of its period of significance, your contemporary goals for functionality, and solid, time-honored design principles.

Every good design needs order, unity, and rhythm. Order, or balance, is the overall framework of a design; it can be achieved by either symmetry or asymmetry. Symmetry is often associated with a more formal landscape; objects are arranged equally around an axis, with one side mirroring the other. In asymmetry, objects are arranged to have an equal, *weighted* balance but without an axial reference; the visual balance is achieved, but the effect is informal or naturalistic. The period and style of your house will dictate whether symmetry or asymmetry is appropriate.

Unity is the choice and arrangement of landscape

1

objects so that the overall composition is harmonious. Harmonious unity characterized the designs of Andrew Jackson Downing and others in the nineteenth century and even earlier; the effect was particularly extolled in writings of early twentieth-century American designers.

Rhythm is another universal design principle that makes a design dynamic by creating movement. Rhythm is achieved by repetition in the landscape. Designers have known for centuries that repeating a pattern, or even a particular plant, makes a design more interesting and vibrant.

What areas will you be designing? The typical American residential landscape has three spaces: a front yard, which is a public area, viewed by everyone; the backyard, which is a more private space, used by the residents; and the side yards, which are either unused or used for storage or as circulation between front and back. In the past, the backyard would have been the service area, where the chores of everyday living were accomplished; it might have included a washing area, a well, a drying yard, and a privy, among other necessities.

Many ideas about landscape design have developed over time. One important idea from the early twentieth century is the concept of outdoor rooms. This concept can

2

1. A trelliswork fence screens the air conditioning units and drying yard in this nineteenth-century landscape. Lawson residence, Virginia. Design by Donald P. Bowman.

2. A traditional-looking rain barrel.

3. Inside the trellis-enclosed drying yard.

3

help you as you design your outdoor spaces. Think in terms of rooms, and your spaces will have a crucial element that make them feel complete: the sense of defined planes of enclosure. The enclosure is not as complete as indoor rooms, of course; it may be actual enclosure from a wall, fence, hedge, or overhead canopy, or it may be implied by a change in materials or grade.

Another long-held concept that is used to improve landscapes is that the outdoor spaces should extend and connect the indoor spaces of the adjacent structures. More important for some historic periods than others, whenever this notion is applied, it helps with the functionality and character of the landscape.

Now you are ready to actually design your historic landscape. You may draw your design plan by hand or on the computer. The preliminary design will lead to the master plan that will eventually be installed. Again, do not worry about creating a perfect professional drawing; it just needs to be good enough for you to understand and follow as you install your landscape. If there are complicated constructed features required, you can have those drawings prepared by a professional landscape designer or landscape architect.

During this process you will want to spend a lot of time thinking about all the facets of your landscape. It should not be a rushed process. Spend as much time as you need to sort out your ideas and maximize your understanding and synthesis of the numerous details you have to consider. Your final design is the guide or map of what will be installed. A planting plan indicates the type, size, and quantity of plants and where they should be located; additional detailed plans (layout plan, grading plan, construction drawings) may be required depending on the scope of the project.

Sometimes contemporary function is at odds with the historical record. Air conditioning units, for example, have a legitimate place, and children's play areas often are deemed a necessity, although not consistent with the historical perspective. This is where some good trelliswork or plant material comes in handy, to screen the anachronistic objects in the landscape. If a "what's old is new again" necessity like a rain barrel is in your plans for sustainabililty, then you should try to use one with a more traditional appearance, like an oak barrel, avoiding the "clash" of a large green vinyl container.

Material Selection

Once the master plan is complete, you must settle on which materials to use for the constructed elements of the design. These hardscape elements include all surfaces—walkways, patios, fences, walls, gates, trellises, pergolas, garden buildings—anything built. Typical materials for the various time periods are detailed in the succeeding chapters. You will need to decide how true you wish to be to the materials that were used in the time of your landscape. Many may still be found, but there may be other choices, providing a similar visual effect, that are more economical, require less maintenance, or are more readily available. For authentic materials, try architectural salvage companies in your area; they are often a good source for period materials. The drawback to this source is that they may not have what you need in the quantities required, and they can be costly. Still, it is worth checking into.

Determining what was typical for both the time period and the region is important in material selection. Often construction materials chosen were based on local availability and custom. If stone was readily available, you might see more stone walls than fences. If trees were in good supply but stone was scarce, people would have built wooden fences. Local custom and heritage also influenced regional style and construction methods used in building hardscapes.

With increasing emphasis on sustainable landscape construction you may be concerned about how this applies to your historic landscape. The good news is that many of the historically used materials are very sustainable. Many are durable and last for centuries. If you use local sources as recommended, you reduce the environmental and economic cost of fossil fuel–based transportation. Selecting to dry-lay patios and walks will allow the surfaces to be more permeable. The use of salvaged materials is a great type of recycling. It is merely a matter of balancing historically appropriate material selection with the need to sustain the environment.

Sources for landscaping materials vary from region to region. Search the Internet for high-quality products from reputable suppliers. You may also want to consult landscape designers or contractors in your area.

1. Picket fence.

2. Wrought iron fence.

1

Fences and walls

In the South and East, early fencing was traditionally of wood. Often the lumber used would have been from local trees, milled on site or nearby; these would have been more durable, rot-resistant species, such as cedar, locust, oak, hickory, cypress, and chestnut. Spruce, pine, and fir were also used. The typical wood varied from region to region; current-day choices will be constrained by availability and cost.

There are many types of wood fences, including split rail, post and rail, picket, stockade, board, and lattice. For some styles, such as picket or stockade, you can purchase premade fence sections; they are easier to install, but there is a limited number of styles from which to choose, and the construction is typically not as good as a hand-built fence. Patterns for replicating historic fence styles are readily available. One thing to remember, when using construction detailing from an older source, is that lumber sizes have changed from what they were in the past; a two-by-four, for example, is now closer to one and a half by three and a half inches. If authenticity and accuracy are impor-

2

tant to you, you can have your lumber custom-milled to exact size; this is an expensive option, however.

In addition to real lumber, there are some very good modern products that have the look of wood. Engineered wood is often more durable and less expensive, and the available selections are increasingly affordable. Plastic or PVC fencing products have also improved in appearance. The better-quality ones look very similar to real wood fences; some do not, however, so be sure to be selective if you choose to go this route. The major advantage to these products is durability and reduced maintenance. A typical painted wood fence will need to be repainted every three to five years depending on your climate, and wood components will deteriorate and need to be replaced as they decay.

Metal fences from earlier periods were usually of wrought iron. Many good companies are still making wrought iron products, so it should be easy to find and support a local concern. Often they will replicate a fence pattern for you from an image or from a sample section of an existing fence, if you are fortunate enough to have one. Of course, custom work will cost more than using stock patterns, and wrought iron is expensive to begin

with. Some less expensive options—aluminum, steel, even vinyl—are very attractive and provide the look of wrought iron, especially when using the simpler styles. Modern powder coating and galvanizing methods used in manufacturing metal fences can also reduce the need to paint.

Walls were made of brick, stone, adobe, or concrete, depending on the region and the period. Adobe was used in the Southwest and West, particularly in areas where lumber was scarce. One of the oldest known building materials, it is made from sand, clay, and sometimes gravel, with hay or grass used as a binder. Traditional surface coatings were mud plaster, lime plaster, whitewash, or stucco. It might be difficult to find traditional builders of adobe since it, like many traditional art forms, is becoming a lost art. A similar look can be had from using a block- or brick-constructed wall covered with stucco.

Brick walls can be made entirely from brick in the traditional way or, as a less expensive alternative, by building a block wall and facing it with brick. True brick is made from clay and was originally cut and formed by hand. Modern bricks can have a slightly different appearance because they are machine-formed and -cut. Old brick was manufactured locally; differences in the firing methods and local clays resulted in distinct color variations. There were also differences in brick sizes before standardization; legal standards were developed in the late eighteenth century but were not fully followed until later. Like lumber, modern brick has changed dimension since earlier times, so you may find the brick to be smaller; this is not usually a big problem unless you are trying to match it up with existing old brick structures. Some manufacturers still produce hand-cut, oversized brick, sometimes referred to as jumbos.

If you are trying to produce an authentic, traditional appearance or match brick to other structures, you will need to do some extra work to find the manufacturers/suppliers in your area, as most brick sellers have limited inventory, and do not stock the older style brick. Another source for old brick can be finding brick from building demolition. But note: the original function of the old brick should match the new use; that is, bricks salvaged from walls should be used only for walls, and bricks taken up from old streets and roads should be used only for paving projects. Also, old brick is often softer than new brick, and you must adjust the type of mortar used to prevent the face of the brick from slagging off; the National Park Service division of Technical Preservation Services has a brief on how to create the proper mortar for old brick.

Stone walls are another traditional, and very durable, type of wall; often they will have endured in the landscape and may just need to be repaired or rebuilt. Stone is another material that varies widely in style and type from region to region. Once again, using local materials is usually the best option for historic accuracy. There are different techniques and patterns for construction, and various ways to lay a stone wall. Walls can be dry laid or mortared; the style you select will depend on what is historically and regionally correct for your site. If you're a do-it-yourself type, you might find a workshop to learn the techniques for laying up a stone wall; inquire at your local historical society or ask at the local stone yard. Contact stone companies for a list of contractors in your area that specialize in building stone walls.

Concrete and concrete block were used for walls by the second half of the nineteenth century; one hundred years later, concrete walls were very common. Both of these materials are readily available, and there are contractors who can build walls to your specifications. Additional wall and fencing materials include bamboo, wattle/twig, and wire.

1

Paving materials

A variety of materials have been used for walkways, drives, and patios over the years. Gravel for drives and paths is available in many sizes and types—crushed and bank-run gravel (called pea gravel in smaller sizes), for instance. The first, being more angular, packs better; the bank-run is more appropriate for older landscapes. Local gravel would have been used, so look for local sources when possible. Keep in mind, too, that (as with common names for plants) gravel types and sizes may have different names in different locales.

Sometimes hay, straw, or pine needles were used for simple paths. Crushed materials, such as brick and slate, were typical in some areas in later periods. Turf was used for paths in many landscape situations, as were packed soil (clay), mulches, and shredded bark.

Brick was used for walkways, patios, and roads. Much of the information about brick in the section on walls also applies to brick for walkways. But again: if you are planning to use old, recycled bricks for your period walkway, make sure that the brick was from a similar past installation. Brick used for structural walls often will not be as permanent on the ground as bricks formerly used for paving streets or sidewalks. The patterns for laying a brick surface varied, with the most common being running bond, herringbone, and basketweave. Regional preferences to pattern did exist, possibly because people copied one another or the local craftsmen preferred (or were adept at) one style over another.

Pavers are often a more economical choice and slightly easier to install than brick. Brick pavers, made from clay, have a thinner depth or face than regular bricks. Pavers made from dyed concrete are variously referred to as pavers, concrete pavers, or modular brick; it is important to be selective when using concrete pavers, as they do vary in quality and appearance.

Stone has long been a favorite choice for surfacing walkways and patios. Limestone, bluestone, slate, sandstone, granite, and marble all have historical use in landscapes. Once again, regional and period differences apply. Flagstone is rock that is split laterally to form paving slabs; originally it was a type of sandstone, but now the term is applied to several stone types. The options for patterns, using varied sizes of stone, are many. For a more geometric or formal application, patterned flagstone is used; this is stone that is cut into regular square and rectangular

2

1. Dry-laid stone wall.

2. Brickwork, basketweave.

3. Brickwork, herringbone.

▶ NEXT SPREAD Brickwork, running bond.

3

shapes. Irregular stone, popular in the early twentieth century in less formal situations, provides a more rustic or natural look that is still sought-after today. For both styles, paving stone can be either mortared or dry laid. Stone pavers with tumbled edges give a naturally worn look to the freshest installation.

Cobblestone is uncut, smooth, round stone used for paving and patios, sometimes in combination with other materials; it can be used in very artistic ways by combining different colors into patterns and images. Granite setts, or Belgian blocks, are broad, rectangular cut stones; they are expensive and sometimes difficult to find but are a beautiful, durable surface when historically appropriate.

Tile is used in milder regions; in cold areas, it might be damaged by freeze-thaw cycles. The most common type is terracotta tile, with ceramic/porcelain tile a close second. Tiles can be glazed or unglazed.

Often new installations look too new to give the historic look you may want for your landscape. There are several techniques for making stone, brick, and concrete surfaces look aged and weathered. The main idea in aging surfaces is to encourage the growth of organisms such as lichens and mosses on the surface. One method is to mix topsoil and compost with water and coat the surface with the resulting mud. Allow the mud to dry and then brush it off, leaving a thin residue for the desired organisms to grow on. Another method is to brush the surface with vinegar; this creates small pits—spaces for organisms to take hold. A method most suitable for shadier areas is to coat the surface with yogurt or buttermilk mixed with soil and ground-up moss; the surface must be kept moist until the moss becomes established on the surface. These techniques can be used in combination.

Brushing with whitewash, paint mixtures, and antiquing glazes can also create an aged look, but it would be best to consult a professional for these processes. Distressing, or lightly chipping areas of the surface may also add a more worn appearance; but again, professionals should be used, lest you get carried away and really damage your surface.

Asphalt or bitumen (asphaltum, in the nineteenth century) is a viscous black petroleum-based substance; it does not become a surfacing material until it is mixed with aggregate. There are several similar processes for creating these surfaces, which have been referred to as asphalt, concrete, macadam, tarmacadam, tarmac, or blacktop, depending on the era and region. These products came into popular use in the early 1900s, typically for roads initially, but residential use grew throughout the century.

A recent development in paving material is stamped and dyed concrete, which can be made to imitate traditional stone and brick; but quality varies widely, so if you chose to use it, make sure you find a contractor whose work most resembles the material you are trying to imitate. While stamped concrete is cheaper in the short term, it may not be as durable or aesthetically pleasing as the more traditional materials.

Many other newly developed products, made to look like stone or brick, are used in both paved surfaces and walls. Most are cheaper and easier to install because they come in uniform sizes that fit or lock together, but most do not look as natural or authentic as the products they imitate. If you choose to use them, you may be compromising the visual quality of your historic landscape. That being said, these products are improving all the time, so better options may be available.

Developing a Plant List

The time will come, as you consider your historic landscape, when you will ask, "What shall I plant?" Choosing appropriate period plants is one of the easiest ways to demonstrate the historical nature of your landscape. Keep in mind regional character and plant communities for your specific area.

For inspiration you will look at your inventory list and identify those plants that remain in your garden as relics of an earlier time. Secondly, your perusal of the primary resources described earlier will add plants to your list. At the end of each chapter in this book, we will include a list of period-appropriate plants for different regions of the country. *Restoring American Gardens* (Adams 2004) is a good resource for additional plant lists.

Sometimes locating the plants that are documented on a plant list can be a challenge. You will need to decide how true you want to be to the historic design in your plant selection. If you cannot find an exact cultivar, are you willing to use a newer cultivar of the same species?

Stone paving, regular pattern.

Stone paving, irregular pattern.

A path of flag- and cobblestone, combined.

Unfortunately, many cultivars of ornamental plants have been the casualties of time and are no longer available. In recent years, several nurseries and seed firms have focused on providing period or heirloom plants; seek them out on the Internet. There are also seed-saver groups that share seeds of species that were found in old gardens.

You might find plants along the roadside or in early cemeteries. Of course, the rule is always to get permission from the owner of the property and then to disturb the plant as little as possible, taking only a few seeds or a small cutting. You might have to take similar steps to ensure the survival of plants that are already in your landscape; it may be necessary to take cuttings and start a new generation of a venerable tree or shrub that is in its twilight years. Maintenance interventions like pruning might improve the health of an old-timer.

We each have a responsibility to assist in preserving the old varieties by planting seeds and cuttings that are important to our own families and in our neighborhoods. Poll your own families and neighbors to find significant plants and preserve them in your landscape. Future generations will thank you for it!

This is a good place to reinforce the hard truth that not all heirloom plants are appropriate for planting in today's gardens. Plants that have proved to be invasive or particularly vigorous might threaten the environment where you live. Purple loosestrife (*Lythrum salicaria*) is an example of an heirloom plant found on fashionable planting plans of the early 1900s that is now on prohibited noxious weed lists in many states; Japanese barberry (*Berberis thunbergii*) is another. Always exclude any plants that might take over, even if they have historic value to your site. The future must be protected as well as the past.

Some plants of the past can be ravaged by pests of the present, which have since arrived on our shores; the American elm and chestnut are classic examples. Other plants, particularly certain trees, are simply no longer in vogue, although they were extremely fashionable a century or two ago. Silver maple and tree-of-heaven, for example, enjoyed popularity in the 1800s but are much maligned today. Try to keep an open mind when making your plant list and attempt to understand what made each plant valuable or beautiful to a previous cultivator. When potentially replacing a species known to have existed in the landscape, we must ask ourselves what purpose the plant originally served and why it was selected and cultivated. Was its form significant, as in the case of the columnar Lombardy poplar or weeping willow? Or perhaps the fruit, flowers, or other ornamental feature was important to the overall design of the garden. Resolving to set aside modern biases and "getting into the head" of the original cultivator or designer can help us make good choices or appropriate substitutions.

Other factors must be considered when choosing plants for the successful landscape. The primary goal is for the plants to function for their intended purpose and thrive in their location. An important consideration in plant selection is to determine which plants are native to a region (or native to regions with conditions similar to those of the site), provided they are historically correct. These plants are more likely to be adapted to the existing conditions and will require less time and materials as well as fewer soil modifications and less irrigation. This is not always the case when a site has been altered significantly from its original conditions by human activity. Another good assurance of plant reliability is to select plants that have a history of succeeding in similar conditions. Fortunately, many of the historic plants that are still available are very reliable garden plants.

It is best if plants can function and thrive with minimum input of labor and water; it goes without saying that any use of chemicals should be kept to an absolute minimum. To determine which plants will be best suited for a particular landscape installation requires an understanding of their physiological needs, growth habits (size, shape, and growth rate), and ability to be adapted to the specific purpose. It also requires a thorough and honest understanding of the site—will the existing site support the plant? Climate, soil type, moisture levels, and human and animal disturbances all determine what plants will grow in a given site.

Cold and heat hardiness maps can give guidance as to which plants will survive in a given region. Again, soil testing should be done to determine pH and nutrient levels as well as the type of soil (clay, sand, and silt), which is a critical predictor of what the drainage might be like. Close observation can also give clues concerning the ability of the soil to retain moisture. The sun and shade patterns you already noted on your site inventory will assure the plants you select for your design receive the proper amount of light.

Be sure to consider the mature sizes of plants; proper spacing at the design phase is crucial to the lasting appeal of your landscape. Overcrowding and under-planting are common mistakes that can reduce its health and beauty. Next, determine the size plant you want to install; this is often a matter of budget versus desire for immediate results. It is sometimes better to use smaller plants and allow them to mature on the site rather than going for larger, more expensive specimens. Another factor in this decision is the availability of labor and equipment.

Plant installation is the last step in the design process. Once completed, you can enjoy your landscape, but do not forget about maintenance! Timely and careful maintenance, especially as plants establish, ensures that your landscape will be enjoyed well into the future. Pruning, weeding, fertilizing, deadheading, mulching, and staking are all still done; it's the frequency of the maintenance techniques which has changed. Our predecessors didn't have the time or probably the energy to achieve our modern standards of perfection—not when the chores of daily living were so labor intensive. Unless you were wealthy and could afford to pay for staff, landscape maintenance would come after the chores need for survival. The quest for the perfect landscape was something few people cared to afford.

Take lawns, for example. Prior to the invention of the lawn mower in 1830, small lawns were mowed with a scythe; larger lawn areas were grazed by livestock, so they were more pasture than lawn. The frequency of cutting the lawn with a scythe was much less than the frequency of mowing we practice today. Early mowers were reel types that required a fair amount of labor. The modern self-propelled and riding mowers created a major change in the way we maintain a lawn. That and the introduction of herbicides and fertilizers in the last half of the twentieth century led to the obsessive quest for the perfect lawn.

Electric or gas-powered hedge trimmers and chainsaws replaced shears and handsaws. Blowers have replaced brooms and rakes. For most of us, the idea of going back to the more labor-intensive ways of doing things would be undesirable, but there are some advantages to the older methods. They are quieter and do not pollute the landscape with fumes. Older pruning techniques tended to respect the natural form of plants in most cases. In past times, there were no pre-emergent herbicides: weeds were controlled with mulches and by hand pulling. This along with the fact there were no string trimmers meant a less manicured look was the norm, and for the serious preservationist, replicating this look for their period landscape may be a goal.

In the past, twigs were commonly used for staking; peas and other vines were tied to trellises with twine made from natural fiber or strips of cloth. Wood stakes followed, and then iron; now, it's fiberglass and pvc. For a period garden to have modern plastic stakes would seem incongruous. But many of the older maintenance methods are tried and true. If you decide to use traditional techniques, old garden magazines and books have a great deal of information. If nothing else, you can use the fact you are using historic methods as an excuse for a less than perfectly maintained landscape.

So now you are ready to tackle your historic landscape! Consult whichever of the following chapters best describes your home or subject residence's era and architectural type, check the case studies and the plant lists for your region for inspiration, and you are really on your way. Remember, always, that contemporary use can seamlessly combine with historic authenticity for a pleasing and functional landscape.

Landscapes of the Colonial Period and New Republic (1620–1820)

1600

1622
Honeybees are introduced into America at Jamestown, Virginia.

1631
Governor John Winthrop orders seeds for his residence in the Massachusetts Bay Colony—our first documentation of such a transaction.

1641
First record of a commercial fruit nursery in the colonies, that of George Fenwick, Saybrook, Connecticut.

1700

C. 1728
Early American botanist John Bartram (1699–1777) plants a garden. The Bartram Garden is the oldest continuous botanic garden in the United States.

1753
Carolus Linnaeus publishes *Species Plantarum,* **describing a new system for naming plants, binomial nomenclature, which we continue to use today.**

1755?
Prince Nursery is established in Flushing, New York; it is the first commercial nursery for which we have an extant catalog (1771).

1785
Arbustrum Americanum: The American Grove—the first botanical treatise by a native American (Humphry Marshall, 1722–1801) on American plants—is published in Philadelphia.

1800

C. 1800
Johnny Appleseed (John Chapman, 1774–1845) begins to distribute apple tree seeds in Ohio and nearby states.

1805
Grant Thorburn establishes the first American seed business in New York.

C. 1815
The first American-bred hybrid rose, 'Champney's Pink Cluster', is discovered in Charleston, South Carolina, creating much excitement among rose fanciers; its parents were *Rosa chinensis* and the musk rose, *R. moschata.*

1900

Architecture Styles

Chances are that not too many people reading this book will have the opportunity to design a landscape for a seventeenth-century house in North America. A few such houses still exist around the United States, but mainly as museums. The first houses in this land were constructed to provide shelter, usually without regard to fashion; they were simple boxes, made of local materials—rock, logs, or timbers in the East, stone or clay in the Southwest. The style of such "folk" houses, built of local materials and reflecting local norms, is termed "vernacular" architecture.

Many eighteenth-century residences survive in eastern cities, particularly in areas where the population grew rapidly. Dutch Colonials were popular in New York and New Jersey, but the Georgian style was the foremost architectural style throughout the English colonies between 1700 and 1780. Houses were simple one- or two-story boxes with a completely symmetrical façade. The five-ranked windows (five windows in a row) were aligned both horizontally and vertically and had many small panes, nine or twelve per sash. The paneled front door was centered and usually topped with a decorative crown. In Georgian houses, the cornice (molding at the junction of wall and roof) was often decorated with small tooth-like protrusions called dentils.

Federal (or Adam) style, which followed in about 1780, was the dominant architectural type until about 1820 in the eastern United States, appearing in other regions of the country as settlers moved westward. Again the windows are symmetrically positioned and five-ranked, but the number of panes per sash is six. A semi-circular or elliptical fanlight highlights the top of the paneled door, which also might have sidelights and an elaborate crown. As in Georgian, the cornice is often decorated with dentils. Many Federal townhouses or attached row houses still survive in Washington, D.C., Boston, Philadelphia, and other cities.

Featured Designer:
Bernard M'Mahon (c. 1775–1816)

THE

AMERICAN GARDENER'S

CALENDAR;

ADAPTED

TO THE CLIMATES AND SEASONS

OF THE

UNITED STATES.

CONTAINING

A COMPLETE ACCOUNT OF ALL THE WORK NECESSARY TO BE
DONE IN THE

KITCHEN-GARDEN,		PLEASURE-GROUND,
FRUIT-GARDEN,		FLOWER-GARDEN,
ORCHARD,		GREEN-HOUSE,
VINEYARD,		HOT-HOUSE, and
NURSERY,		FORCING FRAMES,

FOR EVERY MONTH IN THE YEAR;

WITH AMPLE PRACTICAL DIRECTIONS
FOR PERFORMING THE SAME.

ALSO,

General as well as minute instructions, for laying out, or erecting, each and every of the above departments, according to modern taste and the most approved plans; the ORNAMENTAL PLANTING OF PLEASURE-GROUNDS, in the ancient and modern stile; the cultivation of THORN-QUICKS and other plants suitable for LIVE HEDGES, with the best methods of making them, &c.

TO WHICH ARE ANNEXED,

Extensive CATALOGUES of the different kinds of plants, which may be cultivated either for use or ornament in the several departments, or in rural economy; divided into eighteen separate alphabetical classes, according to their habits, duration, and modes of culture; with explanatory introductions, marginal marks, and their true *Linnæan* or *Botanical*, as well as English names; together with a copious *Index* to the body of the work.

BY BERNARD M'MAHON,
NURSERY, SEEDSMAN, AND FLORIST.

PHILADELPHIA:
PRINTED BY B. GRAVES, NO. 40, NORTH FOURTH-STREET,
FOR THE AUTHOR.
....
1806.

Title page of *The American Gardener's Calendar*
(M'Mahon 1806).

BERNARD M'MAHON IS THE AUTHOR of the first comprehensive gardening book in the United States, *The American Gardener's Calendar*, published in 1806. His book was based on the English model of a month-by-month instruction of all the tasks involved in maintaining a pleasure ground and kitchen garden, as well as orchards, greenhouses, nurseries, and other features of the landscape. M'Mahon influenced the horticultural practices of Thomas Jefferson and was the curator for seeds collected by Lewis and Clark on their 1804–06 "Corps of Discovery" expedition to the Pacific Coast. He is often honored as the father of American horticulture.

Georgian.

Early frame house, Tappan, New York, c. 1750.

Essential Elements of Early American Landscapes

· Fruit trees
· Vegetables, herbs, and flowers grown together in square or rectangular beds
· Garden is enclosed with a fence (most often) or a hedge
· Shade trees

Landscape Design

We can only speculate concerning the appearance of gardens and landscapes for the earliest formative years of our country; records and documentation are rare. Most garden historians believe that both the functional kitchen gardens and any ornamentation of the landscape followed principles learned or observed in the home countries of the colonists.

Early travelers from England and elsewhere observed plants in cultivation and wrote about them. John Josselyn visited New England twice, once in 1638 and again in 1671, and recorded detailed observations about plants and animals he encountered on his travels; thanks to him, we have a record of what plants some colonists grew, even if we do not know exactly how and where they grew them. Plants that Josselyn (1672) wrote about included well-known herbs like dill, sage, garden sorrel, chervil, and winter savory. Some of the flowering plants he observed also belonged in the herbal category in that era, although now we consider them more ornamental—plants like pot marigold (*Calendula officinalis*), eglantine rose (*Rosa rubiginosa*), hollyhock (*Alcea rosea*), gillyflower (*Matthiola incana*), and feverfew (*Tanacetum parthenium*). He also listed plants that did not do well in the northeastern part of the country, for example, rue (*Ruta graveolens*), southernwood (*Artemisia abrotanum*), rosemary (*Rosmarinus officinalis*), and lavender (*Lavandula angustifolia*).

Other writers reassure us that efforts to beautify the landscape with plants were made. William Wood (1634) described Dorchester, Massachusetts, as "well wooded and watered" and wrote of "pleasant Gardens, with kitchen-gardens." Edward Johnson (1654) paints a picture of the settlement as it appeared in 1641:

> Further, the Lord hath been pleased to turn all the wigwams, huts, and hovels the English dwelt in at their first coming, into orderly, fair, and well-built houses, well-furnished many of them, together with orchards filled with goodly fruit trees, and gardens with variety of flowers: There are supposed to be in the Massachusetts Government at this day, neer a thousand acres of land planted for orchards and gardens, besides their fields are filled with garden fruit.

The first garden described on record belonged to Gamaliel Wayte of Boston, who planted a garden in 1642 that was renowned for its fruits and flowering plants (Slade 1895). Governor William Bradford (1654) of the Massachusetts Bay Colony captured in verse some of the cultivated plants he had observed in the landscape:

> All sorts of roots and herbes in gardens grow:
> Parsnips, carrots, turnips, or what you'll sow;
> Onions, melons, cucumbers, radishes,
> Skirrets, beets, coleworts, and fair cabbages.
> Here grow fine flowers many, and, 'mongst those,
> The fair white lily and th' sweet, fragrant rose.

Dutch Colonial.

From inventories and libraries we know that certain English gardening books were present in the colonies during those early years, among them Gerard's *Herball* (1633), *Paradisi in sole, paradisus terrestris* (Parkinson 1629), and *The English Gardener* (Meager 1670). From these and the rare written record, we have gleaned ideas concerning the style and content of the earliest American gardens.

We know that the earliest American gardens were utilitarian. Families cultivated plants they needed for subsistence and medicine. Vegetables, herbs, flowers, and small fruits were all grown together. Fruit trees dotted the landscape. The form of the gardens was geometric—typically a large square or rectangle with rows of plants, or a series of smaller geometric beds within a larger square or rectangle. All gardens were enclosed with a fence or, less frequently, a hedge. Today we refer to the old geometric design style of making beds for gardening as the "ancient style"; the ancient style that was prevalent in the earliest gardens of our country typically demonstrated symmetry.

A 1660 map of Manhattan displays many gardens, some formal, composed of geometric beds. For this map, and other early maps from around the country, we can question whether or not the cartographer or engraver embellished the scene; it is possible that some elements were planned for but never realized. But even if all these gardens did not exist, the illustration clearly demonstrates the ancient garden style of the era and the juxtaposition of garden to house.

Historian U. P. Hedrick (1950) described the early landscapes of New England:

> About small gardens, the garden was a parallelogram bounded by side fences that extended from the corners of the cottage to the road, with the front fence close to the road, the gate in the middle. The fence was commonly of white-washed wooden pickets [and the] flowers were scant in variety—lilies, crown imperials, other bulbs, peonies, pinks and hollyhocks. At the sides of the gate, two shrubs were planted, the usual choice being lilacs or one of the tall-growing roses. The front-yard path had edgings of pinks, irises, sedums, or other perennials that could stand a little trampling.

By the middle of the eighteenth century, landscapes were simple (often a house with a central path, enclosed by a picket fence) and tended to be formal, where resources would allow. Kitchen gardens were often laid out separately and screened from the ornamental areas of the property. In the southern colonies, formality and practicality shaped the terrain; there the geometric style prevailed, featuring a central axis, geometric-shaped beds in squares and rectangles, symmetry and balance in the details of the landscape, and an enclosing fence or hedge.

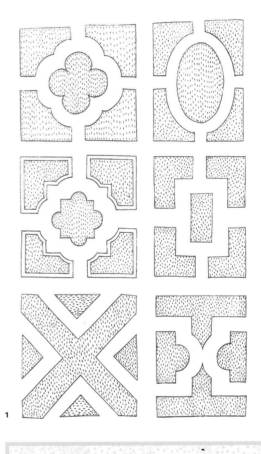

1. Garden beds in the ancient style (Meager 1670). Albert and Mary Small Special Collections Library, The University of Virginia, Charlottesville.

2. "Redraft of the Castello Plan, New Amsterdam in 1660." The Lionel Pincus and Princess Firyal Map Division, The New York Public Library, Astor, Lenox and Tilden Foundations.

3. Picket fences are most often associated with Colonial-style landscapes, such as this one for a Connecticut house built in 1692.

▶ NEXT SPREAD "A north-west prospect of Nassau-Hall, with a front view of the presidents house, in New Jersey," 1764. Rare Books Division, The New York Public Library, Astor, Lenox and Tilden Foundations.

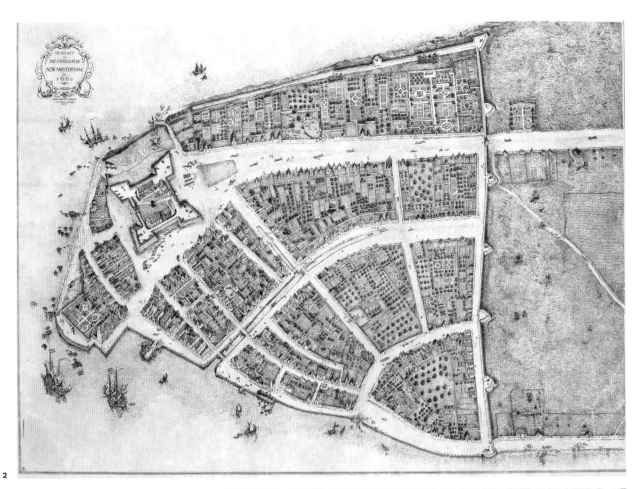

2

3

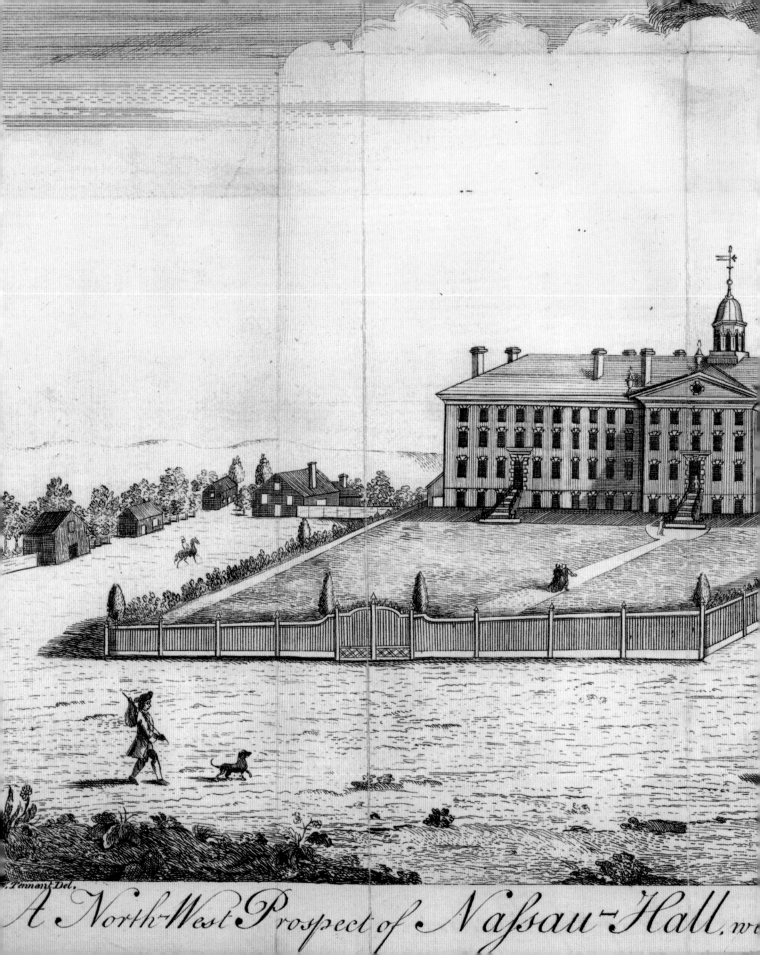

A North-West Prospect of Nassau-Hall, w

Front View of the Presidents House, in New Jersey

H Dawkins Sc.

Flower gardens from pleasure grounds

As this country developed over the seventeenth and eighteenth centuries, grand estates were constructed, mainly along the Atlantic coastal region. Although this book does not consistently cover the elaborate landscapes of the wealthy, about which much already has been written, looking at those estates helps us to understand the design styles and attitudes that continue to influence the American landscape ideal.

A pleasure ground is "an extensive garden, laid out in a liberal taste, and embellished according to nature, where both nature and art are so united, as to form one grand scene" (An Old Gardener 1822). The idea of a pleasure ground began in England and migrated to North America with the settlers, most of whom did not have the time or resources for such garden affectations, but, of course, there were exceptions. By the first decade of the 1800s, at least one book concerned the design of extensive pleasure grounds: M'Mahon (1806) advised gardeners to install a grassy lawn in front of the house with trees, shrubs, and flowers in clumps and thickets to form its boundaries.

> Each boundary must be planted with a choice variety of ornamental trees and shrubs, deciduous and ever-greens, arranged principally in several clumps; some consisting of lofty trees, others being entirely of shrub kinds, and some consisting of trees, shrubs, and herbaceous plants together: in all of which, arrange the taller growing kinds backward, and the lower forward, according to their gradation of height; embellishing the front with more curious low flowering shrubs, and ever-greens, interspersed with various herbaceous flowering perennials, all open to the lawn and walks.

The walkways in the M'Mahon landscape were serpentine in form, and the prescribed material for them was grass or gravel. He included description of other areas, for example a "wilderness" composed of "winding mazes or labyrinths." The landscape could feature a grotto or temple in the English landscape tradition. He also mentions topiary forms, ruins, bridges and artificial rivers, rock-work, and shell-work. Interestingly M'Mahon (1806) also allowed for some adherence to the ancient style of gardening, particularly the use of geometric forms for flowerbeds.

> Another part shall appear more gay and sprightly, displaying an elegant flower-ground, or flower garden, designed somewhat in the parterre way, in various beds, borders, and other divisions, furnished with the most curious flowers; and the boundary decorated with an arrangement of various clumps, of the most beautiful flowering shrubs, and lively ever-greens, each clump also bordered with a variety of the herbaceous flowery tribe.

In order to maintain order and symmetry in a flower garden, writers proposed different edging material. They mentioned dwarf English boxwood (*Buxus sempervirens* 'Suffruticosa') and, although no evidence of its early use has been found in New England, where it is only marginally hardy, it was the iconic edging plant for the southern region. Other recommended edging plants included thrift (*Armeria maritima*), pinks (*Dianthus*), London pride (*Saxifraga*), and even strawberries with their runners removed. William Cobbett (1821) described "the spot for flowers" in gardens, as he saw them during his travels in America: "The smaller kinds, and even the small shrubs, such as roses, dwarf honey-suckles, and the like, may be planted by the sides of the broad walks in the kitchen garden, or a little piece of ground may be set apart for the purpose."

Kitchen gardens

Early American gardens were primarily kitchen gardens. Herbs and vegetables were not segregated but rather grew together, in geometric beds. Flowers, particularly easily-grown-from-seed annuals, grew among the more practical plants. Perennial vegetables like asparagus and rhubarb might occupy a bed of their own. Bush fruits (currants, gooseberries, blueberries, raspberries) were often in long narrow beds that outlined or surrounded the vegetable beds.

The grouping of fruit trees in an orchard was essential. Historians have pointed out that early fruit trees, mainly apples and pears, were often cultivated not so much for table use as to make alcoholic cider. Early nurseries always initiated their businesses with the sale of fruit trees. In fact, we know that the stability of a community was guaranteed when these trees were being sold to adorn the landscape and nurture the body and spirit.

Raised beds at Plimoth Plantation, Massachusetts.

It is often reported that the colonists constructed raised beds in their kitchen gardens, piling the soil into eight- to twelve-inch heaps and enclosing the beds with boards, saplings, or rocks. While this type of cultivation makes sense in order to ensure good drainage (and we know it was a practice in England), for this book we could find no documentation to confirm this style of garden making in early American kitchen gardens. Lack of evidence does not mean it was not done; it merely indicates that perhaps no one recorded it at a time when written or pictorial documentation for anything is rare.

Trees and shrubs

In the early years of the nation, the first step in order to construct a house often involved clearing the building site of trees. The second step, following the construction of the house, was to replant trees of value to the homeowner. Most landscapes were simple. Fruit trees were a necessity. Large deciduous trees and evergreens were placed strategically near the house for shade and/or general ornamentation. In the case of the Lombardy poplar (*Populus nigra* 'Italica'), its decorative value overrode its negligible value as a shade tree. A traveler in Virginia, Morris Birkbeck, stated in 1818, "The Lombardy poplar is a favorite accompaniment of the best mansions, rising in gloomy columns to a great height above the surrounding forest" (Lockwood 1931).

M'Mahon (1806) offered advice on the placement of trees. He recommended that deciduous and evergreen trees, such as the Lombardy poplar, eastern red cedar (*Juniperus virginiana*), and straight-trunked tulip tree (*Liriodendron tulipifera*), be placed along driveways and avenues, in either a single or a double row. Many long, old driveways particularly in the South, even to the present time, illustrate this practice. In that era as now, trees and shrubs were situated on the lawn either as single specimens or in small groups. A "thicket," according to M'Mahon, was a thoughtful combination of deciduous trees with shrubs interspersed between them.

Landscape Features

Paths and driveways

Path and driveway materials varied by location. For walkways, dirt or grass was the default material. Gravel, if it was available, was another good path material; Meager (1670) described such walks in his portrayal of the kitchen garden. M'Mahon (1806) allowed that grass walks were more comfortable to walk upon in the summer time but believed overall that gravel-walks "should lead all around the pleasure-ground, . . . so as to have dry and firm walking, at all times of the year; for frequently, but particularly in winter, and in wet weather, grass-walks are very uncomfortable and even unhealthy to walk on." By the eighteenth century, crushed oyster shells were seen in the coastal areas; other materials included bricks, crushed brick or tile, and even a composition material. The paths in the c. 1765 garden of William Faris of Baltimore consisted of a mixture of gravel, oyster shells, sand, and pulverized bricks (Sarudy 1998). It makes sense that gardeners typically used whatever inexpensive materials were available.

> Walks are either of grass or gravel [and their] number and breadth . . . determined by the quantity of ground allotted; but it is better that they be few and wide, than many and contracted. If the garden be small, one good walk all around will be sufficient. If long and narrow, the cross walks should not be many; six or eight feet is not too wide in a moderate sized garden. [Gravel walks] should be preferred, and if possible, accomplished (Gardiner and Hepburn 1826).

"The Seat of Mr. John Stevens," Hoboken, New Jersey, 1808. Emmet Collection, Miriam and Ira D. Wallach Division of Art, Prints and Photographs, The New York Public Library, Astor, Lenox and Tilden Foundations.

"Davis' Clearing 1 ½ mile South West of Piqua, Ohio." Print Collection, Miriam and Ira D. Wallach Division of Art, Print and Photographs, The New York Public Library, Astor, Lenox and Tilden Foundations.

Fences and hedges

Most gardens were enclosed with a fence. Fences were varied, from the more practical board or paling fences to decorative iron railings and simple, uniform pickets. A type of early fence that is frequently used to illustrate the colonial period is the rail fence. However, Gardiner and Hepburn (1826) spoke against it—and for the wall of stone or brick:

> In this country, board fences and palings are most in use. Rail fences ought to be avoided, as they are easily surmounted by idle or thieving men, and mischievous boys, while they admit the entrance of hogs and dogs at the bottom. [G]ood brick and stone walls are not only the most ornamental and useful, but, in the end, the cheapest. They impart a general warmth to the atmosphere they inclose, break the force of boisterous winds, and contribute to accelerate the maturation of fruits, and the growth of vegetables.

Hedges were less frequent. Such "live-fences" were the normal practice to enclose the landscape in England, and observers in this country lamented the lack of general interest here in making extensive hedges. Writers made the argument that a hedge could be utilitarian as well as beautiful and recommended shrubs for the "outward" view like hawthorn (*Crataegus*) as well as shrubs and trees for the "internal" view like privet (*Ligustrum*), yew (*Taxus*), boxwood (*Buxus sempervirens*), and eastern red cedar (*Juniperus virginiana*).

An unusual type of "fence," the ha-ha, had its origins in the English landscape tradition. A ha-ha was a sunken ditch five or six feet deep and ten to twenty feet wide. The purpose of the ha-ha was to provide an unbroken sweep of scenery, often focusing on animals in a field, while providing an unseen barrier for the animals to cross into the living space of the property. The first mention of a ha-ha in America was at Stratford Hall in Virginia in 1730; this type of enclosure was suitable only for extensive estates.

1

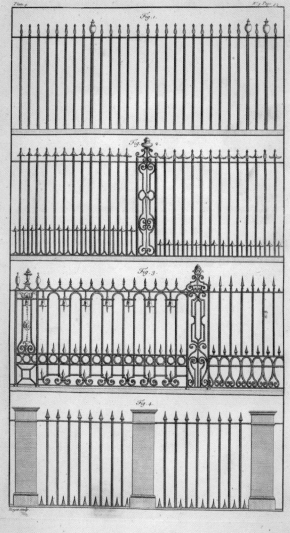

2

3

4

5

1. The worm fence, so called for its appearance of slithering across the property.

2. Examples of iron railing, 1756. Art and Architecture Collection, Miriam and Ira D. Wallach Division of Art, Prints and Photographs, The New York Public Library, Astor, Lenox and Tilden Foundations.

3. A board fence sets off the "ancient house" of Mr. Daniel Fenn, built in Stockbridge, Massachusetts, in 1737 (Barber 1839).

4. Rail fence along the Blue Ridge Parkway, Virginia.

5. A ha-ha fence provides, invisibly, a barrier to the cows.

1

Seating

Outdoor seating for rest and repose was as much a necessity in earlier times as it is today. An advertisement placed
in the *Baltimore Daily Repository* of 9 January 1791 read
in part, "Garden Seats, made and painted to particular
directions" (Lockwood 1931). Robert Sutcliff (1811), visiting Burlington, New Jersey, in 1805, wrote in his journal
on 5 June of that year, "It is very common here to have
benches, facing each other, on the outside of their houses,
at the doors, under the shade of trees planted in the
streets, where [people] frequently sit enjoying the fresh
breeze, and the shade."

Garden accessories

Sundials graced many early American gardens; old
wooden fence posts, boulders, and even parts of cemetery
monuments all made good pedestals for them (Earle 1901).
Once while visiting an old Virginia estate garden along
the James River, we spotted a sundial from the eighteenth
century, but such treasures are few and far between, and
few records, much less the accessories themselves, survive
from this era. The inventory of the eighteenth-century

Governor's Palace in Williamsburg, Virginia, does list lead
vases as ornaments in the formal garden (Israel 1999),
and perhaps the large East Coast estates utilized these and
other features (urns, trellises, pergolas) in the ornamentation of their landscapes and gardens.

Trellises and arbors for the support of vines would
have been simple in the colonial world. An arbor might
be arched over the gate of a picket fence and covered with
old roses. Simple wooden trelliswork might guide trumpet creeper (*Campsis radicans*) up the side of a privy or
support clematis next to the front door of the residence.
Many gardens had old straw beehives, or skeps. These
are difficult to find today; most are imported from third
world countries, but a few local craftsmen continue to
make them for their ornamental value, and indeed, they
do add a charming cottage-look to the garden. But most
modern beekeepers skip the skeps: they want their colony
to be healthy, and it is not so easy to inspect for disease or
parasites in a skep.

Dovecotes were also a feature of early American
gardens, particularly in the South; a circular brick dove-
cote existed at Shirley Plantation in Virginia as early as
1686 (Hill 1995). These structures were decorative in the
landscape, and their residents were eventually food for
colonial tables.

1. Wooden garden benches, 1798. Picture Collection, The New York Public Library, Astor, Lenox and Tilden Foundations.

2. Eighteenth-century sundial, Virginia.

3. Sundial in the garden of Mary Washington (Earle 1901).

4. A dove surveys the world from his ornamental perch.

5. Bee skeps in the colonial tradition.

2

3

4

5

Southern view of Conway.

1

RESIDENCE OF J. C. NEWHALL,
CONWAY, FRANKLIN CO., MASS.

2

Case Studies

Circa 1790 house, Conway, Massachusetts

The house in this study has a long and colorful history. Originally built as a modest frame dwelling, it was by the end of the century enlarged to serve as a tavern for the town of Conway, Massachusetts. A second transformation took place as the demographics of the region changed, and by the second half of the 1800s the house was part of a successful dairy farm. It was a little over a century later, in 1985, that John and Jan Maggs came upon the then-dilapidated structure. It was the perfect answer to their quest for a restorable historic house. After many years spent painstakingly restoring its interior, they began to explore options for the landscape.

The initial plan called for a formal fenced front garden (as depicted in the 1879 engraving) and a more primitive rail fence to surround an adjacent field. The front path would be centered with the restored Connecticut Valley doorway and geometric beds would contain an assortment of colorful flowers. Bernard M'Mahon would have congratulated the Maggses for this choice: he advised that when the ancient geometric style was implemented in a landscape, it should adhere to a central axis, and that the main straight walk should always extend from the front door at right angles to all other walks. He also described the placement of a parterre in the front of the house as "a spacious level plot of ground, divided into many partitions, of different figures and dimensions; by means of edgings or lines of dwarf-box, & c. or by verges of grass-turf, and tracks of sand, fine gravel, shell, and scroll-work" (M'Mahon 1806).

By the time we met the Maggs family, the garden had been in place for twenty years; many plants had been replaced over the years, and others had matured beyond their bed edging. It badly needed a facelift. They asked us to provide a new, more formal planting plan for the garden, one with an atmosphere that would suit the era of the house's original construction. They requested that both herbaceous plants and shrubs be used and that at least two of the existing plants, gasplant (*Dictamnus albus*) and goatsbeard (*Aruncus dioicus*), remain in the new design. Personal taste stipulated that there be no daisies and no

3

4

1. Engraving of Conway (Barber 1839).

2. Illustration of Conway (*The History of the Connecticut River Valley* 1879).

3. Maggs residence.

4. A nineteenth-century sundial is the focal point of the center bed.

5. Of gasplant, Neltje Blanchan (1909) wrote, "It will flash at dusk, on still summer eve, if a lighted match is brought near."

5

yellow flowers. Also, we were to choose plants that could be utilized for cut flowers.

We selected dwarf heirloom fruit trees to give structure and balance to the garden. These apple and pear trees, on dwarf rootstocks, will mature at five feet tall. They are placed in the center of each of the four large beds and underplanted with strawberries or grass pinks (*Dianthus plumarius*), or both. *Dianthus* 'Rose de Mai' is a nice heirloom selection for the underplanting, since it tends to be evergreen and blooms two times during the season. Primary colors are cool blue/purples and warm red/oranges, with some white to rest the eye. An underplanting of spring bulbs could include *Crocus vernus*, period selections (remembering "no yellows") of daffodils such as *Narcissus poeticus* var. *recurvus* (old pheasant's eye), and tulips such as *Tulipa clusiana* and *T. sylvestris*. With the addition of

bulbs, there would be flowers in bloom from April through September in this zone 5b garden.

Surrounding the large beds is an edging of clipped dwarf lavender (*Lavandula angustifolia*); an alternative edging material might be lavender cotton (*Santolina chamaecyparissus*), although the yellow flowers would have to be pruned. Early garden designers often recommended that thrift (*Armeria maritima*) be used as an edging plant, but modern gardeners report that it does not hold its shape uniformly. The center bed already has a focal point, a sundial on a pedestal, surrounded with a groundcover of thyme and pinks. Other choices for garden structure could be an evergreen clipped as a short topiary, or a trellis supporting everlasting pea (*Lathyrus latifolius*) or some other vine.

Planting plan for the Maggs garden, definitely in the ancient style: smaller geometric beds within a larger square or, as here, a rectangle; with gravel paths.

Construction of garden beds.

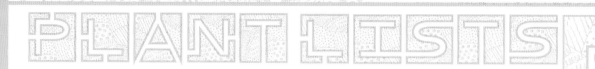

PLANT LISTS

* Please check for possibility of invasiveness in your locale.

** Plant is from the period but not necessarily listed in extant resources for the region.

These earliest ornamental annuals, perennials, vines, and bulbs are known to have been cultivated somewhere in America before 1750; the regional breakdowns that follow this first general list are for plants in the years between 1750 and 1820.

Achillea millefolium
yarrow

Aconitum napellus
aconite

Alcea rosea
hollyhock

Anemone coronaria
windflower

Aquilegia vulgaris
columbine

Aster novae-angliae
New England aster

Calendula officinalis
pot marigold

Callistephus chinensis
China aster

Dianthus caryophyllus
carnation

Digitalis purpurea
foxglove

Erysimum cheiri
wallflower

Fritillaria imperialis
crown imperial

Galanthus nivalis
snowdrop

Hedera helix*
English ivy

Iris germanica
German bearded iris

'Florentina'
Florentine iris

Lathyrus latifolius
everlasting pea

Lilium candidum
Madonna lily

Lilium superbum
Turk's cap lily

Lunaria annua*
honesty

Narcissus
daffodil

Nerine sarniensis
Guernsey lily

Paeonia
peony

Papaver orientale
oriental poppy

Papaver somniferum
opium poppy

Phlox paniculata
perennial phlox

Phlox subulata
moss phlox

Polianthes tuberosa
tuberose

Primula veris
cowslip

Ricinus communis
castor bean

Tanacetum parthenium
feverfew

Tulipa
tulip

Viola tricolor
Johnny-jump-up

Yucca filamentosa
Adam's needle

NEW ENGLAND

Trees

Cercis canadensis
redbud

Cornus florida
dogwood

'Rubra'
red-flowering dogwood

Crataegus crus-galli
hawthorn

Juniperus virginiana
eastern red cedar

Larix decidua
larch

Liriodendron tulipifera
tulip tree

Populus nigra 'Italica'
Lombardy poplar

Shrubs

Buxus sempervirens
boxwood

Chionanthus virginicus
fringe tree

Kalmia latifolia
mountain laurel

Syringa ×persica
Persian lilac

Syringa vulgaris
lilac

Perennials and biennials

Alcea rosea
hollyhock

PLANT LISTS

* Please check for possibility of invasiveness in your locale.

** Plant is from the period but not necessarily listed in extant resources for the region.

Amberboa amberboi
yellow sweet sultan

Antirrhinum majus
snapdragon

Aquilegia vulgaris
columbine

Campanula medium
Canterbury bells

Cerinthe major
honeywort

Dianthus barbatus
sweet William

Dianthus caryophyllus
carnation

Dianthus plumarius
grass pink

Emilia coccinea
Flora's paintbrush

Erysimum cheiri
wallflower

Hedysarum coronarium
French honeysuckle

Hesperis matronalis*
dame's rocket

Hyssopus officinalis
hyssop

Lavandula angustifolia
lavender

Lavatera arborea
tree mallow

Lupinus
lupine

Lychnis coronaria
rose campion

Oenothera
evening primrose

Origanum majorana
marjoram

Thymus ×citriodorus
lemon thyme

Annuals

Amaranthus caudatus
love-lies-bleeding

Consolida ambigua
larkspur

Cynoglossum officinale
hound's tongue

Dianthus chinensis
China pink

Gomphrena globosa
globe amaranth

Lunaria annua*
honesty

Matthiola incana
gillyflower

Mesembryanthemum crystallinum
ice plant

Papaver somniferum
opium poppy

Ricinus communis
castor bean

Satureja hortensis
summer savory

Scabiosa atropurpurea
mourning bride

Scabiosa stellata
starry scabious

Tagetes erecta
African marigold

Tagetes patula
French marigold

Roses

Rosa gallica 'Versicolor'**
rosa mundi

Rosa 'Great Maiden's Blush'**

Rosa rubiginosa**
eglantine rose

Bulbs

Colchicum autumnale
autumn crocus

Gladiolus communis subsp. *byzantinus***
cornflag

Ornithogalum umbellatum*
star of Bethlehem

Ranunculus asiaticus
Persian buttercup

Tulipa
tulip

'Duc van Tol'**

'Keizerskroon'**

sylvestris**

Trees

Abies balsamea
balsam fir

Acer rubrum
red maple

Acer saccharum
sugar maple

Aesculus pavia
red buckeye

Aralia spinosa
Hercules' club

Catalpa speciosa
northern catalpa

Cornus florida
dogwood

Gleditsia triacanthos
honey locust

Juniperus virginiana
eastern red cedar

Liriodendron tulipifera
tulip tree

Magnolia acuminata
cucumber tree

Magnolia tripetala
umbrella magnolia

Pinus strobus
white pine

Platanus occidentalis
sycamore

Populus nigra 'Italica'
Lombardy poplar

Robinia pseudoacacia
black locust

Sassafras albidum
sassafras

Taxodium distichum
bald cypress

Thuja occidentalis
arborvitae

Tilia americana
basswood

Shrubs

Amelanchier canadensis
Canadian serviceberry

Calycanthus floridus
Carolina allspice

Chionanthus virginicus
fringe tree

Clethra alnifolia
summersweet

Colutea arborescens
bladder senna

Euonymus americanus
strawberry bush

Hamamelis virginiana
witch hazel

Hibiscus syriacus
rose of Sharon

Kalmia latifolia
mountain laurel

Laburnum anagyroides
golden chain

Lindera benzoin
spicebush

Magnolia virginiana
sweet bay magnolia

Philadelphus coronarius
mock orange

Prunus dulcis
sweet almond

Robinia hispida
rose acacia

Syringa vulgaris
lilac

Viburnum opulus 'Roseum'
snowball

Perennials and biennials

Aquilegia vulgaris
columbine

Asclepias tuberosa
butterfly milkweed

Baptisia australis
false indigo

Chelone glabra
turtlehead

Comptonia peregrina var. *asplenifolia*
sweet fern

Dianthus barbatus
sweet William

Dianthus caryophyllus
carnation

Dodecatheon meadia
shooting star

Echinacea purpurea
purple coneflower

Hemerocallis lilioasphodelus
lemon lily

Hibiscus moscheutos
rosemallow

Iris xiphium
Spanish iris

Lobelia cardinalis
cardinal flower

Lobelia siphilitica
blue cardinal flower

Lychnis chalcedonica
Maltese cross

Monarda didyma
beebalm

Phlox paniculata
perennial phlox

Podophyllum peltatum
May apple

Spigelia marilandica
Indian pink

Annuals

Amaranthus tricolor
Joseph's coat

Carthamus tinctorius
false saffron

Chrysanthemum
winter pink

Clarkia amoena subsp. *lindleyi*
evening primrose

Dianthus chinensis
China pink

Heliotropium arborescens
cherry pie

Hibiscus trionum
flower-of-the-hour

Impatiens balsamina
balsam

Nigella damascena
love-in-a-mist

Reseda odorata
sweet mignonette

Ricinus communis
castor bean

Viola tricolor
Johnny-jump-up

Roses

Rosa gallica 'Versicolor'
rosa mundi

Rosa 'Great Maiden's Blush'

Rosa palustris
swamp rose

Rosa 'Red Damask'

Rosa rubiginosa
eglantine rose

Rosa 'York and Lancaster'

PLANT LISTS

* Please check for possibility of invasiveness in your locale.

** Plant is from the period but not necessarily listed in extant resources for the region.

Vines

Apios americana
potato bean

Bignonia capreolata
crossvine

Campsis radicans
trumpet creeper

Clematis crispa
American bluebells

Lathyrus latifolius
everlasting pea

Lonicera sempervirens
trumpet honeysuckle

Bulbs

Anemone coronaria
windflower

Fritillaria imperialis
crown imperial

Hyacinthus orientalis
hyacinth

   'Roman Blue'**

Lilium candidum
Madonna lily

Lilium martagon
Turk's cap lily

Lilium superbum
Turk's cap lily

Narcissus
daffodil

'Albus Plenus Odoratus'**
double poet's narcissus

'Campernelle'**

moschatus**
swans-neck daffodil

Polianthes tuberosa 'Flore Pleno'
double tuberose

Sprekelia formosissima
Jacobean lily

Tulipa
tulip

   'Duc van Tol'**

   'Keizerskroon'**

   sylvestris**

Zephyranthes atamasca
rain lily

SOUTHERN

Trees and shrubs

Buxus sempervirens 'Suffruticosa'
dwarf English boxwood

Erica
heath

Magnolia grandiflora
magnolia

Melia azedarach*
chinaberry

Nerium oleander
oleander

Populus nigra 'Italica'
Lombardy poplar

Viburnum tinus
laurustinus

Perennials and biennials

Campanula medium
Canterbury bells

Convallaria majalis
lily-of-the-valley

Dianthus barbatus
sweet William

Erysimum cheiri
wallflower

Iris persica
Persian iris

Primula auricula
primrose

Primula ×polyantha
primrose

Solidago
goldenrod

Annuals

Adonis aestivalis
summer pheasant's eye

Amberboa moschata
sweet sultan

Callistephus chinensis
China aster

Consolida ambigua
larkspur

Impatiens balsamina
balsam

Kochia scoparia*
summer cypress

Matthiola incana
gillyflower

Papaver somniferum
opium poppy

Pelargonium**
geranium

Reseda odorata
sweet mignonette

Scorpiurus vermiculatus
one-flowered caterpillar

Tagetes erecta
African marigold

Tagetes patula
French marigold

Viola tricolor
Johnny-jump-up

Roses

Rosa centifolia
moss rose

Rosa chinensis
China rose

Rosa cinnamomea
cinnamon rose

PAGE 5 OF 5

Rosa 'Maiden's Blush'

Rosa moschata
musk rose

———————————————

Bulbs

Anemone coronaria
windflower

Crocus
crocus

   'Cloth of Gold'**

Hyacinthus orientalis
hyacinth

   'Roman Blue'**

Narcissus
daffodil

   'Albus Plenus Odoratus'**
   double poet's narcissus

   'Campernelle'**

   'Grand Primo'**

   *moschatus***
   swans-neck daffodil

   *pseudonarcissus***
   Lent lily

Nerine sarniensis
Guernsey lily

Polianthes tuberosa
tuberose

Ranunculus asiaticus
Persian buttercup

Tulipa
tulip

   'Duc van Tol'**

   'Keizerskroon'**

   *sylvestris***

3

Landscapes of the Early to Mid-Nineteenth Century (1820–1860)

1800

1823

Botanist David Douglas makes his first visit to Oregon Country; two years later, William Prince, of Flushing, New York, offers *Mahonia aquifolium* (Oregon grape) for an astronomical twenty-five dollars in his nursery's catalog.

1830

First lawn mower patent issued to Edwin Beard Budding in Great Britain. Lawn mower reaches the United States in the 1860s.

1834

Elm leaf beetle arrives in North America. This pest attacks all species of elm (*Ulmus*), weakening the trees and making them vulnerable to disease.

1842

First production of superphosphate fertilizer in Great Britain; it is available in the United States by the 1850s.

1850

1858

Frederick Law Olmsted and Calvert Vaux design New York City's Central Park.

1857

Gregor Mendel, "father of genetics," begins his pea experiment.

1859

Henry Shaw establishes the Missouri Botanical Garden.

1900

Architecture Styles

The early to mid-nineteenth century was a period of growth in the United States. Many portions of the country's transportation infrastructure were then under construction, making the business of building homes and planning and planting landscapes more feasible for many people. Roads had been nothing more than horse trails, but by the 1830s a turnpike system began. Waterways continued to be the most efficient means of transportation: by 1843 an established line of steamships traveled between England and the major ports of Boston, New York, and Philadelphia; canals served the interior. And railroads slowly enmeshed the country; between 1850 and 1860, the distance covered by lines of track increased more than three hundred percent.

Architectural styles looked to the past for inspiration. Federal-style residences continued to be popular in some areas of the country. Greek Revival, Gothic Revival, and Italianate houses dotted the landscape. Vernacular examples of these styles were everywhere; these were houses that combined details of the fashionable architecture or capitalized on the traditions and materials that were available in their own locality, thereby making unique folk structures.

Greek Revival architecture was the most popular style in the United States between 1830 and 1860—so popular, in fact, that it was called the "National Style." Concentrations of this style occur mainly east of the Mississippi River, although the California Gold Rush assured examples as far west as San Francisco. Taking inspiration from the ruins of Greek temples, Greek Revival houses are generally front-gabled (the vertical triangular shape formed by a double sloping roof) and have a porch with classically detailed columns; they are further distinguished by wide, plain frieze boards under the eaves and cornice (Langhart 1999).

Gothic Revival homes were characterized by a steeply pitched roof and windows with a pointed or Gothic arch at the top; usually there was a one-story porch, and the gables often had richly ornamented bargeboards (boards that hang from the end of the roof). Most of these houses

Featured Designer:
Andrew Jackson Downing (1815–1852)

Andrew Jackson Downing.

ANDREW JACKSON DOWNING is generally counted among the most influential designers in U.S. landscape history. He established and edited the periodical *The Horticulturist* and wrote several books for an eager audience of homeowners and gardeners in America, who were just beginning to develop an American perspective on the landscape that obscured lines of class and wealth. Chief among these was *A Treatise on the Theory and Practice of Landscape Gardening, Adapted to North America* (1841), an eloquent argument for artistic landscape design principles based on European precedent. An ardent horticulturist, Downing included recommendations for many plants, emphasizing trees in his designs and commentaries.

were built between 1840 and 1880, in rural rather than urban areas. By contrast, a low-pitched roof with decorative brackets on the eaves was the dominant feature of Italianate houses. These houses have tall narrow windows, often with decorated crowns, and sometimes include a square cupola or tower on the roof. Although many of these houses were constructed in cities, the design inspiration for them came from the informal rural farmhouses of Italy.

Essential Elements of Downing-style Landscapes

- Lawn
- Trees singly and in groups
- Circular or elliptical bed of flowers and/ or shrubs in view of a window
- Large urns and vases
- Kitchen garden screened from view
- Fruit trees, grapes
- Rustic bench
- Vines

Landscape Design

These four decades of the nineteenth century were marked by the continuing development of an American consciousness in landscape gardening. The geometric style could still be found as well as the irregular, more naturalistic English landscape style; often a landscape included elements of both.

Our featured designer, Andrew Jackson Downing, was one of several who sought to Americanize the fashions of European garden-makers. His popular *Treatise* (1841) and *Cottage Residences* (1842), both of which went through several editions, described and illustrated his landscape ideals (and although he claimed to write for both the gentry and the craftsman, his ideals were for the most part too fashionably elaborate for the average worker). Downing's general approach to the landscape distinguished between "the Beautiful" and "the Picturesque" in nature: the Beautiful promoted the gentle side of nature, featuring soft,

Greek Revival.

Gothic Revival.

undulating outlines and harmonious composition, while the Picturesque echoed the power and violence inherent in nature, with irregular outlines and abrupt imagery.

Downing's elaborate two-acre design for a "cottage-villa" illustrates the nineteenth-century attitude toward the residential landscape and many of the features he himself considered essential. For example, Downing always recommended screening the service areas and has done so here by the use of a privet ("prim") hedge enclosing both the vegetable garden at left and the orchard on the right. As an additional camouflage, he adds extensive flower borders encircling the great oval of lawn at the rear, so that the view from the house would be completely ornamental.

Flowerbeds, each recommended to host one genus of flower, dot the landscape; Downing recommended verbenas and petunias, for their showiness and their long bloom time. Roses too might have been planted in these beds. Trees and shrubs combined to form the perimeter boundary and were arranged in more naturalistic style within the landscape composition. The driveways and walking paths are all curvilinear. In the front of the house there is a driveway circle to accommodate carriages in the most efficient manner.

Maintaining a lawn in Downing's time was a time-consuming duty, and this design features quite a large lawn area. Unfortunately, although the lawn mower had been invented in England by this time, it did not become available in the United States until the 1860s.

Frequent mowing is necessary to insure that velvet-like appearance so much admired in English lawns. To perform this operation neatly, the mower must be provided with a scythe the blade of which is very broad, and hung nearly parallel to the surface of the lawn (Downing 1842).

Italianate.

Portions of this design for a "cottage-villa" could serve even today (Downing 1842).

Flower gardens

Flower gardens were of several different types during this period. Squares and circles cut out of the lawn were gaining in a popularity that reached its crescendo during the Victorian period. Sometimes these beds were edged in boxwood, thrift (*Armeria maritima*), or other uniform plants. J. J. Thomas (1848) described a geometric flower garden in the pages of Downing's *The Horticulturist*:

> A practice much admired and becoming prevalent, is the formation of circular and elliptical flower beds in closely shaven turf. . . . Each of these beds is often entirely occupied with a single variety, densely planted, and affording, at the proper season, a truly rich display of flowers. It is believed that an improvement may be made by planting a few different flowers in the same bed, not for promiscuous intermixture or to present strong contrasts, but to exhibit a rich blending of colours, slightly variant, or to place together several plants of similar habit of growth.

Although flowerbeds of this period frequently contained a showy display of annuals or bulbs, Thomas recommended combining perennials like yellow daylilies with oriental poppies, orange daylilies, and a double crimson peony. Another of his planting recommendations was the quartet of gasplant (*Dictamnus albus*), both purple and white, joined with blue baptisia and the yellow and red of Canadian columbine (*Aquilegia canadensis*).

Whatever its size or shape, "neatness should be the prevailing characteristic of a flower-garden, which should be so situated as to form an ornamental appendage to the house; and when circumstances will admit, placed before windows exposed to a southern or south-eastern aspect." The goal was an effect of unity, of "one beautiful whole": "In a small flower-garden, viewed from the windows of the house, this effect is best produced by beds, or borders, formed on the side of each other, and parallel to the windows from whence they are seen" (Breck 1858).

More extensive flower gardens were found on larger estates. Robert Buist (1839) recommended that a large area be enclosed with serpentine walks "as would allow an agreeable view of the flowers when walking for exercise." Buist theorized that "the arrangement of a flower garden is rather a matter for the exercise of fancy, than one calling for the application of refined taste. [A] design should be kept in view that will tend to expand, improve, and beautify the situation." For his choice of plants, Buist called for a good selection of perennials: "They are lasting ornaments; and when judiciously selected, will give yearly gratification. In making a choice, a view should be to have those that flower abundantly, are of free growth, beauty, and continuation of bloom."

Downing (1841) distinguished between two main forms: a flower garden might be either "a place exclusively devoted to the cultivation of flowers" or "an architectural flower-garden." An artistic arrangement of plants, sculpture, urns, and vases, the architectural flower garden complemented the formality and symmetry of the accompanying residence. The urns could remain empty or be filled with stiff vertical plants like *Yucca*, *Agave*, or *Aloe*. Downing specified that boxwood be used to border the beds to give them a uniform appearance and that shrubs and perennials be chosen more for their ornamental foli-

1. **A balustrade fence.**

2. In this design, a low, vine-covered balustrade fence surrounds a formal octagonal flower garden; at the angles of the fence are pedestals for urns or vases (Downing 1842).

3. The front flower garden "of the late Col. Marinus Willett," including shrubs, annuals, perennials, and even some architectural agaves, illustrates a more vernacular approach (*Valentine's Manual* 1854). Emmet Collection, Miriam and Ira D. Wallach Division of Art, Prints and Photographs, The New York Public Library, Astor, Lenox and Tilden Foundations.

2

3

age than for their blooms—a very modern thought! He also spoke of the "French flower garden" as one of intricate design and reputedly installed a fanciful parterre in this style at his own residence in Newburgh, New York. Downing's own flower garden was described as follows:

> A small space laid out in seven circular beds; the center one nearly twice as large as the outer ones: these were all filled with plants: a running rose in the center of the large bed, and the outer edge planted with fine phloxes, Bourbon roses, & c., the other six beds were all filled with similar plants excepting the running rose, which would be of too vigorous growth for their smaller size (Hovey 1841).

Always a popular component of the flower garden, the rose gained even more prominence during this period. Buist (1854), in the introduction to the fourth edition of his book on roses, wrote thus: "We had no anticipation of the popularity it [his book] was to enjoy, neither had we conceived that the germ of rose culture was at that period ready to burst forward in luxuriant grandeur." Roses, whether in the flower garden or in a garden solely of roses, were often featured in landscapes of this era. In particular 'Champney's Pink Cluster', celebrated for its long bloom season, was "universally cultivated" (Buist 1854); clearly it would be a wonderful period addition to the landscape in areas where it is hardy. It and other Noisettes, as this hybrid group is known, remain popular to this day, in zone 6 and above.

Climbing roses had particular landscape value to Downing. One of his recommendations was the 'Queen of the Prairies' rose, a Hybrid Setigera known in the United States before 1843. Lady Banks' rose could be found in white or yellow and grew vigorously in the southern regions of the country. Climbing roses can be used now, as they were then, on pillars, fences, and trelliswork.

The rockery or rock garden

Often an elaborate flower garden would have an area designed for the cultivation of plants among the rocks. Such a feature was termed the rockery. "For a small garden one collection of rocks or stones, with a walk around it, will be sufficient; but when a person has some fancy, a variety of beds or collections may be made with winding walks around them" (Breck 1858).

> In extensive pleasure grounds the rockery has a good effect when placed distinct from the flower garden, and near a rustic arbor, ornamental bridge, or seat; and if placed by the side of a retired walk, near the lawn or grass plot, it has an easy effect. The materials should be rough stones, and good rich earth; the base to be laid with stones, and then a quantity of soil; this method may be pursued until the whole is completed. When finished, it should have, as much as possible a natural appearance and a ridge-like shape (Sayers 1838).

Downing (1841) cautioned against the irresponsible construction of rockeries in areas where they did not blend in with the landscape, reminding his readers that the object of rockwork or a rockery was to produce a scene from nature, using the appropriate setting, rocks, and plants, and not to make "a barbarous mélange, or confused pile of stones mingled with soil, and planted over with dwarfish plants." He advised that by studying rock placement in natural areas, one could learn how to imitate the art. The rockeries of this era would look more primitive and rough than rock gardens of the twentieth century.

Kitchen gardens

Growing fruits and vegetables for the family's table was a universal activity in this epoch. Although the economic practicality cannot be argued, some writers also bestowed on this practice a healthy morality that separated the cultivators from the non-cultivators:

> I consider a good garden not only as contributing largely to the sustenance and health of the family, but as a pretty good indication of the taste, comfort and refinement of its inmates. Nothing is more conducive to health and rational enjoyment than fresh fruits and vegetables, gathered or plucked at maturity from one's own garden (Buel 1837).

The kitchen garden typically was a square or rectangle in the ancient style, enclosed by a fence (the taller, the better) to keep out marauders, both human and other species.

The rockery (Downing 1841).

Pickets often were mentioned; occasionally a writer might suggest a living hedge, perhaps of Osage orange (*Maclura pomifera*) or a vigorous rose, to provide the enclosure. The garden itself might simply be rows of vegetables, or it might have been composed of smaller geometric beds with paths in between and another path encircling the garden; paths were dirt or grass. Vegetables and herbs were grown together. Asparagus and other perennial vegetables usually had their own space or bed; tree or bush fruits often filled the outer perimeter beds.

Fertility was considered—"A farmer's garden should be near the farmyard, for the convenience of the manure" (Hooper 1839)—and the art of making compost was well documented. Gardeners were advised to combine garden soil with surface loam from pastureland, including the turf. These were to be mixed thoroughly with well-rotted animal dung and allowed to sit, exposed to the weather, for several months, the pile being turned every five or six weeks.

Practically speaking, the following advice from *New England Farmer* could be applied to any residential situation with good effect:

> [A] farmer can make a beautiful garden . . . anywhere; among the rocks, upon the steep declivity, he can form a terrace; by the side of the brook, around the pond, or along the borders of the marsh, he can make beautiful flowers spring up. He can plant flowering shrubs, or climbing vines, or fruit-bearing trees. He can form beds of rich vegetables, and borders of roses, or pinks and verbenas. He can arrange them in straight lines, or curved lines. He can form them into parallelograms or squares, into circles or ellipses, into triangles or hexagons, into any form that may please his fancy, or best suit the nature of his ground. He may so arrange the vegetable forms that spring from the soil, and which are beautiful in themselves, and so combine their shade and hues, as to increase and brighten the beauty of the whole. And he can set the picture in a beautiful frame. He can surround his garden with trees—evergreens, forest trees and fruit trees, so arranged as to give shade to those plants that require it and to protect all from the cold winds. By doing a little at a time, by adding one improvement after another, and one beauty after another, every farmer may, in a few years, create a beautiful scene around him that will amply reward all of his pains (Editor 1856b).

Trees and shrubs

According to Downing (1841), the grouping of trees (however large or small their number) for a natural perspective was the main challenge of the landscape gardener:

> [The chief care is] *not* to place them in any regular or artificial manner . . . but so to dispose them, as that the whole may exhibit the variety, connection, and intricacy seen in nature. . . . Trees of medium and smaller size should be so interspersed with those of larger growth, as to break up all formal sweeps in the line produced by the tops of their summits, and occasionally low trees should be planted on the outer edge of the mass, to connect it with the humble verdure of the surrounding sward.

Foundation plantings are historically inappropriate for houses of this era. Whether to keep such plantings or to remove them will be a decision facing many owners of houses built between 1820 and 1860.

Pruning won't do it: for an authentic period landscape, these boxwoods should be removed. West's tavern (1843), Gravel Hill, Virginia.

"Residence of the Hon. Daniel F. Tiemann," with trees arranged for natural effect—and a marked absence of foundation plantings *(Valentine's Manual* 1858). Emmet Collection, Miriam and Ira D. Wallach Division of Art, Prints and Photographs, The New York Public Library, Astor, Lenox and Tilden Foundations.

Landscape Features

Paths and driveways

Writers of this period urged readers to "be content with tasteful simplicity (A. D. G. 1855) and, in that spirit, most agreed that the most appropriate material for walks and driveways was gravel. The gravel must be tamped down with the use of a roller and the grass edgings should be kept neatly cut with an "edging iron." Downing's advice was that gravel should be used for driveways and paths near the house, while grass paths might be utilized elsewhere.

> The best walks are composed of small stones, oyster-shells, coarse gravel, or broken bricks, covered with five or six inches of fine gravel. Ground oyster shells are sometimes used, also granite chips which make fine, hard walks; but these substances are too brilliant for the eye in a sunny-day, and on that account are objectionable. A reddish free-stone color has a better effect (Sayers 1838).

> A gravelled walk is as apparently a work of art as a building, its outline should therefore be accurately defined. It should appear brimfull of gravel; there is nothing disfigures a walk or conveys so meagre an expression as deep raw edgings, looking as if they had been cut with a plough (Saunders 1855).

Regarding the shape of the walkway, common sense prevailed. For a short space, designers recommended a straight line. If there was more room for flourish, then some curves might be incorporated.

> If the distance between the entrance gate and the house be small, you must be content with a straight walk from the one to the other; but this should be relieved, and its necessary stiffness somewhat modified, by curved side-walks, branching from the main walk near the front door, and running back to the vegetable garden in the rear of the house. Where the space is a little greater, the straight walk should not be tolerated. It may be curved in various ways, as taste may suggest (Wells 1858).

A farm cottage with curved pathways (Editor 1856b).

Fences and hedges

Board fences were not the most decorative of fences, but they functioned as enclosures very ably. In fact, many writers of the era invoked rustic design as a way to transition smoothly from nature to the man-made landscape. Drawings of rustic fences (and furniture) occupied the pages of the fashionable gardening periodicals; rustic fencing made of cedar in particular lent a "wild character" to those areas not immediately adjacent to the house, and such fences continue to be created and used to this day.

Where stones were plentiful in the agricultural fields, as in the Northeast, they were used to set boundaries or make an enclosure:

> In making stone fences, the stones should be of good size, and so broken as to bind well; be well put up,

Rustic fence (*The Horticulturist* 1853).

"A picturesque gate" at Wodenethe, the residence of H. W. Sargent, Esq. (*The Horticulturist* 1856).

Iron and masonry sets off the front yard, but a stone fence marks the property line. Residence of E. Powers, Phillipston, Pennsylvania, c. 1860. Robert N. Dennis Collection of Stereoscopic Views, Miriam and Ira D. Wallach Division of Art, Prints and Photographs, The New York Public Library, Astor, Lenox and Tilden Foundations.

Vine creeping up the façade of an 1851 brick
house, heavily shaded by trees.

Board fence at a Greek Revival house,
location unknown, c. 1855.

pinned with care, and have a dry and deep foundation, to guard against the effects of frost. They should be wide at the bottom, and tapering upwards, and securely tapped at top. Where the stones are handy to haul, a fence of this kind will not cost a great deal more than a worm fence (Hooper 1839).

Hedges became more frequent and were often a topic of discussion, among agricultural writers especially. Constructed of shrubs and small trees, these made perfect enclosures when wood and/or stone was in short supply, providing beauty, protection, and screening in residential landscape settings as well as being useful for delineating larger agricultural landscapes. John Warder (1858) of Cincinnati, Ohio, was an avid hedge-maker; he recommended rose of Sharon (*Hibiscus syriacus*) for "one of the quickest and most effective screens [for it] strikes readily from cuttings, grows rapidly, and furnishes a succession of variously

colored flowers during the mid-summer, when few shrubs are in bloom." As for trees, Warder singled out beeches, birches, and hornbeams (*Carpinus*) for mention, "all notable for the exceeding beauty and feathery lightness of their foliage." Other favorite hedging plants were barberry (*Berberis*), privet (*Ligustrum*), mock orange (*Philadelphus coronarius*), lilac (*Syringa vulgaris*), and roses (in the case of roses, a wire trellis was added to provide support); boxwood (*Buxus sempervirens*) was not hardy enough to be used in the North but was ubiquitous in many southern landscapes of the period.

1. Advertisement for hedge makers (Warder 1858).

2. An ornamental gate in the Gothic style (Thomas 1858).

3. Picket fences were popular from coast to coast. Residence, perhaps Lansing, Michigan, c. 1860.

4. Double-flowered varieties of rose of Sharon, a favorite hedge plant, were known in American gardens since 1800. Weltz Nursery, Wilmington, Ohio, c. 1900.

5. Ornamental hedges at the home of Nicholas William Stuyvesant, New York (*Valentine's Manual* 1857). Picture Collection, The New York Public Library, Astor, Lenox and Tilden Foundations.

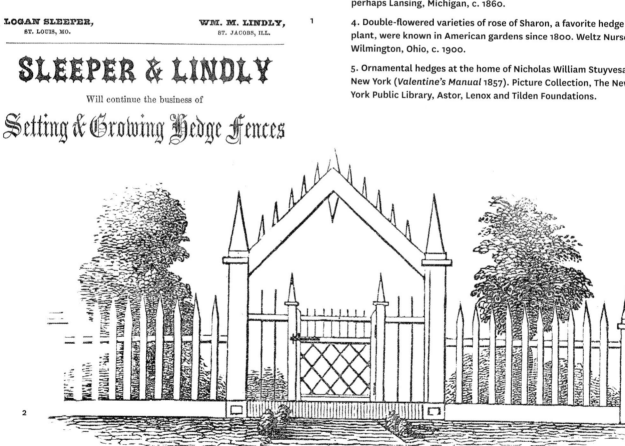

LOGAN SLEEPER,
ST. LOUIS, MO.

WM. M. LINDLY,
ST. JACOBS, ILL.

1

SLEEPER & LINDLY

Will continue the business of

Setting & Growing Hedge Fences

2

3

4

THE RESIDENCE of N.W. STUYVESANT,
which formerly stood in 8th Street, between 1st & 2d Avenues.

5

Seeting

Benches, chairs, and settees in the mid-nineteenth century
might have been of several types, including ironwork and
rustic style. Wrought iron had some advantages over cast
iron; it was "less liable to be broken," yet it was lighter than
cast iron and therefore "much more easily moved from
place to place" (Barry 1853). Seating in the rustic style
was often a do-it-yourself affair: "In a retired part of the
garden a rustic seat may be formed, over and around which
honeysuckles, and other sweet and ornamental creepers
and climbers, may be trained on trellises, so as to afford a
pleasant retirement" (Breck 1858). Indeed, every landscape
setting, of any era, needs appropriate seating in order for
the gardener and visitors to take time to "smell the roses."

1. A wrought iron tree bench in four parts, "adapted to be fixed
under the shade of a tree" (Barry 1853).

2. Rustic table (Thomas 1858).

3. Another tree bench, this time of wood (Thomas 1858).

4. A wrought iron bench, "greatly admired for its elegant
appearance and the comfort and ease of its seat" (Barry 1853).

1

2

3

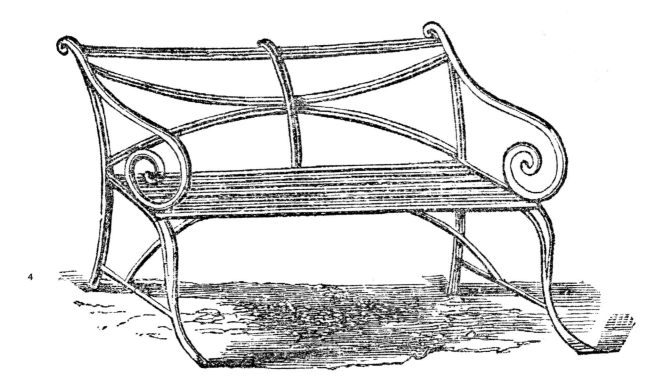

4

Garden accessories

In brief, the use of trellises prevailed, as vines were common plants for adornment of houses, gardens, and even, as we just read, rustic retreats.

> Vines are never planted by architects, masons, carpenters or those who build a cottage, but always by those that live in it, and make it truly a home, and generally by the mother or daughter, whose very planting of vines is a labor of love offered up on the domestic altar. [It follows] that vines on a rural cottage always expresses domesticity and the presence of heart (Downing 1850b).

Supports for cypress vine and other climbers that would not completely cover the trellis were themselves designed to be ornamental, "to add to the appearance" (Thomas 1858). Writers described various other types of support, including using a pillar of cedar with holes bored through it at regular intervals for the vine to pass through; an adaptation of such a pillar called for wooden rods to be driven through the holes to guide the vine. But with such contraptions came the first injunctions against a neighbor's choices and gentle, general calls for simplicity:

> As in all other matters requiring taste, we often see great errors made in the introduction of garden ornaments. How common is it to see elaborate carpenter-work, painted a brilliant green or dazzling white painful to look upon, supporting a slender climber, when a simple cedar pole with perhaps a few wires would have been a much cheaper and better support. . . . As a general thing, simple rustic work made of the limbs of trees with the bark on, worked into simple and appropriate designs, is the most appropriate, though we have observed some pretty designs in iron (Barry 1853).

Whether of cast iron, plaster, or Roman cement, vases and urns continued to play a part in gardens, formal and informal. Downing (1842) reminded his readers that "all vases, urns, or other sculptured ornaments for gardens or grounds, should be placed on proper pedestals."

1

2

3

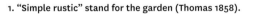

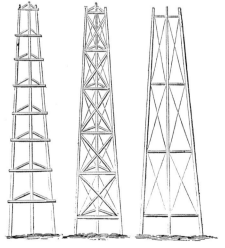

1. "Simple rustic" stand for the garden (Thomas 1858).

2. Rustic pedestal and matching pot (Thomas 1858).

3. "A covered arbour like this is agreeable at all seasons of the year, when a walk in the garden is sought after" (An Amateur 1850).

4. Ornamental trellises (Thomas 1858).

4

Case Studies

Obviously architecture and garden styles vary geographically as well as chronologically so, for this period, we decided to include a discussion of three approaches to landscape design in three discrete locations: co-author Laura Burchfield's own Federal farmhouse in Ohio, an urban New Orleans Creole cottage, and a Georgia farmhouse with some distinctive Greek Revival features.

1842 Federal farmhouse, Circleville, Ohio

The architecture of the Burchfield residence combines elements of the Federal style with later Italianate details. It was built in 1842 by a man who reputedly modeled it on his grandfather's house back in Virginia. Ownership of the property changed several times since; it was vacant for many years in the twentieth century, and a fire destroyed most of the structure in 2000. But Laura and her husband, Jim, have painstakingly restored it to its original appearance. It stands on 192 acres, of which about ten are used by the family for their daily activities.

Owners Jim and Laura Burchfield wanted their home to have a "country estate" feeling, with details evoking the elegance and prosperity of the past; and since our featured designer Downing's books were so influential during the early development of this property, his precepts were taken as the primary guide in their approach to their rural landscape. Downing (1841) extolled the virtues of the *ferme ornée*, or ornamental farm, calling it "a pretty mode of combining something of the beauty of the landscape garden with the utility of the farm"; and again, "[The] cardinal points within the bounds of a country residence are (taking health and pleasant locality for granted,) convenience, comfort—or social enjoyment—and beauty." Fortunately the existing driveway, which curved and flirted with views of the house along its .9 mile length, was in line with his recommendation: "The Beautiful in Landscape Gardening . . . is produced [in] walks and roads, by easy flowing curves, following natural shapes of the surface, with no sharp angles or abrupt turns" (Downing 1841). A brick walkway, discovered underground around the house, had already been restored.

The lawn continues to be a starting point for many property owners in the twenty-first century, and Downing (1846) provided guidance in that department as well, although his ideal lawn would have been maintained with scythe and animals during his era.

> [With] a *lawn, and large and massive trees, one has indeed the most enduring sources of beauty in a country residence.* Perpetual neatness, freshness and verdure in the one; ever expanding beauty, variety and grandeur in the other—what more does a reasonable man desire of the beautiful around him in the country? Must we add flowers, exotic plants, fruits? Perhaps so, but they are all, in an ornamental light, secondary to trees and grass, where these can be had to perfection.

Speaking of the primary attribute of trees, a site inventory revealed an old Norway maple hybrid on the northwest side of the Burchfields' house and several ancient hackberries. Specimen trees in the new design include tulip tree (*Liriodendron tulipifera*) and a *Magnolia grandiflora*, thoughtfully placed near the house for protection from the cold Ohio winter. As for "social enjoyment," Jim and Laura entertain frequently, and so an outdoor stone dining terrace was constructed along the length of the house on the north side; a balustrade wall and symmetrical placement of urns in a built landscape helps convey a sense of the past.

Vegetables and fruits for the table are ably produced in the designed kitchen garden, which is entered on the east by a gate covered with an arbor planted with climbing roses and clematis. In the center is a sundial surrounded by a circle of brick planted in thyme. The four central beds are planted with vegetables that must be rotated annually; the outer beds, along the picket fence, are planted with herbs and longer-lasting crops, such as asparagus. On the west side is another gate that leads out, through a small pergola planted with grapes, to the orchard; rustic benches under the pergola provide a relaxing place in the summer and fall. Small fruits are planted along the outside west fence, gooseberries and currants with a groundcover of strawberries.

An artificial waterfall that cascades gently down the side of a small hill to the north of the house follows the advice of Downing (1841): "[In] no way is the peculiar stillness of the air, peculiar to the country, more pleasingly broken, than by the melody of falling water." Downing went on in his *Treatise* to describe the construction of a waterfall. His most pointed advice was that the resulting fall should look absolutely natural in its surroundings by the use of strategically placed rocks: "The simplest or most monotonous view may be enlivened by the presence of water in any considerable quantity; and the most picturesque and striking landscape will, by its addition, receive a new charm, inexpressibly enhancing all its former interest." The Burchfield water feature consists of an upper pond, with lilacs for a backdrop, and a lower pond, with a small stream running between them. The stream is a rubber liner, and rocks from the property, primarily fieldstones in various sizes, line the bottom, arranged in such a way that they create ripples and pooling areas along

its path. The water recirculates through two-inch buried PVC tubing from a recirculating pump placed in the lower pond. So although this feature *looks* historically correct, it was constructed using modern technology.

Finally, Laura wished to have an ornamental flowering display in front of the house. The rose was an important flower for this era (as it had been before and would continue to be into the future), so the front yard features a rose border. The roses will provide color and fragrance for the summer season, and the beds are in view of the front windows, as is appropriate for the period. Many times it is the plants in the landscape as much as the structure and layout of the property that help to fix it concretely within a certain time period and frame of reference. The smell of old-fashioned roses offers that benefit to many gardens in heirloom landscapes.

1. Kitchen garden beds.

2. Kitchen garden with sundial and vine-covered arbor.

3. New Orleans residence.

4. "There are many quiet, snug little gardens and delicious retreats, scattered here and there, through [New Orleans] and its suburbs, giving a little variety to the ungainly masses of brick and mortar" (Sylvanus 1851). Carl Axtel Hedin, Plan Book 25, Folio 20 (025.20), 20 November 1849. Clerk of Civil District Court, Notarial Archives Division, New Orleans, Louisiana.

1

2

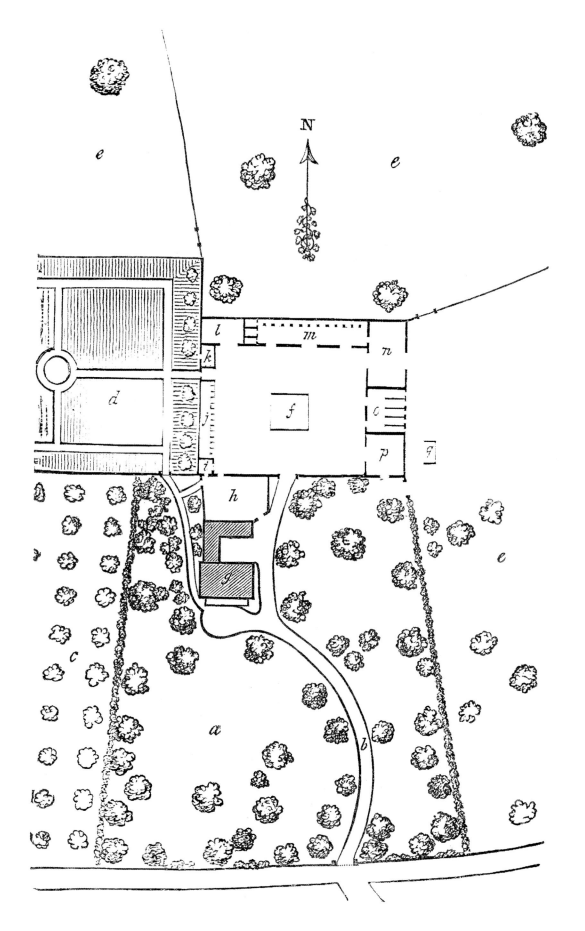

1. Virginia creeper (*Parthenocissus quinquefolia*) covers the south face of the Burchfield residence, anchoring it to the landscape and providing cooling insulation in the summer; it is also kinder to old brick and mortar than English ivy (*Hedera helix*).

2. The property is composed primarily of cultivated farm fields, which make for lovely seasonally shifting views.

3. Kitchen garden detail, showing main axil paths of reclaimed brick and secondary paths of red crushed gravel.

4. Burchfield master plan.

5. *Ferme ornée* (Downing 1841).

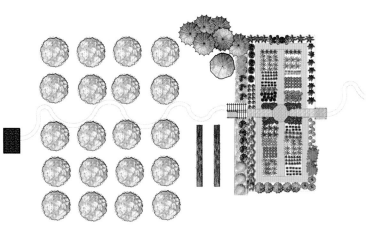

3

4

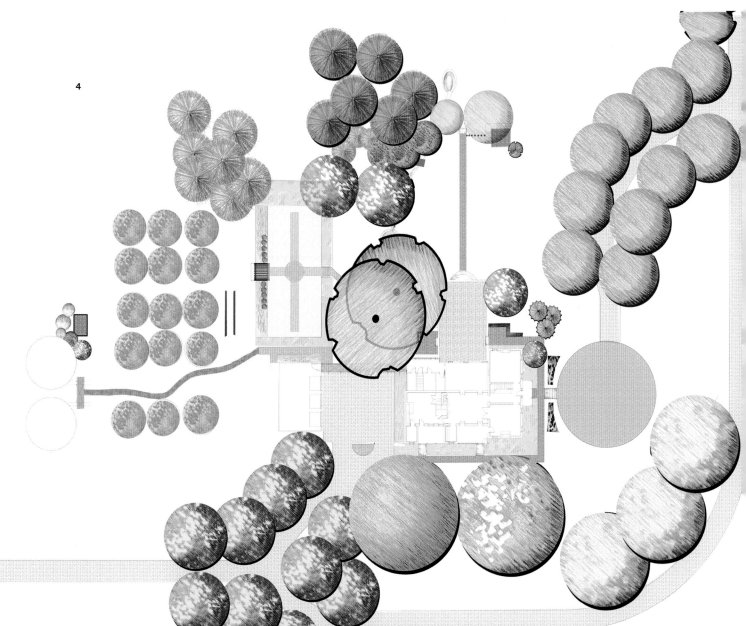

Circa 1850 Creole cottage, New Orleans

Our next case study is located in the Garden District of New Orleans, an area characterized by houses of several different architectural types, including Greek Revival and Italianate. The historical influences typically came from the northeastern seaboard of the United States; but this particular property more closely resembles those in the neighboring French Quarter, with its pervasive French flavor. It features a back courtyard with a geometric design, as opposed to having an expanded lawn like many of its neighbors.

It was the custom when selling a property in nineteenth-century New Orleans to supply a colored illustration of the house and grounds in the real estate ad. Many of these excellent period images survive in the collection of the New Orleans Notarial Archives, providing valuable insight into landscape trends during this period. In the era of the cottage's construction, a traveler described a nearby garden:

3

> Great numbers of tree-like oleanders, eugenias, jasmines, pomegranates, and myrtles, with their dark, somber foliage, gave a stateliness and grandeur to the scenery, while their blossoms spread a delicious fragrance around, and their branches afford shelter to the mocking-bird (Paulsen 1846).

In the late 1980s, David and Lynn Adams completely renovated the landscaping of their 30 × 40.5 ft. courtyard. The flowerbeds, fountain, and herringbone brick paving remained for the desired effect, but many of the original plantings had either disappeared in the intervening years or become overgrown; other writers have noted how quickly the vegetation in New Orleans grows and how rapidly shade is produced, which, of course, is a bonus for this hot, tropical environment.

The owners asked the designers to provide a new planting plan featuring period flowers that would withstand the challenges of the summer heat and also thrive in the shade now provided by mature trees. Startling focal points from the early days of this garden were retained: the two enormous, mature light pink-flowered crepe myrtles (*Lagerstroemia indica*) that flanked the back wall, rising to

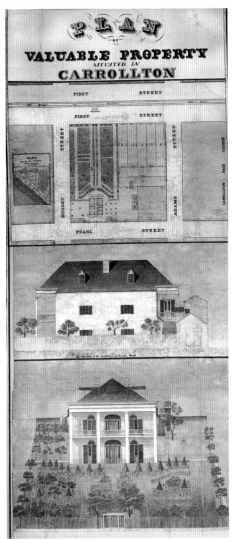

4

a height of approximately fifty feet. Another area of focus in the design was the water feature: the plantings needed to draw the eye to the fountain and at the same time camouflage the modern plastic lining of the water basin. Fragrance is a frequently described attribute of nineteenth-century New Orleans landscapes, so care was also taken to provide delicious aromas that would contribute to the sensual aspect of this enclosed space. The planting plan featured heavily scented plants like *Gardenia jasminoides* (Cape jasmine) and *Osmanthus fragrans* (tea olive); and three specimens of a period shrub, *Rhododendron indicum* (Chinese azalea), were added at each side of the water feature.

Essential Elements of Mid-1800s New Orleans Landscapes

· Enclosure
· Geometric bed shapes
· Water feature
· Mature trees
· Fragrant plants

1

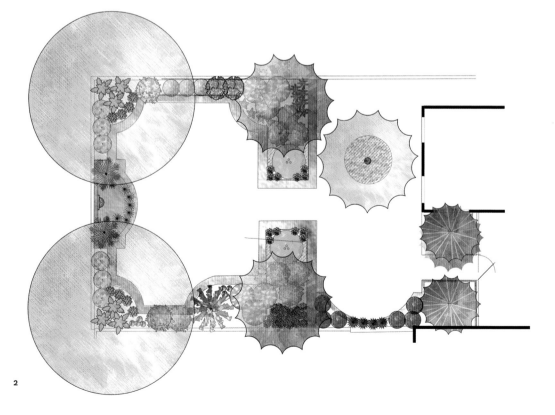

2

3

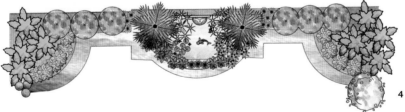

4

1. Enormous crepe myrtles anchor the courtyard plantings.

2. Design for a New Orleans courtyard garden.

3. Typically New Orleans: this "snug little garden" has a water feature and a regional calling card: iron seating.

4. Planting plan for fountain area.

1818 Greek Revival farmhouse, Eatonton, Georgia

The Greek Revival style of architecture that was prevalent in the antebellum South and other sections of the country is frequently associated with the nineteenth century. Though elsewhere, the loose imitation of nature was increasingly in vogue, the antebellum Greek Revival plantation homes of the southern states continued most often to be surrounded by stately formal gardens designed in the ancient style. A common landscape feature of many of these homes was an elaborate rectangular boxwood garden, with geometric beds crisply edged by dwarf English boxwood (*Buxus sempervirens* 'Suffruticosa'). The centers of these beds were planted with flowering shrubs, lilies, bulbs such as hyacinths, or annuals. Crepe myrtles, southern magnolias, or eastern red cedars often provided vertical interest. The formal gardens were adjacent to the residence; more naturalistic plantings would be installed at a greater distance from the house.

Outbuilding (c. 1850), Eatonton, Georgia.

Hitchcock-Garner residence.

Jim designed this picket fence to harmonize with the house and the site.

Old roses cloak a picket fence that encloses the traditional kitchen garden.

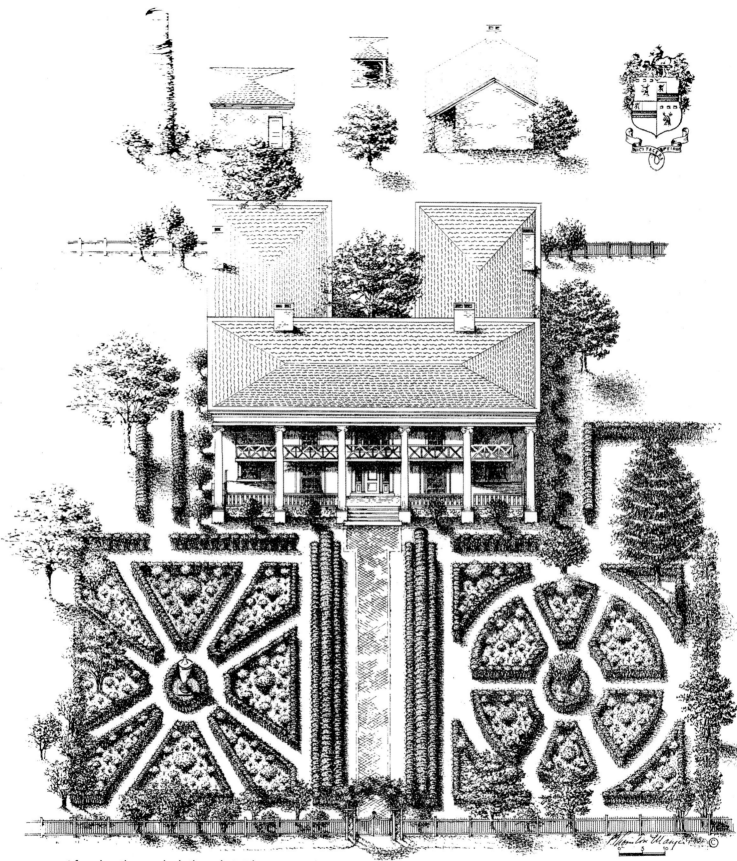

A formal southern garden in the ancient style
(*Garden History of Georgia* 1933).

Old brick pathway.

Garden History of Georgia (1933) gives a description of a garden at Valley View in Bartow County as it is thought to have appeared between 1848 and 1863. Hedges of *Prunus caroliniana* (Carolina laurel cherry) and boxwood lined the central walk, while dwarf boxwood lined the borders. Roses, lilies, narcissus, and violets brought fragrance to the garden, and locusts and cedars provided architectural structure, containment, and shade.

When Susan Hitchcock and Jim Garner purchased their c. 1818 antebellum house in Eatonton, both the house and the gardens were in need of major renovation. The site inventory revealed several plants thought to be original to the property, including boxwood, Japanese rose (*Kerria japonica*), camellias, crepe myrtle, and old-fashioned petunias. A large area adjacent to the house was the home of many spring-flowering bulbs that also might have bloomed in the early years of the residence. A shed on the property is thought to date to the 1850s.

To give a period "feel" to the landscape, the owners settled upon a simple, heirloom-plant-focused approach. They decided not to install a formal geometric garden, such as might have existed for such a house in Middle Georgia; a naturalistic garden would best fit their lifestyle. But they also wanted to emphasize the timelessness of the garden. With this in mind, they used brick from an old chimney to make weathered-looking pathways and incorporated rocks found on the property to outline some of the flowerbeds. Flowering shrubs and perennials abound at this site, many from the period of the construction of the house.

Jim, a horticulturist, and Susan, a historic landscape preservation specialist, may be trusted to suggest some favorite period plants for a Middle Georgia garden in the mid-1800s: heirloom roses, daffodils, *Iris albicans*, boxwood (both dwarf and American), Deodar cedar, *Magnolia grandiflora*, gardenias, camellias, tea olive (*Osmanthus*), banana shrub (*Michelia figo*), crepe myrtle, snowball (*Viburnum opulus* 'Roseum' or *V. macrocephalum*), hydrangeas, petunias, daylilies (*Hemerocallis*), and four o'clock (*Mirabilis jalapa*).

The heirloom rose 'Zéphirine Drouhin' scents the air in the Hitchcock-Garner kitchen garden.

PLANT LISTS

* Please check for possibility of invasiveness in your locale.

** Plant is from the period but not necessarily listed in extant resources for the region.

NEW ENGLAND

Trees

Abies balsamea
balsam fir

Acer rubrum
red maple

Aesculus hippocastanum
horse chestnut

Catalpa speciosa
northern catalpa

Cercis canadensis
redbud

Cladrastis kentukea
yellowwood

Fagus sylvatica
European beech

Gymnocladus dioicus
Kentucky coffee tree

Picea abies
Norway spruce

Salix babylonica
weeping willow

Shrubs

Aesculus parviflora
bottlebrush buckeye

Calycanthus floridus
Carolina allspice

Chionanthus virginicus
fringe tree

Clethra alnifolia
summersweet

Hydrangea quercifolia
oakleaf hydrangea

Kalmia latifolia
mountain laurel

Symphoricarpos albus
snowberry

Syringa laciniata
fringe-leaf lilac

Syringa ×persica
Persian lilac

Viburnum trilobum
cranberrybush

Perennials and biennials

Aconitum napellus
aconite

Baptisia australis
false indigo

Belamcanda chinensis
blackberry lily

Campanula pyramidalis
chimney bellflower

Centranthus ruber
Jupiter's beard

Dianthus superbus
superb pink

Echinacea purpurea
purple coneflower

Liatris scariosa
blazing star

Linum perenne
flax

Lupinus polyphyllus
bigleaf lupine

Monarda didyma
beebalm

Papaver orientale
oriental poppy

Physostegia virginiana
false dragonhead

Rudbeckia hirta
black-eyed Susan

Viola odorata
sweet violet

Annuals

Ageratum houstonianum
flossflower

Amaranthus caudatus
love-lies-bleeding

Ammobium alatum
winged everlasting

Callistephus chinensis
China aster

Centaurea cyanus
bachelor's buttons

Cleome hassleriana
spider flower

Consolida ambigua
larkspur

Dianthus chinensis
China pink

Viola grandiflora
pansy

Viola tricolor
Johnny-jump-up

Roses

Rosa banksiae
Lady Banks' rose

Rosa glauca
red-leaved rose

Rosa 'Maiden's Blush'

Rosa 'Quatre Saisons'
four seasons rose

Rosa 'York and Lancaster'

Vines

Apios americana
potato bean

Campsis radicans
trumpet flower

Lonicera sempervirens
trumpet honeysuckle

Wisteria frutescens
American wisteria

Bulbs

Dahlia atropurpurea
species dahlia

PLANTLISTS

* Please check for possibility of invasiveness in your locale.

** Plant is from the period but not necessarily listed in extant resources for the region.

Fritillaria imperialis
crown imperial

Hyacinthus orientalis
hyacinth

Lilium lancifolium
tiger lily

Narcissus
daffodil

　'Orange Phoenix'

　poeticus
　pheasant's eye

Tulipa
tulip

　'Couleur Cardinal'**

MIDDLE ATLANTIC

Trees

Abies balsamea
balsam fir

Acer rubrum
red maple

Aesculus hippocastanum
horse chestnut

Catalpa bignonioides
Indian bean

Cornus florida
dogwood

Gleditsia triacanthos
honey locust

Gymnocladus dioicus
Kentucky coffee tree

Ilex aquifolium
English holly

Juniperus virginiana
eastern red cedar

Koelreuteria paniculata
golden rain tree

Liriodendron tulipifera
tulip tree

Magnolia macrophylla
large-leaved magnolia

Pinus strobus
white pine

Populus nigra 'Italica'
Lombardy poplar

Ptelea trifoliata
hop tree

Robinia pseudoacacia
black locust

Salix babylonica
weeping willow

Sorbus aucuparia
European mountain ash

Thuja occidentalis
arborvitae

Tilia platyphyllos
European linden

Tsuga canadensis
hemlock

Ulmus glabra
Scotch elm

Shrubs

Aesculus parviflora
bottlebrush buckeye

Amorpha fruticosa
wild indigo

Calycanthus floridus
Carolina allspice

Chionanthus virginicus
fringe tree

Cotinus coggygria
purple smoke tree

Daphne mezereum
February daphne

Halesia tetraptera
silver bell

Hibiscus syriacus
rose of Sharon

Hydrangea quercifolia
oakleaf hydrangea

Kerria japonica 'Pleniflora'
double-flowered Japanese rose

Laburnum anagyroides
golden chain

Magnolia virginiana
sweet bay magnolia

Mahonia aquifolium
Oregon grape

Philadelphus coronarius
mock orange

Syringa ×persica
Persian lilac

Syringa vulgaris
lilac

Viburnum opulus 'Roseum'
snowball

Perennials and biennials

Alcea rosea
hollyhock

Armeria maritima
thrift

Baptisia australis
false indigo

Convallaria majalis
lily-of-the-valley

Delphinium elatum
bee larkspur

Dodecatheon meadia
shooting star

Filipendula ulmaria
meadowsweet

Hemerocallis lilioasphodelus
lemon lily

Hibiscus laevis
halberdleaf rosemallow

Iris germanica 'Florentina'
Florentine iris

Iris pallida
Dalmatian iris

Linum perenne
flax

Lychnis coronaria
rose campion

Paeonia 'Festiva Maxima'
peony

Phlox paniculata
perennial phlox

Physostegia virginiana
false dragonhead

Primula auricula
primrose

Senna marilandica
Maryland cassia

Tanacetum parthenium 'Flore Pleno'
double feverfew

Annuals

Dianthus chinensis
China pink

Helianthus annuus
sunflower

*Ipomoea coccinea**
morning glory

Myosotis arvensis
forget-me-not

Reseda odorata
sweet mignonette

Tagetes lucida
Mexican marigold

Viola grandiflora
pansy

Viola tricolor
Johnny-jump-up

Roses

Rosa 'Charles de Mills'

Rosa gallica 'Versicolor'
rosa mundi

Rosa 'Great Maiden's Blush'

Rosa rubiginosa
eglantine rose

Rosa 'Tuscany'

Vines

Apios americana
potato bean

Aristolochia macrophylla
Dutchman's pipe

Campsis radicans
trumpet creeper

Lonicera sempervirens
trumpet honeysuckle

Passiflora lutea
yellow passion vine

Wisteria frutescens
American wisteria

Bulbs

Allium moly
yellow garlic

Anemone coronaria
windflower

Crocus 'Cloth of Gold'**
crocus

Fritillaria imperialis
crown imperial

Hyacinthus orientalis 'Marie'
hyacinth

Lilium superbum
Turk's cap lily

Narcissus
daffodil

　'Albus Plenus Odoratus'
　double poet's narcissus

　bulbocodium
　hoop petticoat daffodil

　jonquilla
　jonquil

　'Orange Phoenix'

Tulipa
tulip

　'Couleur Cardinal'**

　'General Ney'**

　'Mabel'**

SOUTHERN

Trees

Cedrus deodora
Deodar cedar

Cedrus libani
cedar of Lebanon

Cupressus funebris
weeping cypress

Ginkgo biloba
maidenhair tree

Juniperus communis 'Hibernica'
Irish juniper

Juniperus communis 'Suecica'
Swedish juniper

Juniperus sabina
savin

Laurus nobilis
sweet bay

Magnolia denudata
Yulan magnolia

Magnolia grandiflora
southern magnolia

Magnolia macrophylla
large-leaved magnolia

Paulownia imperialis
empress tree

Photinia serrulata
evergreen photinia

Platycladus orientalis
Chinese arborvitae

Taxodium distichum
bald cypress

Taxus baccata 'Fastigiata'
Irish yew

Thuja occidentalis
arborvitae

Shrubs

Buxus sempervirens
boxwood

PAGE 4 OF 7

* Please check for possibility of invasiveness in your locale.

** Plant is from the period but not necessarily listed in extant resources for the region.

Camellia japonica
camellia

Euonymus japonicus
Japanese spindle tree

Gardenia jasminoides
Cape jasmine

Hibiscus rosa-sinensis
Chinese hibiscus

Jasminum
jasmine

Kerria japonica
Japanese rose

Michelia figo
banana shrub

Myrtus communis
sweet myrtle

Nerium oleander
oleander

Osmanthus fragrans
tea olive

Philadelphus coronarius
mock orange

Prunus laurocerasus
cherry laurel

Punica granatum
pomegranate

Spiraea cantoniensis
double white bridal wreath

Spiraea prunifolia
bridal wreath

Viburnum tinus
laurustinus

Weigela florida
weigela

Perennials and biennials

Alcea rosea
hollyhock

Antirrhinum majus
snapdragon

Aquilegia vulgaris
columbine

Belamcanda chinensis
blackberry lily

Chrysanthemum
winter pink

Dianthus barbatus
sweet William

Dianthus deltoides
maiden pink

Dianthus plumarius
grass pink

Digitalis purpurea
foxglove

Erysimum cheiri
wallflower

Linum perenne
flax

Lychnis chalcedonica
Maltese cross

Pelargonium
geranium

Phlox paniculata
perennial phlox

Senna marilandica
Maryland cassia

Viola odorata
sweet violet

Annuals

Amaranthus tricolor
Joseph's coat

Calendula officinalis
pot marigold

Callistephus chinensis
China aster

Celosia argentea var. *cristata*
crested cockscomb

Consolida ambigua
larkspur

Dianthus chinensis
China pink

Impatiens balsamina
balsam

Mirabilis jalapa
four o'clock

Papaver somniferum
opium poppy

Tagetes erecta
African marigold

Tagetes patula
French marigold

Verbena ×hybrida
verbena

Roses

Rosa 'Archiduc Charles'

Rosa 'Baltimore Belle'

Rosa 'Bon Silene'

Rosa 'Bougère'

Rosa 'Champney's Pink Cluster'

Vines

Campsis grandiflora
trumpet creeper

Ipomoea quamoclit*
cypress vine

Lablab purpureus
hyacinth bean

Lonicera periclymenum 'Belgica'
monthly honeysuckle

Momordica balsamina
balsam apple

Wisteria sinensis*
Chinese wisteria

Bulbs

Canna indica
Indian shot

Crinum
swamp lily

Hippeastrum
amaryllis

Hyacinthus orientalis 'Marie'
hyacinth

Lilium candidum
Madonna lily

Narcissus jonquilla
jonquil

Narcissus poeticus
pheasant's eye

Narcissus pseudonarcissus
Lent lily

Zantedeschia aethiopica
calla lily

GREAT LAKES

Trees

Abies balsamea
balsam fir

Acer saccharinum
silver maple

Aesculus glabra
Ohio buckeye

Catalpa speciosa
northern catalpa

Cercis canadensis
redbud

Diospyros virginiana
persimmon

Magnolia acuminata
cucumber tree

Populus alba
white poplar

Robinia pseudoacacia
black locust

Salix babylonica
weeping willow

'Crispa'

Sorbus aucuparia
European mountain ash

Shrubs

Cotinus coggygria
purple smoke tree

Hibiscus syriacus
rose of Sharon

Kerria japonica 'Pleniflora'
double-flowered Japanese rose

*Ligustrum vulgare**
privet

Philadelphus coronarius
mock orange

Symphoricarpos albus
snowberry

Symphoricarpos orbiculatus
Indian currant

Syringa vulgaris
lilac

Viburnum opulus 'Roseum'
snowball

Perennials and biennials

Alcea rosea
hollyhock

Antirrhinum majus
snapdragon

Aquilegia canadensis
Canadian columbine

Campanula medium
Canterbury bells

Convallaria majalis
lily-of-the-valley

Delphinium elatum
bee larkspur

Dianthus plumarius
grass pink

Dictamnus albus
gasplant

Digitalis grandiflora
great-flowered foxglove

Echinacea purpurea
purple coneflower

Filipendula ulmaria
meadowsweet

Hosta plantaginea
plantain lily

Lobelia cardinalis
cardinal flower

Lupinus polyphyllus
bigleaf lupine

Lychnis chalcedonica
Maltese cross

Lychnis coronaria
rose campion

Paeonia 'Festiva Maxima'
peony

Paeonia suffruticosa
tree peony

Papaver orientale
oriental poppy

Phlox paniculata
perennial phlox

Phlox subulata
moss phlox

Tanacetum parthenium
feverfew

Annuals

Dianthus chinensis
China pink

Salvia splendens
scarlet sage

Verbena ×hybrida
verbena

Viola grandiflora
pansy

Viola tricolor
Johnny-jump-up

Roses

Rosa 'Baltimore Belle'

Rosa 'Champney's Pink Cluster'

Rosa 'Harison's Yellow'

PLANT LISTS

* Please check for possibility of invasiveness in your locale.

** Plant is from the period but not necessarily listed in extant resources for the region.

Rosa 'Hermosa'

Rosa 'Lamarque'

Vines

Campis radicans
trumpet creeper

Lathyrus latifolius
everlasting pea

Lonicera sempervirens
trumpet honeysuckle

Parthenocissus quinquefolia
Virginia creeper

Wisteria sinensis*
Chinese wisteria

Bulbs

Fritillaria imperialis
crown imperial

Gladiolus communis subsp. *byzantinus*
cornflag

Hyacinthus orientalis 'Marie'
hyacinth

Lilium lancifolium
tiger lily

Narcissus bulbocodium
hoop petticoat daffodil

Polianthes tuberosa
tuberose

Tulipa
tulip

'Couleur Cardinal'**

'General Ney'**

'Mabel'**

CENTRAL STATES & GREAT PLAINS

Trees

Abies balsamea
balsam fir

Aralia spinosa
Hercules' club

Catalpa speciosa
northern catalpa

Juniperus virginiana
eastern red cedar

Maclura pomifera
Osage orange

Pinus rigida
pitch pine

Pinus strobus
white pine

Populus alba
white poplar

Salix babylonica
weeping willow

Sorbus americana
American mountain ash

Thuja occidentalis
arborvitae

Shrubs

Calycanthus floridus
Carolina allspice

Chaenomeles speciosa
Japanese quince

Cotinus coggygria
purple smoke tree

Hibiscus syriacus
rose of Sharon

Ligustrum vulgare*
privet

Morella cerifera
wax myrtle

Prunus dulcis
sweet almond

Robinia hispida
rose acacia

Syringa vulgaris
lilac

Viburnum opulus 'Roseum'
snowball

Perennials and biennials

Achillea millefolium
yarrow

Achillea ptarmica
sneezewort

Antirrhinum majus
snapdragon

Belamcanda chinensis
blackberry lily

Filipendula ulmaria
meadowsweet

Hemerocallis lilioasphodelus
lemon lily

Hosta plantaginea
plantain lily

Lychnis chalcedonica
Maltese cross

Paeonia 'Festiva Maxima'
peony

Phlox paniculata
perennial phlox

Platycodon grandiflorus
balloon flower

Tanacetum parthenium
feverfew

Yucca filamentosa
Adam's needle

Annuals

Catharanthus roseus
Madagascar periwinkle

Cuphea ignea
cigar plant

Heliotropium arborescens
cherry pie

Lantana camara
lantana

Pelargonium graveolens
rose-scented geranium

Petunia ×atkinsiana
petunia

Portulaca grandiflora
moss rose

Salvia splendens
scarlet sage

Verbena ×hybrida
verbena

Viola grandiflora
pansy

Vines

Campsis radicans
trumpet creeper

Lonicera sempervirens
trumpet honeysuckle

*Wisteria sinensis***
Chinese wisteria

Bulbs

Lilium lancifolium
tiger lily

Narcissus
daffodil

'Albus Plenus Odoratus'**
double poet's narcissus

'Orange Phoenix'**

'Van Sion'

Tulipa
tulip

'Couleur Cardinal'**

'General Ney'**

'Mabel'**

Built in 1887

Antoinette Norris
Mrs. F. C. Norris
Rowland

Mrs. J. M. Norris (grandma)
J. M. Norris (grandpa)
Walter Norris
F. C. Norris

F. C. Norris Residence 19th Ave & Buckeye Road

4

American Victorian Landscapes

(1860–1900)

1850

1868

First U.S. patent on a reel lawn mower is issued to Amariah Hills of Connecticut.

1869

Gypsy moth accidentally introduced near Boston.

1871

First patent on an American lawn sprinkler; hose reels, nozzles, and sprinklers are widely available by 1900.

1876

W. Atlee Burpee founds his seed company in Philadelphia.

1875

1891

New York Botanical Garden opens in the Bronx.

1893

World's Columbian Exposition opens in Chicago. The architecture and landscaping of the White City is credited with inspiring the "City Beautiful" movement so popular throughout the eastern United States at the turn of the century.

1894

Japanese Tea Garden in San Francisco's Golden Gate Park begins inspiring a generation to use details of Asian garden design.

1899

American Society of Landscape Architects (ASLA) is established in New York.

1900

This era opens with the country at war. The Civil War would continue to occupy the nation's heart and soul for four long years. Landscape design and garden making were not at the forefront of the national consciousness during the 1860s; economic times were difficult following the war, and major depressions in 1873 and 1893 left many people unemployed. Still, there was rapid growth in the areas of industry and transportation, which contributed to a boom in housing. As the years passed, more and more enthusiasm was directed toward the making of functional—and ornamental—landscapes: "Decorative Planting [is] the art of picture making and picture framing, by means of the varied forms of vegetable growth" (Scott 1870).

Architecture Styles

Queen Victoria of England reigned from 1837 to 1901, and her name is used to describe the American architectural style of buildings constructed between 1860 and 1900. Victorian architecture took advantage of trends and changes in housing construction techniques and the increased range of transportation options. Structures featured multifaceted shapes and details derived from classical and medieval prototypes. Second Empire, Queen Anne, Folk Victorian, and Richardsonian Romanesque are all sub-styles of Victorian architecture.

Most people recognize Queen Anne houses as those with bay windows. Towers are an imposing feature of some, and most have porches with finely turned supports. The walls might have different types of siding, giving Queen Anne houses a multitextural appearance. Folk Victorian houses are simpler examples of the Queen Anne style; the house is much less ornate and the main recognizable feature is the porch with spindlework and trim.

The main distinguishing feature of Second Empire architecture—so named because it imitated French style during the reign of Napoleon III, France's "Second Empire"—is the mansard roof, a dual-pitched hipped roof with dormer windows on a steep lower slope. Second Empire houses were particularly popular in the Midwest and on the East Coast between 1860 and 1880.

Featured Designer:
Frank J. Scott (1828–1919)

Frank J. Scott.

INDUSTRIALIZATION IN URBAN areas motivated those who could afford it to move where the air was cleaner—farther away from the city centers. Frank J. Scott of Toledo, Ohio, was one of the first landscape architects to work with these new "suburban" properties. He is often credited with instilling in Americans an appreciation for the lawn as a symbol of community, an "emerald carpet" connecting the residences in a neighborhood. His 1870 design classic, *The Art of Beautifying Suburban Home Grounds of Small Extent*, inspires gardeners to this day.

Houses in the Richardsonian Romanesque style, named for noted Boston architect Henry Hobson Richardson, are always of masonry and usually feature stonework. A wide, rounded arch at each entryway is another key feature. This style was used more often for commercial buildings than for private residences; it reached the height of its popularity in the 1890s.

Essential Elements of American Victorian Landscapes

· Lawn in front yard
· At least one large shade tree in front yard
· Carpet bedding
· Vines on house and/or porch
· Kitchen garden with square or rectangular beds at rear of property
· Fruit trees
· Weeping specimen tree
· Trees and shrubs at perimeter of property
· Cast iron fences and accessories

Landscape Design

Judging from the prominence of gardening books and magazines that not only continued to circulate but proliferated during these four decades, an avalanche of information was offered to the residents of houses, large and small, with the message that one should make a plan for one's residence and then implement it. Although most of the literature dealt with residential landscapes of varying sizes and locations, there was an increased awareness of the need for guidelines for smaller urban and suburban properties.

Landscape design continued to illustrate the principal ideals of Andrew Jackson Downing: that is, the juxtaposition of an informal, ornamental area with geometric beds for functional plantings like vegetables, fruits, and herbs.

Queen Anne.

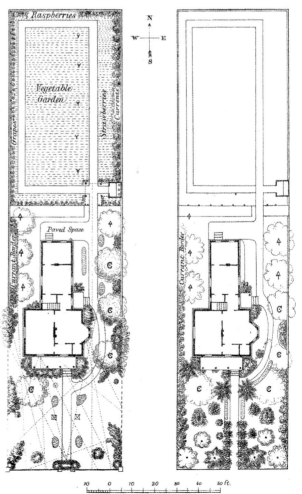

"Crowded and Open Grounds Compared, on a Cottage Lot of fifty feet front" (Scott 1870).

Second Empire.

Richardsonian Romanesque.

In Downing's time, the geometric beds would be at the rear of the house; beside them would be a yard for drying clothes and any other service areas, including privy. In Victorian landscapes, however, geometric beds for ornamentals were also inserted in the midst of more naturalistic plantings at the front of the house—the adage "more is better" was the rule of the day. Historians in recent years have criticized the gaudy nature of the Victorian landscape; but even the designers of the period seem to have been aware of a cultural penchant for excessive ornamentation, and cautionary advice crops up everywhere in their writings. Scott (1870) illustrates two landscapes, one that shows restraint in its use of plants and the other that in ten years will be a "mass of agglomerated and tangled verdure."

Scott and others recommended that trees and shrubs should play an important role in helping to screen undesirable vistas, provide all-season decoration, and delineate property boundaries. Every designer urged the placement of at least one large tree for shade in the front yard, often mentioning the purple-leaved variety of beech (*Fagus*

sylvatica 'Purpurea'). The challenge then as now was to be familiar with the plant materials and to know and understand their growth habits and mature size. Many landscape designs also featured at least one weeping tree, often a weeping willow (*Salix babylonica*) or a weeping beech (*F. sylvatica* 'Pendula').

A porch covered in vines and climbing plants was a common feature of the residences; a porch might even have supported several different vines—wisteria, clematis, a climbing rose—grown together. Porches were also important as a place to grow more plants, in containers that ranged from tin cans to elaborate urns to rustic baskets. Hanging baskets, containing a mixture of colorful and trailing plants, also adorned porches. The Boston fern (*Nephrolepis exaltata*) so often associated with Victorian parlors was introduced into cultivation in the late nineteenth century and did not become an important feature of porches until the twentieth century.

In 1880 *Vick's Monthly Magazine* described an ideal landscape treatment for a house with "towers and gables,

A cottage at Newburgh, New York, with a trellis at the side already covered in vines and the columns of the porch prepared to be so (Vaux 1867).

and curious porches, and strange windows." An extensive lawn was important, unbroken except for an occasional specimen tree for shade and ornament. Clumps of shrubs were spaced along the boundary of the property. A few flowerbeds were located in the view from windows, either in the ribbon style (long narrow strips and coils) or a circular bed of subtropical plants. This latter might be composed of castor bean (*Ricinus communis*) or cannas in the center, followed by a ring of *Colocasia esculenta*, with an edging of coleus. A simple border with favorite flowers for cutting (China asters, zinnias, gillyflower, sweet peas) might be located in the back of the house.

The gardens of the early row houses in New York, Boston, Philadelphia, and other East Coast cities forced compromises with regard to the use of space and the functionality of the area. Six designs for embellishing city yards appeared in *American Gardening* magazine in 1894. Each back garden space was forty by twenty feet, and the

use of one or two simple geometric figures gave form and function to the area. The first approach in the design of these properties was to cover the fence with a vine like the native trumpet honeysuckle (*Lonicera sempervirens*) or Virginia creeper (*Parthenocissus quinquefolia*). The designer suggested that annuals be planted in all sunny spots, preferably started from seed to keep costs down. Shady sites were host to native ferns such as the maidenhair (*Adiantum pedatum*) or to clumps of lily-of-the-valley (*Convallaria majalis*). The finishing touch was a large urn in each front yard.

Senator W. P. Jackson Residence,
Salisbury, Md

1

2

BED OF SUB-TROPICAL PLANTS.

3

4

1. House with "towers and gables, and curious porches,"
c. 1900.

2. An exclamation point of castor bean (*Ricinus communis*)
recalls the subtropical bedding of the Victorian age.

3. Subtropical bedding (Editor 1880b).

4. Another circular flowerbed, punctuated this time by
Canna indica.

▶ NEXT SPREAD Still life (potted plants and people) on a
porch, c. 1890.

Flower gardens

Probably the most recognized (and often vilified) features
of Victorian landscaping were the bedding schemes so
popular both in the United States and in Europe. Bedding
consisted of arranging plants, usually annuals and tender
perennials or tropicals, in designs cut out of the lawn
and meant to be viewed from a window, porch, or other
elevated post. It required "besides good taste in arranging
colors harmoniously, judgment to select those kinds that
will continue in bloom the whole season, withstanding the
summer drought, and that will harmonize in habit and
growth with one another" (Hints for May 1863). Carpet
bedding usually involved simple geometric figures such
as circles or ovals, or it might have entailed an intricate
cutout design for a tapestry effect.

Urn filled with bold foliage and colorful flowers (Editor 1880c).

Carpet bedding patterns (Editor 1881).

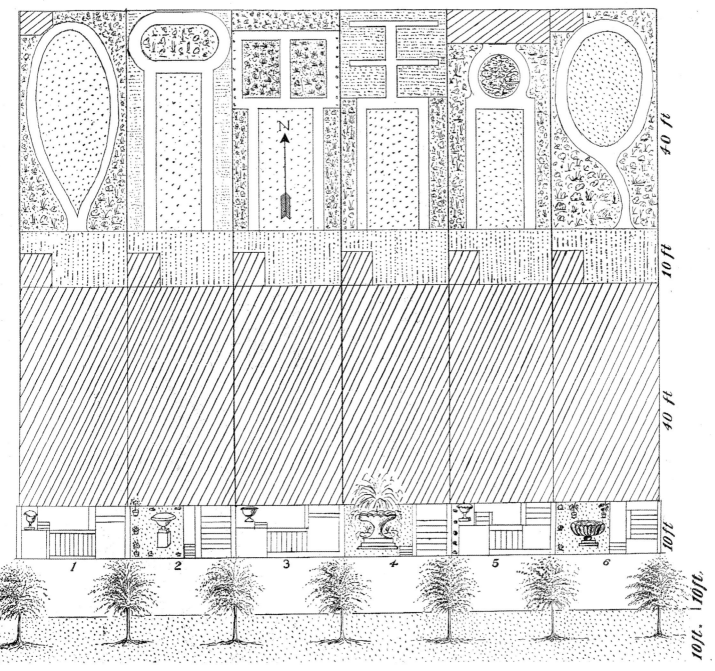

"Suggestions for Laying Out a City Garden" (Editor 1894).

1

2

Bedding schemes emphasized contrasting color, either of flowers or of foliage. Color schemes were vivid and simple—red, white, and blue; purple, yellow, and red. The plants had to be uniform in habit and maintain their ornamental features throughout the season. Sometimes a multiseason effect was achieved by planting hyacinths, tulips, and other bulbs for springtime color, followed with annuals and foliage plants to last until the first frost. Bedding required strict attention to maintenance, and it was relatively expensive. Owners of small properties were encouraged to adopt the style on a simple scale by cutting only one or two simple designs in their lawns and filling them with colorful annuals.

Bedding schemes were also popular in public or commercial sites, where the costs associated with their upkeep were more readily absorbed. From train stations to public institutions, passersby could enjoy the drama of a vivid floral picture. Not everyone enjoyed the flamboyant carpet bedding, according to one reader of *Vick's Monthly Magazine*: "I have heard it sarcastically called by some of the old-school gardeners the 'scarlet fever and yellow jaundice style' in allusion to so many red Geraniums and yellow Calceolarias being used" (J. B. 1881).

Awareness grew that by cultivating hardy herbaceous perennials in the garden, one could enjoy lower maintenance and overall lower costs than those associated with the bedding schemes, and orderly borders of herbaceous perennials slowly became a more common feature of the landscape. Elias Long (1893), noting "the increasing attention that this class of plants is now attracting," advised that perennial borders be placed at the foundation of the house and that the beds themselves be characterized by wavy lines as opposed to straight to give the illusion of more space devoted to the flowers. Often in designs, one would see graphic designations for flowerbeds, particularly along the sides of paths or along the boundaries of a property.

1 & 2. Period hyacinths 'Bismarck' (1875) and 'Chestnut Flower' (1880). Photos courtesy of Old House Gardens–Heirloom Bulbs, Ann Arbor, Michigan.

3. A lushly planted bed (Butz 1886).

4. Bedding scheme at Eagle Mound, Dayton, Ohio, 1880.

3

618 Flower Garden, Eagle Mound, Nat'l Military Home, Ohio.

4

The path borders typically called for both annuals and perennials to provide a floral display.

Subtropical gardening was a distinctive subcategory of bedding. In these beds, the form and size of the foliage was more important to the visual impact of the bed than color or flowers. Savvy gardeners in America began practicing this garden style in the late 1800s.

> There is a growing taste for additional bold picturesque effects—something suggestive of the stately grandeur of luxuriant tropical vegetation. . . . This taste has led to the introduction into gardens of large-leaved so-called "subtropical" foliage plants, the characteristics of which, nobility of form and habit, luxuriant growth, and exuberant and graceful leafage, render them of high decorative value, either grown as specimens or boldly grouped (Henderson 1901).

Many of the tender plants used in this style of gardening required a greenhouse or other overwintering facility. Plants for subtropical effect included agaves, amaranthus, angel wings, cannas, castor bean, coleus, elephant ears, sago palm, swamp lily, and yucca. Ornamental grasses with pleasing foliage effect such as selections of Japanese silver grass (*Miscanthus sinensis* 'Variegatus' and 'Zebrinus'), ravenna grass, pampas grass (*Cortaderia selloana*), and bamboo came into favor at this time. In photos of the era, one often sees a house with a single pot or urn containing a tropical plant, often elephant ears, in the front yard—visual testimony to the seduction of the prevailing fashion.

The "old-fashioned" or grandmother's garden also came into being at this time.

> An old-fashioned garden appeals to the mind as well as the eye, and whether formal or informal has about it something individual suggested by the mind of the owner. Its very tangles have a meaning and its stiffness a significance. . . . The plants of an old-fashioned garden were beloved, and are still justly beloved, for beauty or fragrance or for picturesque effect (Sargent 1895).

Plants for the grandmother's garden were those that had been cherished over the years by succeeding generations of gardeners. C. S. Sargent recommended peonies,

1. Subtropical bedding (Editor 1880b).

2. Ornamental grasses and palms frame three generations of the Norris family at their 1887 residence, Phoenix, Arizona, 1892.

3. A rose on a pillar (Parsons 1869).

4. A vernacular backyard garden featuring tender, potted rex begonias and mixed borders of annuals, perennials, and tropicals, c. 1900.

1

lilies, and roses, and also beebalm (*Monarda didyma*), sweet William (*Dianthus barbatus*), grass and maiden pinks (*D. plumarius, D. deltoides*), Maltese cross (*Lychnis chalcedonica*), Canterbury bells (*Campanula medium*), phlox, four o'clock (*Mirabilis jalapa*), pansies, and buttercups (*Ranunculus*).

As they had for centuries, roses graced many gardens of the Victorian era. A rose on a pillar might have been the centerpiece of a bedding scheme, a climbing rose might have covered a porch trellis or arbor, or a Hybrid Perpetual rose might have bloomed continuously among herbaceous perennials in a border or in the foreground of a shrubbery. More elaborate gardens of the Victorian era sometimes boasted a *roseraie*—an entire garden devoted to this cherished flower.

2

3

4

Kitchen gardens

Victorian writers and designers called for the separation of the kitchen garden from the rest of the ornamental landscape, believing it "injudicious . . . to mix flowers with the vegetables" (Sanders 1877). In fact, with the increased availability of fresh fruits and vegetables in the market-place, not every family elected to have a kitchen garden on their private grounds. Those who did had to keep certain considerations in mind:

> Upon small places the kitchen-garden should be as far from the house as the grounds will admit, and well fenced in. . . . A perfect square is the best shape, but a quadrangle oblong figure is good. The size will be in proportion to the extent of the grounds and the number of the family. . . . The best, cheapest, most lasting and beautiful fence for it is an osage-orange hedge. . . . A garden enclosed with such a hedge, and locked gates, and the gardener and owner only having keys, the best fruits of our climate can be grown without molestation (Elder 1861).

Typically, central beds were reserved for herbs and vegetables, and small fruits were planted in surroundings beds. A Victorian innovation that continues to the present was the strawberry barrel: oak barrels filled with strawberry plants provided vertical gardens that could be located in sunny sites throughout the property for a delectable product. A utility area was often located adjacent to the garden; here, one could pile and "cook" compost, or perhaps build a shed in which to keep tools and sashes, covers, pea-stakes, and other supplies. This area was enclosed and often screened by shrubs like lilacs, hydrangeas, or rose of Sharon (*Hibiscus syriacus*).

Nearly every design published by a professional landscape designer during this era featured fruit trees. Apples, peaches, cherries, and pears contributed springtime loveliness with their blossoms and harvest-time productivity with their fruit. Many residential landscapes had room for at least one fruit tree; if space was at a premium, espaliered fruit trees could be cultivated on the walls of an outbuilding, the back of the house, or on a fence.

Victorian gardeners marveled at the idea of strawberries planted in an oak barrel (Buckeye Woman 1882).

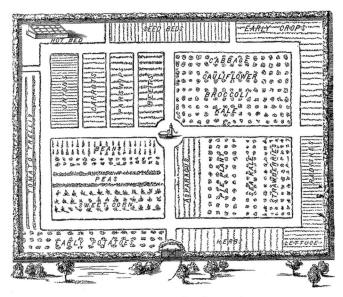

A practical design for a kitchen garden (Sanders 1877).

Fruit trees are both practical and beautiful, as here,
in full May bloom, in the side yard of a home in Natick,
Massachusetts, 1889.

Espaliered fruit trees.

Trees and shrubs

The tradition from earlier times to place a shrub here and
there around the house, maybe under a window or on a
corner, continued; often these were fragrant: roses, lilacs
(*Syringa*), or mock orange (*Philadelphus coronarius*). But
residential photos from the late nineteenth century rarely
show any foundation planting, at least as we would recognize it; the majority of houses, in fact, entirely lack major
front yard plantings.

Designers initially began promoting the idea of planting shrubs and small trees around the foundation of the
house, as opposed to the perimeter of the property, in the
form of a belt. Some modern historians say that this was
one way to hide high Victorian building foundations; oth-

ers view it as an attempt to provide a transition between
the natural and constructed landscape—a view that took
fierce hold during the Arts and Crafts period. For whatever reason—a nurseryman trying to sell more plants, a
garden writer touting the latest fashion—the suggestion
that homeowners place (mainly) woody plants in such a
strategic position became more frequent.

Charles Eliot (1891) provided an early design for
foundation plantings, one that was simple in aspect but
intricate in the number and variety of shrub and perennial
species it contained. The plant list (twenty-five in number)
included broadleaved evergreens like rhododendrons and
kalmia; deciduous flowering shrubs such as forsythia, spirea, and viburnum; conifers like junipers, arborvitae, and
dwarf white pine; and a plethora of perennials, including
lilies, peonies, foxgloves, and oriental poppies.

"The building may be connected with the ground and the appearance of nakedness removed by massing shrubs along the bases of the walls or piazzas" (Eliot 1891).

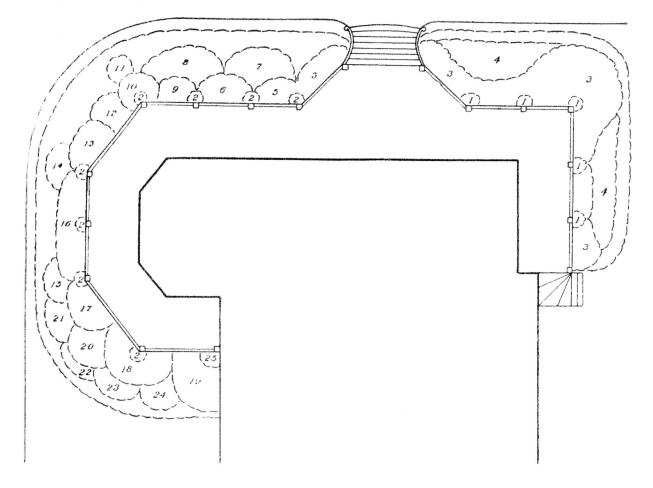

Lawns

Many credit our featured designer, Frank Scott, with instituting the American obsession with the front lawn. Lawns had been important components of earlier landscapes, and certainly the new availability of lawnmowers, although expensive at Scott's time, simplified the maintenance perspective. But his approach added to the concept of a lawn the element of community connection. The essential feature of Scott's neighborhood plan was this: "that *back of a line ten or twelve feet from the front street, to the foot-step of the porches, there shall be no shrub or tree planted on any of the fronts*; and only those species of flowers which do not exceed six to nine inches in height" (Scott 1870). He was poetic in his observation, calling grass "a close-fitting green robe thrown over the smooth form of the earth, through which every undulation is revealed, and over which the sunlight will play as upon velvet, and the shadows of environing objects be clearly outlined as upon a floor."

Other writers joined Scott in extolling the virtues and the positive appearance of a green lawn: "The main part of the lawn should be left unbroken by any tree or shrub, as a general rule, and if any tree is admitted it should be only an occasional fine specimen, like a Purple Beech, or Magnolia, or Cut-Leaved Birch" (Editor 1878b).

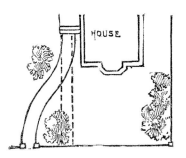
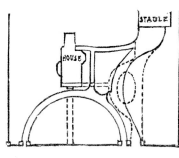

Designs to illustrate how paths may be curved in the front yard (Long 1893).

A community sidewalk of flagstone, Trumansburg, New York, c. 1875. Robert N. Dennis Collection of Stereoscopic Views, Miriam and Ira D. Wallach Division of Art, Prints and Photographs, The New York Public Library, Astor, Lenox and Tilden Foundations.

Landscape Features

Paths and driveways

The question of whether a path should be curved or straight raged on. Elias Long (1893) offered gentle guidance: "When the door of the house is twenty or more feet from the entrance gate, curves may usually be introduced by having the gate not directly in front of the house, but a little to one side." Many designers took the practical approach that stated for a very small urban lot, walks should be straight, beginning at the front gate and approaching the entrance of the house. The width of a front walk was between four and five feet.

> Have no useless paths. . . . Make the necessary paths to the public road short and direct, with only curve enough to break the outline. Often the best line of direction is that taken by a person naturally when walking over the course (Anon. 1888).

If the property was large enough to support curves and winding paths and roads, homeowners often chose that form to enhance their pleasure grounds. Drawings from the period illustrate driveways with gentle curves, not the partial arcs that modern architects tend to recommend: "Communication roads or walks leading from the gate to the house . . . should, if possible, have a graceful, almost direct curve so as not to create a desire to shorten the distance between the two objects by making a track through the lawns" (Weidenmann 1870).

Materials for paths and drives varied by region and availability. Gravel was the default in most places. Concrete too was very common, and bricks continued their long history. Writers often recommended flagstones for walkways and asphalt for drives. In the eastern United States flagstones were usually of bluestone, a type of sandstone quarried in Ohio and New York, among other places. According to our featured designer, "Solid stone flagging, if neatly dressed, is of course preferable for walks to gravel, and will be used where it can be afforded" (Scott 1870).

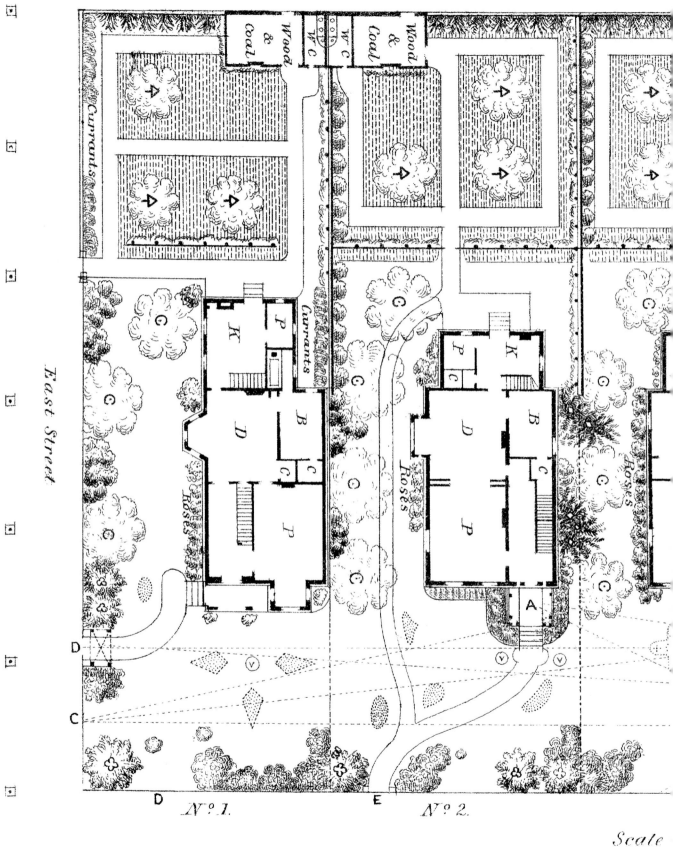

East Street

Wood & Coal

W C

W C

Wood & Coal

Currants

Currants

Roses

Roses

Roses

D

C

D   Nº 1.

E   Nº 2.

Scale

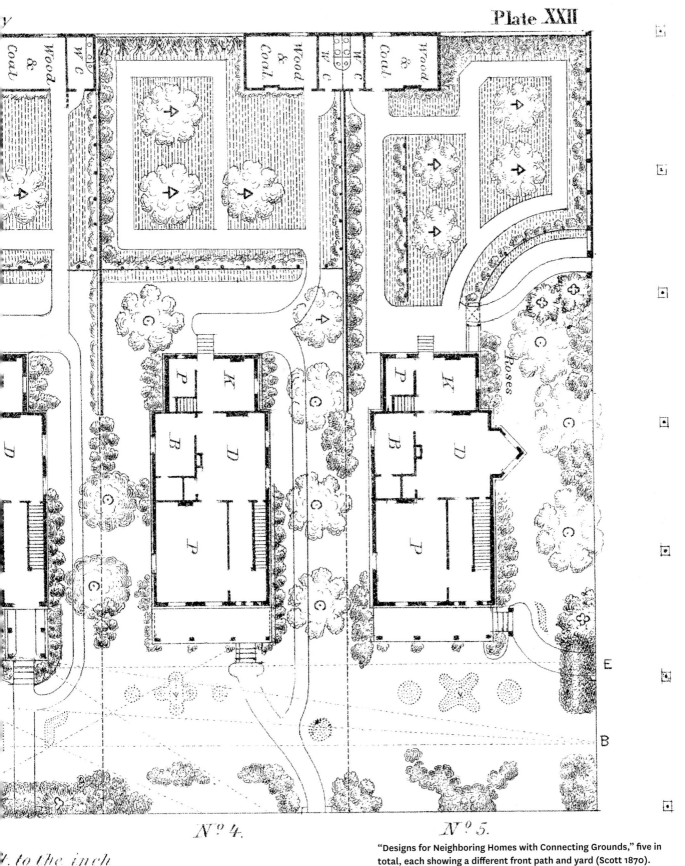

Plate XXII

№ 4.

№ 5.

"Designs for Neighboring Homes with Connecting Grounds," five in
total, each showing a different front path and yard (Scott 1870).

An iron fence encloses this yard in Berlin, Pennsylvania.

Concrete coping separates this property from the public street and sidewalks (Editor 1878a).

1. Two coping wall designs, one concrete block and the other carved stone, border this property (note too the weeping tree next to the house), c. 1890.

2. A wooden picket fence, designed to give an impression of intricate ironwork, Massachusetts, c. 1880. Robert N. Dennis Collection of Stereoscopic Views, Miriam and Ira D. Wallach Division of Art, Prints and Photographs, The New York Public Library, Astor, Lenox and Tilden Foundations.

Fences and hedges

A Victorian landscape innovation was the use of a concrete coping to delineate property boundaries from the public street and sidewalks. Stone and brick walls, and iron and picket fences also continued to be used for the purpose. Fences were designed as much for their decorative value as for enclosure, screening, or other special function; in fact, some writers recommended that fences have a certain transparent quality, framing the yard beyond. Iron fences, whether of wire or rail, excelled in this, with fanciful forms and space between the rails and posts. Picket fences continued apace but were beginning to have their detractors, among them Jacob Weidenmann (1870): "Picket fences are sufficiently used everywhere, but are objectionable for truly ornamental purposes. They are costly, requiring, if well kept, annual painting, frequent repairs, and rebuilding; and if kept in the best order, are repulsive, as well as stiff and unnatural."

Hedges crisscrossed the country from coast to coast. Plant materials included hemlock, privet, and spirea, or even Cherokee rose (*Rosa laevigata*) in the South. An article in *Vick's Monthly Magazine* described how to use hedges to screen a row of townhouses from the street; again, the notion of transparency figures in: "Flowering shrubs are planted in masses to screen the grounds, while they are not so tall as to cut off the view from the windows, and openings between the groups admit of views from the streets" (Editor 1883b). *Vick's* went on to list recommended shrubs (lilacs, mock orange, snowballs, Japanese quince), advising readers to either choose among them or include them *all*, for an attractive hedge.

Coping in front of a California house, c. 1890.

Low, uniform hedging encloses a California front yard, with simple wire trellises for roses and vines, c. 1900.

An ornate picket fence encloses the yard of the Hon. A. J. Clark, Massachusetts, c. 1880.

Wire fence (and a belt of cannas fronting the porch), Arabella Street, New Orleans, Louisiana, c. 1890.

Seeting

Benches and outdoor seating were of varied types and materials during the Victorian era. Stone was expensive but "perhaps the most beautiful, certainly the most durable, material for garden seats," and stone benches "may be made curving or straight, and of a length to suit the place to be occupied" (Long 1893). Ornate "wicker work" chairs and tables of rattan and cane, now proudly and artfully made in the United States, began an unprecedented sixty-year run of popularity on covered porches in about 1870. Traditional wooden rustic seating remained in vogue, and cast iron outdoor furniture was increasingly popular, with many pieces featuring natural designs of stylized ferns, twining vines, and such. Many of the latter have become classics, and reproductions are readily available. Make use of them: it remains our challenge, as gardeners, to take the time to sit back, relax, and enjoy our natural surroundings!

1. A Gothic settee is "best adapted where Gothic architecture prevails" (Thomas 1877).

2. "A garden seat of stone or marble" (Long 1893).

3. Rustic wooden chair (*Vick's Floral Guide* 1874).

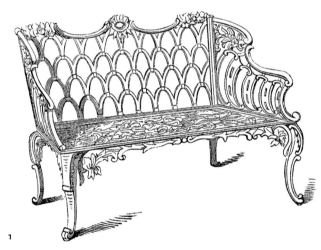

1

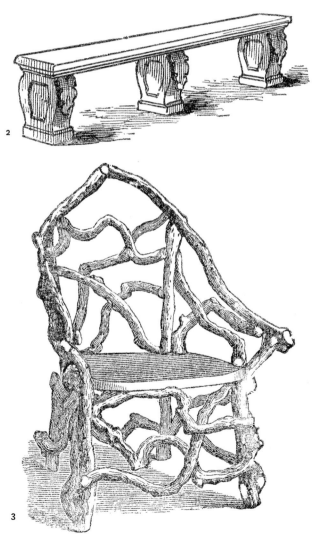

2

3

4

4. Formal people arrayed on informal seating at the Gesster residence, Valley Road, Orange, New Jersey, c. 1860. Robert N. Dennis Collection of Stereoscopic Views, Miriam and Ira D. Wallach Division of Art, Prints and Photographs, The New York Public Library, Astor, Lenox and Tilden Foundations.

5 & 6. Vines even crept their way into seating, as a motif: cast iron morning-glory chair and grape settee (Thomas 1877).

5

6

Garden accessories

Whenever and wherever vines are important to the landscape, trellises and pergolas become mandatory, and in the American Victorian landscape, vines were an essential element, providing shade, flowers, and fragrance: it was not unusual to see a house entirely clothed in a vigorous vine like Virginia creeper (*Parthenocissus quinquefolia*) or Boston ivy (*P. tricuspidata*). Trelliswork might be fancy or plain, made of wooden lathes and rustic in nature or more ornamental; or a homeowner might simply use wire or string to guide the climbing plants on their path skyward. Such means to support and guide vines did not change much over the decades.

Urns and vases, whether of iron, wood, or terracotta, were an important focal point in many gardens. Styles ranged from formal to very rustic and naturalistic. Some vases containerized the bedding scheme designs that dominated the era. Urns and vases made of cast iron and in the classic style added a formal touch to the landscape; however, writers cautioned against the excessive use of urns, vases, statuary, and other architectural adornments, particularly for smaller places. "Few, if any, [such] should be allowed. They are pretentious, artificial, and not in keeping with a natural style of the best landscape gardening" (Parsons 1891).

Artful rustic stands, with bowls, had become very common; Frank Scott (1870) recommended ivy and other trailing foliage plants, especially those with variegated leaves, for them. These, and baskets too, came in many sizes; they were used in the garden, on the porch, or even in the parlor. Fountains also had become more common, with writers for *Vick's* and other magazines lamenting the overpopularity of those that emphasized elaborately wrought cast iron or masonry over the pure sound and appearance of the water.

1. A simple fountain with a naturalistic pedestal of stones (Elliott 1881).

2. Sixteen-dollar three-bowl rustic stand (*B. K. Bliss' Descriptive Seed Catalogue* 1869).

3. A full vase of cascading plants was much more desirable than a partially filled container (*Vick's Floral Guide* 1874).

4. An urn filled with foliage plants and encircled by a garden of succulents satisfied the penchant for bedding (Thomas 1881).

1

2

3

4

5

5. An arch at left, a trellis at right, but a simple potted geranium in a fantastically rustic single-bowl stand takes pride of place in this photograph, possibly Mississippi, c. 1885.

6. An ornamental trellis (Vaux 1867).

6

The porch of a Victorian house was a place for relaxing, tending potted plants, and viewing the street life, c. 1895.

Iron fence on a stone wall, Pottsville, Pennsylvania, c. 1880.

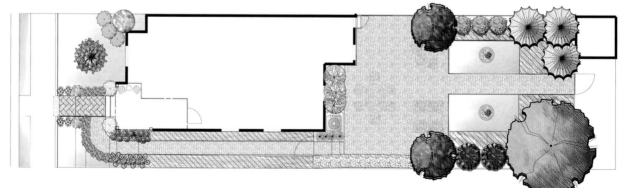

Dawson-Kehlmeier preliminary master plan.

Case Studies

1890 Folk Victorian house, Columbus, Ohio

Victorian Village, an area just north of the Columbus downtown area characterized by houses built in the late nineteenth century, has experienced a renaissance over the last decade, with new homeowners renovating previously neglected houses. Carlon Dawson and Michael Kehlmeier purchased their house there in 2007 and after extensive interior renovations decided to address the landscape.

The lot is typically urban: narrow but deep. The small front yard faces a busy thoroughfare; the backyard is long and backs to an alley. Carlon and Michael have somewhat different tastes when it comes to the landscape. Carlon prefers a more traditional approach, and Michael has a more eclectic sense of style. They determined that the front yard would be a more traditional Victorian garden area, in keeping with the architecture of the house and style of the neighborhood. The backyard, while having some aspects of the period in form and layout, would be devoted to entertaining and include areas for modern sculpture. Both wanted little or no lawn.

Carlon and Michael enjoy sitting on the front porch, and it is a major focal point from the street, so we included it in the landscape plans. An eighteen-inch-high brick wall, for stability, was added along the front of the property, and topped with an iron fence, to add height; the brick entry walk, which leads straight to the front porch, is entered through an ornamental iron gate. Previous owners added the metal porch pillars in the 1940s; these will be replaced with replicas of the originals (and they will still support vines). Beside the porch, the pre-existing Boston ivy is being encouraged to clothe the house once more; this will help anchor it to the landscape and add to the appearance that it is truly an unchanged Victorian house. A couple of comfortable period chairs, a small table, and a few containers and hanging baskets will complete the porch.

The walkway leading to the porch is lined with old-fashioned plants (mophead hydrangeas, peonies, variegated weigela) with staggered bloom periods for a long season of interest. Two *Spiraea ×vanhouttei*, the quintessential Romantic shrub, flank the steps to the front porch. On the southeast corner of the front, the role of specimen

Dawson-Kehlmeier residence.

shade tree is played by a saucer magnolia (*Magnolia ×sou-langeana*). On the west side, the circular flowerbed creates a perfect period view from the front window of the house; this bed can be changed annually or seasonally but should always include a tall, exclamation-point of a centerpiece plant—hollyhock, for example. At the corner of the house, a lilac and zebra grass (*Miscanthus sinensis* 'Zebrinus') balance the magnolia and provide structure and framing; the zebra grass could be replaced with small conifers for winter interest.

In the backyard we designed a large brick patio for entertaining. It is a flexible area, suitable for both small intimate dinners and large gatherings of people. The main large dining table takes advantage of the partial cover of a small vine-covered arbor; the existing grapes will be trained and paired with clematis. In the eastern rear corner is one of the new disease-resistant hybrids of American elm (*Ulmus americana*); these modern cultivars are not heirloom, but they do impart the visual quality of the popular nineteenth-century tree. There is also a kitchen garden, a single large rectangular bed for growing vegetables, a change from the preliminary master plan. And—a mark of the period—the perimeter beds are planted with shrubs (Carolina allspice, snowberry, rhododendrons) for lower maintenance; there is plenty of room for Michael to tuck in some sculpture, which the herbaceous underplantings can be tailored to enhance. Two fruit trees are included for beauty and function; planted urns and containers will further soften and ornament the patio. The overall effect of the backyard landscape plan is a gracious mix of old and new.

1

1. Backyard detail.

2. *Miscanthus sinensis* 'Zebrinus' (*Storrs and Harrison Co. Nursery Catalogue* 1894).

3. Front yard detail.

2

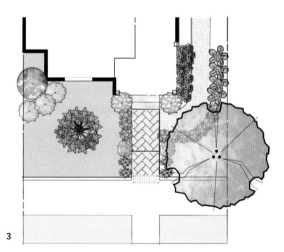

3

PLANT LISTS

PAGE 1 OF 9

* Please check for possibility of invasiveness in your locale.

** Plant is from the period but not necessarily listed in extant resources for the region.

NEW ENGLAND

Trees

Abies balsamea
balsam fir

Acer saccharum
sugar maple

Cercis canadensis
redbud

Cladrastis kentukea
yellowwood

Larix decidua
larch

Liriodendron tulipifera
tulip tree

Picea abies
Norway spruce

Pinus nigra
Austrian pine

Salix babylonica
weeping willow

Thuja occidentalis
arborvitae

Shrubs

Calycanthus floridus
Carolina allspice

Chaenomeles japonica
Japanese quince

Chionanthus virginicus
fringe tree

Cotinus coggygria
purple smoke tree

Epigaea repens
trailing arbutus

Prunus dulcis
sweet almond

Symphoricarpos albus
snowberry

Viburnum opulus 'Roseum'
snowball

Weigela florida
weigela

Perennials and biennials

Aquilegia canadensis
Canadian columbine

Aurinia saxatilis
golden alyssum

Bellis perennis
English daisy

Campanula medium
Canterbury bells

Centranthus ruber
Jupiter's beard

Convallaria majalis
lily-of-the-valley

Dodecatheon meadia
shooting star

Gypsophila paniculata
baby's breath

Hesperis matronalis*
dame's rocket

Iberis sempervirens
candytuft

Lychnis chalcedonica
Maltese cross

Myosotis palustris
forget-me-not

Platycodon grandiflorus
balloon flower

Tanacetum parthenium
feverfew

Annuals

Callistephus chinensis
China aster

Consolida ambigua
larkspur

Dianthus chinensis
China pink

Phlox drummondii
annual phlox

Ricinus communis
castor bean

Verbena ×*hybrida*
verbena

Viola grandiflora
pansy

Viola tricolor
Johnny-jump-up

Zinnia elegans
zinnia

Roses

Rosa 'Alfred Colomb'

Rosa 'American Beauty'

Rosa 'Anna De Diesbach'

Rosa 'Baltimore Belle'

Rosa 'Mme. Plantier'

Vines

Adlumia cirrhosa
mountain fringe

Apios americana
tuberous-rooted wisteria

Clematis virginiana
American white clematis

Lathyrus odoratus
sweet pea

  'America'**

  'Senator'**

Parthenocissus quinquefolia
Virginia creeper

Bulbs

Chionodoxa lucillae
glory of the snow

Crocus vernus
crocus

  'King of the Striped'**

PLANT LISTS

* Please check for possibility of invasiveness in your locale.

** Plant is from the period but not necessarily listed in extant resources for the region.

Hyacinthus orientalis
hyacinth

   'City of Haarlem'

Lilium canadense
Canada martagon lily

Lilium speciosum 'Rubrum'
crimson banded lily

Narcissus
daffodil

   'Mrs. Langtry'**

   'Rip Van Winkle'**

   'Sir Watkin'**

   'W. P. Milner'

Tulipa
tulip

   'Clara Butt'**

   marjoletti

   turkestanica

MIDDLE ATLANTIC

Trees

Cedrus deodora
Deodar cedar

Chamaecyparis pisifera 'Plumosa'
Sawara cypress

   'Plumosa Aurea'
   golden Sawara cypress

Cladrastis kentukea
yellowwood

Cryptomeria japonica
Japanese cedar

Magnolia denudata
Yulan magnolia

Magnolia ×soulangeana
saucer magnolia

Picea abies
Norway spruce

Prunus persica 'Plena'
double-flowering peach

Quercus robur
English oak

Taxus baccata 'Fastigiata'
Irish yew

Shrubs

Calycanthus floridus
Carolina allspice

Chaenomeles japonica
Japanese quince

Cotinus coggygria
purple smoke tree

Deutzia gracilis
slender deutzia

Hibiscus syriacus
rose of Sharon

Rhododendron
rhododendron, azalea

Spiraea prunifolia
bridal wreath

Syringa vulgaris
lilac

Viburnum opulus 'Roseum'
snowball

Perennials and biennials

Alcea rosea
hollyhock

Antirrhinum majus
snapdragon

Aurinia saxatilis
golden alyssum

Bellis perennis
English daisy

Campanula medium
Canterbury bells

Cortaderia selloana*
pampas grass

Delphinium elatum
bee larkspur

Dianthus barbatus
sweet William

Digitalis purpurea
foxglove

Lychnis chalcedonica
Maltese cross

Myosotis palustris
forget-me-not

Phlox paniculata
perennial phlox

Platycodon grandiflorus
balloon flower

Viola odorata
sweet violet

Annuals

Ageratum houstonianum
flossflower

Amaranthus tricolor
Joseph's coat

Callistephus chinensis
China aster

Consolida ambigua
larkspur

Dianthus chinensis
China pink

Gaillardia pulchella var. *picta*
blanket flower

Petunia ×atkinsiana
petunia

Verbena ×hybrida
verbena

Viola grandiflora
pansy

Viola tricolor
Johnny-jump-up

Roses

Rosa 'Cramoisi Supérieur'

Rosa 'Gloire de Dijon'

Rosa 'Hermosa'

Rosa 'Lamarque'

Rosa 'Mme. Bravy'

Vines

Adlumia cirrhosa
mountain fringe

Aristolochia macrophylla
Dutchman's pipe

Cardiospermum helicacabum*
balloon vine

Lablab purpureus
hyacinth bean

Lathyrus latifolius
everlasting pea

Bulbs

Allium moly
yellow garlic

Colchicum autumnale
autumn crocus

Fritillaria imperialis
crown imperial

Hyacinthus orientalis
hyacinth

Lilium auratum
gold-band lily

Lilium lancifolium
tiger lily

Narcissus
daffodil

'Mrs. Langtry'**

'Rip Van Winkle'**

'Sir Watkin'**

'W. P. Milner'

Tulipa
tulip

'Clara Butt'**

'Elegans Alba'**

'Elegans Rubra'**

SOUTHERN

Trees

Acer saccharinum
silver maple

Aesculus hippocastanum
horse chestnut

Albizia julibrissin*
mimosa

Cupressus funebris
weeping cypress

Cycas revoluta
sago palm

Ginkgo biloba
maidenhair tree

Juniperus communis 'Hibernica'
Irish juniper

Juniperus communis 'Suecica'
Swedish juniper

Lagerstroemia indica
crepe myrtle

Magnolia acuminata
cucumber tree

Magnolia grandiflora
southern magnolia

Melia azedarach*
chinaberry

'Umbraculiformis'
umbrella tree

Paulownia imperialis
empress tree

Picea abies
Norway spruce

Platycladus orientalis
Chinese arborvitae

Prunus caroliniana
Carolina laurel cherry

Thuja occidentalis
arborvitae

Tilia platyphyllos
European linden

Shrubs

Calycanthus floridus
Carolina allspice

Camellia japonica
camellia

Eriobotrya japonica
loquat

Gardenia jasminoides
Cape jasmine

Hibiscus rosa-sinensis
Chinese hibiscus

Hibiscus syriacus
rose of Sharon

Hydrangea macrophylla 'Otaksa'
Japanese hydrangea

Mahonia aquifolium
Oregon grape

Michelia figo
banana shrub

Nerium oleander
oleander

Osmanthus fragrans
tea olive

Pittosporum tobira
pittosporum

Rhododendron indicum
Chinese azalea

Spiraea cantoniensis
double white bridal wreath

Spiraea prunifolia
bridal wreath

Syringa vulgaris
lilac

Trachelospermum jasminoides
confederate jasmine

Viburnum opulus 'Roseum'
snowball

Vitex agnus-castus
chaste tree

Weigela florida
weigela

PLANT LISTS

* Please check for possibility of invasiveness in your locale.

** Plant is from the period but not necessarily listed in extant resources for the region.

Perennials and biennials

Alcea rosea
hollyhock

Antirrhinum majus
snapdragon

Begonia
begonia

Bellis perennis
English daisy

Campanula medium
Canterbury bells

*Cortaderia selloana**
pampas grass

Dianthus barbatus
sweet William

Dicentra spectabilis
bleeding heart

Digitalis purpurea
foxglove

Erysimum cheiri
wallflower

Hibiscus coccineus
scarlet rose-mallow

Mimulus moschatus
musk plant

Myosotis palustris
forget-me-not

Paeonia
peony

'Baroness Schroeder'**

'Festiva Maxima'**

'Monsieur Jules Elie'**

Pelargonium
geranium

Phlox paniculata
perennial phlox

Phygelius capensis
Cape fuchsia

Primula sinensis
Chinese primrose

Tanacetum parthenium
feverfew

'Flore Pleno'
double feverfew

Annuals

Ageratum houstonianum
flossflower

Amaranthus tricolor
Joseph's coat

Catharanthus roseus
Madagascar periwinkle

Cuphea ignea
cigar plant

Heliotropium arborescens
cherry pie

Impatiens balsamina
balsam

Lobelia erinus
edging lobelia

Lobularia maritima
sweet alyssum

Mesembryanthemum crystallinum
ice plant

Pelargonium
geranium

Petunia ×atkinsiana
petunia

Phlox drummondii
phlox

Reseda odorata
mignonette

Salvia splendens
scarlet sage

Solenostemon scutellarioides
coleus

Tropaeolum majus
nasturtium

Verbena ×hybrida
verbena

Viola grandiflora
pansy

Viola tricolor
Johnny-jump-up

Zinnia elegans
zinnia

Roses

Rosa 'Chromatella' ('Cloth of Gold')

Rosa 'Général Jacqueminot'

Rosa laevigata
Cherokee rose

Rosa 'Louis Philippe'

Rosa 'Maréchal Niel'

Rosa 'Safrano'

Rosa 'Souvenir de la Malmaison'

Vines

Clematis 'Jackmanii'
Jackman's clematis

Cobaea scandens
cathedral bells

Gelsemium sempervirens
Carolina jasmine

*Hedera helix**
English ivy

*Ipomoea purpurea**
morning glory

*Ipomoea quamoclit**
cypress vine

Jasminum nudiflorum
winter jasmine

Lonicera flava
yellow trumpet honeysuckle

Lonicera periclymenum 'Belgica'
monthly honeysuckle

*Wisteria sinensis**
Chinese wisteria

Bulbs

Caladium bicolor
angel wings

Canna indica
Indian shot

Colocasia esculenta
elephant ears

Crinum
swamp lily

Dahlia
dahlia

Hyacinthus orientalis
hyacinth

Hymenocallis rotata
spider lily

Lilium auratum
gold-band lily

Lilium speciosum
Japanese lily

  'Album'
  white Japanese lily

  'Rubrum'
  crimson banded lily

Narcissus
daffodil

  'Mrs. Langtry'**

  'Rip Van Winkle'**

  'Sir Watkin'**

  'W. P. Milner'**

Polianthes tuberosa
tuberose

Sprekelia formosissima
Jacobean lily

Zantedeschia aethiopica
calla lily

GREAT LAKES

Trees

Abies balsamea
balsam fir

Acer saccharinum
silver maple

Betula pendula 'Laciniata'
cut-leaf birch

Catalpa speciosa
northern catalpa

Fagus sylvatica
European beech

  'Purpurea'

Fraxinus americana
white ash

Larix decidua
larch

Picea abies
Norway spruce

Pinus strobus
white pine

Pinus sylvestris
Scotch pine

Sorbus aucuparia
European mountain ash

Thuja occidentalis
arborvitae

Tilia platyphyllos
European linden

Tsuga canadensis
hemlock

Shrubs

Berberis vulgaris
'Atropurpurea'*
purple-leaf barberry

Calycanthus floridus
Carolina allspice

Chaenomeles speciosa
Japanese quince

Chionanthus virginicus
fringe tree

Cotinus coggygria
purple smoke tree

Deutzia gracilis
slender deutzia

Hibiscus syriacus
rose of Sharon

Philadelphus coronarius
mock orange

Spiraea ×billardii
Billard's spirea

Spiraea prunifolia
bridal wreath

Syringa vulgaris
lilac

Viburnum opulus 'Roseum'
snowball

Perennials and biennials

Achillea ptarmica
sneezewort

Alcea rosea
hollyhock

Antirrhinum majus
snapdragon

Campanula medium
Canterbury bells

Convallaria majalis
lily-of-the-valley

Delphinium formosum
showy larkspur

Dianthus barbatus
sweet William

Dicentra spectabilis
bleeding heart

Hosta plantaginea
plantain lily

Iberis sempervirens
candytuft

Lychnis chalcedonica
Maltese cross

Myosotis palustris
forget-me-not

Papaver orientale
oriental poppy

Phlox 'Miss Lingard'
perennial phlox

Tanacetum parthenium
feverfew

PLANT LISTS

* Please check for possibility of invasiveness in your locale.

** Plant is from the period but not necessarily listed in extant resources for the region.

Annuals

Ageratum houstonianum
flossflower

Chrysanthemum
winter pink

Consolida ambigua
larkspur

Heliotropium arborescens
cherry pie

Pelargonium
geranium

Petunia ×atkinsiana
petunia

Salvia splendens
scarlet sage

Solenostemon scutellarioides
coleus

Verbena ×hybrida
verbena

Viola grandiflora
pansy

Viola tricolor
Johnny-jump-up

Roses

Rosa 'Baltimore Belle'

Rosa 'General Washington'

Rosa 'Mme. Plantier'

Rosa 'Queen of the Prairies'

Rosa 'Seven Sisters'

Vines

Cobaea scandens
cup-and-saucer vine

Hedera helix*
English ivy

Lathyrus odoratus
sweet pea

Lonicera sempervirens
trumpet honeysuckle

Parthenocissus quinquefolia
Virginia creeper

Parthenocissus tricuspidata
Boston ivy

Passiflora caerulea
passion vine

Wisteria sinensis*
Chinese wisteria

Bulbs

Caladium bicolor
angel wings

Canna indica
Indian shot

  'America'**

  'Florence Vaughan'**

Colocasia esculenta
elephant ears

  'Fontanesii'

Dahlia
dahlia

  'Kaiser Wilhelm'**

  'Nellie Broomhead'**

  'Union Jack'**

Fritillaria imperialis
crown imperial

Hyacinthus orientalis
hyacinth

  'Chestnut Flower'**

  'City of Haarlem'**

Lilium auratum
gold-band lily

Lilium lancifolium
tiger lily

Lilium speciosum
Japanese lily

  'Album'
  white Japanese lily

  'Rubrum'
  crimson banded lily

Narcissus
daffodil

  'Mrs. Langtry'**

  'Rip Van Winkle'**

  'Sir Watkin'**

  'W. P. Milner'

Tulipa
tulip

  'Clara Butt'**

  'Peach Blossom'**

CENTRAL STATES & GREAT PLAINS

Trees

Abies balsamea
balsam fir

Acer saccharinum
silver maple

Aesculus hippocastanum
horse chestnut

Betula pendula 'Laciniata'
cut leaf weeping birch

Catalpa speciosa
northern catalpa

Fraxinus americana
white ash

Juniperus virginiana
eastern red cedar

Morus alba 'Tatarica'
Russian mulberry

Picea abies
Norway spruce

Pinus nigra
Austrian pine

Pinus sylvestris
Scotch pine

Thuja occidentalis
arborvitae

Tilia americana
basswood

Shrubs

Calycanthus floridus
Carolina allspice

Chaenomeles japonica
Japanese quince

Cotinus coggygria
purple smoke tree

Hibiscus syriacus
rose of Sharon

Lonicera tatarica*
shrub honeysuckle

Philadelphus coronarius
mock orange

Spiraea prunifolia
bridal wreath

Syringa vulgaris
lilac

Viburnum opulus 'Roseum'
snowball

Weigela florida
weigela

Perennials and biennials

Alcea rosea
hollyhock

Antirrhinum majus
snapdragon

Bellis perennis
English daisy

Campanula medium
Canterbury bells

Dianthus barbatus
sweet William

Dianthus plumarius
grass pink

Dicentra spectabilis
bleeding heart

Linum perenne
flax

Lychnis chalcedonica
Maltese cross

Myosotis palustris
forget-me-not

Paeonia
peony

'Baroness Schroeder'**

'Festiva Maxima'**

'Monsieur Jules Elie'**

Phlox 'Miss Lingard'
perennial phlox

Sedum sieboldii
Siebold's sedum

Tanacetum parthenium
feverfew

'Aureum'
golden feather

Yucca filamentosa
Adam's needle

Annuals

Ageratum houstonianum
flossflower

Catharanthus roseus
Madagascar periwinkle

Cuphea ignea
cigar plant

Gazania splendens
gazania

Heliotropium arborescens
cherry pie

Pelargonium ×hortorum
geranium

'Crystal Palace Gem'**

Petunia ×atkinsiana
petunia

Salvia splendens
scarlet sage

Verbena ×hybrida
verbena

Viola grandiflora
pansy

Roses

Rosa 'Baltimore Belle'

Rosa 'Harison's Yellow'

Rosa 'Mme. Plantier'

Rosa 'Queen of the Prairies'

Rosa 'Seven Sisters'

Vines

Campsis radicans
trumpet creeper

Lonicera sempervirens
trumpet honeysuckle

Parthenocissus quinquefolia
Virginia creeper

Parthenocissus tricuspidata
Boston ivy

Wisteria sinensis*
Chinese wisteria

Bulbs

Canna indica
Indian shot

Dahlia
dahlia

'Kaiser Wilhelm'**

'Nellie Broomhead'**

'Union Jack'**

Gladiolus
sword lily

Hyacinthus orientalis
hyacinth

'Chestnut Flower'**

'City of Haarlem'**

Lilium auratum
gold-band lily

Lilium lancifolium
tiger lily

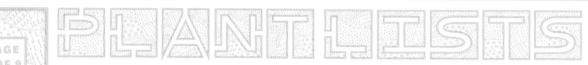

* Please check for possibility of invasiveness in your locale.

** Plant is from the period but not necessarily listed in extant resources for the region.

Lilium speciosum
Japanese lily

'Album'
white Japanese lily

'Rubrum'
crimson banded lily

Narcissus
daffodil

'Mrs. Langtry'**

'Rip Van Winkle'**

'Sir Watkin'**

'W. P. Milner'**

Polianthes tuberosa
tuberose

Tulipa
tulip

'Clara Butt'**

marjoletti

turkestanica

FAR WEST & MOUNTAIN STATES

Trees

Albizia julibrissin*
mimosa

Chamaecyparis lawsoniana
Lawson's cypress

Chilopsis linearis
desert willow

Cordyline australis
cabbage tree

Cupressus macrocarpa
Monterey cypress

Eucalyptus globulus*
blue gum

Juniperus virginiana
eastern red cedar

Lagerstroemia indica
crepe myrtle

Magnolia grandiflora
southern magnolia

Melia azedarach*
chinaberry

'Umbraculiformis'
umbrella tree

Pinus radiata
Monterey pine

Platanus occidentalis
sycamore

Platycladus orientalis
Chinese arborvitae

Populus alba
white poplar

Populus nigra 'Italica'
Lombardy poplar

Schinus molle
Peruvian peppertree

Sequoiadendron giganteum
redwood

Thuja occidentalis 'Aurea'
golden arborvitae

Trachycarpus fortunei
windmill palm

Shrubs

Chaenomeles japonica
Japanese quince

Chaenomeles speciosa
Japanese quince

Erythrina crista-galli
coral tree

Euonymus japonicus
Japanese spindle tree

Gardenia jasminoides
Cape jasmine

Hibiscus syriacus
rose of Sharon

Ligustrum ibota
Japanese privet

Ligustrum ovalifolium*
California privet

Nerium oleander
oleander

Punica granatum
pomegranate

Spiraea cantoniensis
double white bridal wreath

Spiraea prunifolia
bridal wreath

Syringa vulgaris
lilac

Viburnum opulus 'Roseum'
snowball

Viburnum tinus
laurustinus

Weigela florida
weigela

Yucca whipplei
Our Lord's candle

Perennials and biennials

Alcea rosea
hollyhock

Arundo donax 'Versicolor'
striped reed

Bellis perennis
English daisy

Chrysanthemum
winter pink

Convallaria majalis
lily-of-the-valley

Cortaderia selloana*
pampas grass

Cymbopogon citratus
lemon grass

Dianthus caryophyllus
carnation

Miscanthus sinensis*
Japanese silver grass

'Variegatus'
variegated Japanese silver grass

'Zebrinus'
zebra grass

Paeonia suffruticosa
tree peony

Phlox 'Miss Lingard'
perennial phlox

Phormium tenax
New Zealand flax

   'Variegata'

Saccharum ravennae
ravenna grass

Viola odorata
sweet violet

Yucca filamentosa
Adam's needle

Annuals

Callistephus chinensis
China aster

Eschscholzia californica
California poppy

Heliotropium arborescens
cherry pie

Impatiens balsamina
balsam

Matthiola incana
gillyflower

Pelargonium
geranium

Petunia ×atkinsiana
petunia

Reseda odorata
sweet mignonette

Solenostemon scutellarioides
coleus

Verbena ×hybrida
verbena

Viola grandiflora
pansy

Viola tricolor
Johnny-jump-up

Roses

Rosa 'Géant des Batailles'

Rosa 'Général Jacqueminot'

Rosa 'Homère'

Rosa 'La France'

Rosa 'Maréchal Niel'

Rosa 'Paul Neyron'

Rosa 'Perle des Jardins'

Vines

Akebia quinata
chocolate vine

Campsis grandiflora
Chinese trumpet creeper

Campsis radicans
trumpet flower

Clematis 'Jackmanii'
Jackman's clematis

*Hedera helix**
English ivy

Lonicera periclymenum 'Belgica'
monthly honeysuckle

Lonicera sempervirens
trumpet honeysuckle

Pandorea jasminoides
bower plant

Parthenocissus quinquefolia
Virginia creeper

Parthenocissus tricuspidata
Boston ivy

Passiflora caerulea
passion vine

Vigna caracalla
snail flower

*Wisteria sinensis**
Chinese wisteria

   'Alba'

Bulbs

Agapanthus africanus
blue African lily

Calochortus luteus
yellow mariposa lily

Canna indica
Indian shot

   'Florence Vaughan'

Crinum
swamp lily

Dahlia
dahlia

   'Kaiser Wilhelm'**

'Nellie Broomhead'**

'Union Jack'**

Dichelostemma congestum
ookow

Hyacinthus orientalis
hyacinth

   'Bismarck'**

   'Chestnut Flower'**

   'City of Haarlem'**

Lilium candidum
Madonna lily

Lilium humboldtii
California lily

Lilium pardalinum
California tiger lily

Polianthes tuberosa
tuberose

Zantedeschia aethiopica
calla lily

Eclectic Landscapes
(1900–1930)

C. 1900

Chestnut blight (*Endothia parasitica*) attacks chestnut trees in New York. By 1940, most American chestnuts (*Castanea dentata*) are gone.

1916

Japanese beetles are discovered in a New Jersey nursery; the National Park Service is established.

1919

First gasoline-powered lawn mower manufactured in United States.

1920s

Swimming pools become a common feature in residential landscapes.

1914–18

World War I prompts the creation of victory gardens.

1922

American Horticultural Society is founded in Washington, D.C.

1928

Dutch elm disease is discovered in New England after elm bark beetles arrive in a shipment of wood from The Netherlands.

1900

1910

1920

1930

Architecture Styles

Residential building styles proliferated across the United States in the early years of the twentieth century. Constructing houses for the middle class was a burgeoning industry, and contemporary domestic architecture styles varied from the predominantly coastal Arts and Crafts (Craftsman) bungalow to the Prairie-style homes of the upper Midwest to the Colonial Revival houses that filled newly constructed suburbs across the country. Other prominent styles were Tudor Revival, Mission Revival, Beaux Arts, and Neoclassical. In addition to these high styles of architecture, one could find many hybrids and modifications based on local customs and availability of materials. Pre-fabricated houses became available during this period; the most famous was the Sears Modern Home, which sold more than seventy thousand units from 1908 to 1940. Sears houses were in ready-to-assemble kits that were shipped via rail; the recent innovations of dry wall construction (instead of plaster walls) and asphalt roof shingles (instead of wood or slate) made the Sears house an affordable option for many American families.

Arts and Crafts/Craftsman

The Arts and Crafts movement in nineteenth-century England, the emergence of which was strongly associated with William Morris, was in part a philosophical reaction against industrialization. Appreciation for handicrafts, local materials, and admiration for manual labor and craftsmanship were hallmarks of this progressive way of thinking, which turned—always—to the natural world for its design inspiration. Many credit William Robinson with initiating a gardeners' Arts and Crafts style, an approach that attempted to undo the flamboyance and exaggerations of the Victorian bedding style and fully replace it with more naturalistic effect. Designers for large manor houses in England installed landscapes that emphasized the connection between dwelling and garden and created garden "rooms" as an extension of the house. Robinson's The *Wild Garden* (1870) remains popular to this day (including a

California bungalow.

2009 expanded edition by Rick Darke, published by Timber Press); *The English Flower Garden* (1883), another of his books, was also very influential in its time.

Another famous spokesperson of this movement was English designer and garden writer Gertrude Jekyll. A painter, Jekyll started to design gardens later in her life after her eyesight began to decline. She is credited with introducing the idea of using color theory to enhance the design of a garden. Jekyll advised using a mixed palette of bulbs, shrubs, perennials, and annuals to compose a mixed border in a painterly fashion. Her gardens exhibited color harmony and seasonal ornamentation. She collaborated with architect Edwin Lutyens to design garden rooms and borders for fashionable estates in England and also designed three gardens for American clientele, although she never visited this country. As the author of several best-selling gardening books, she excited gardeners on both sides of the Atlantic.

And just how mixed was that palette? The Craftsman's ethic on plant choice is best summed up in this quote:

> As regards the grounds—the "garden" in its wider sense—they will assuredly be most beautiful, interesting, and enjoyable when both native and foreign plants have been used in tasteful combination (Van Rensselaer 1903).

In the United States, the Arts and Crafts movement crossed economic boundaries, widely influencing middle-class architecture and renewing interest in many crafts, including the making of furniture and pottery. In

October 1901, Gustav Stickley published the first issue of *The Craftsman Magazine*, which promoted many details for a way of life that emphasized "beauty, simplicity, and efficiency."

The bungalow, a ubiquitous American architecture style during this period, originated in Pasadena, California; it is best exemplified in the work of the architectural firm Greene and Greene. Thousands of bungalows survive in many American cities today, exhibiting the Arts and Crafts philosophy of craftsmanship, simplicity, and using local materials. They typically are one-story buildings with a low-pitched gabled roof. Roof material varies, from slate to wood shingles to terracotta, Mission-style tiles. Roof rafters are usually exposed, with decorative beams and braces under the gables; tapered square columns often support the roof. Porches are always featured. Larger homes in this style might have two stories of contrasting surface material—for example, stucco on one level and river rock on another.

Essential Elements of Arts and Crafts Landscapes

- Simple forms
- Harmonious elements
- Pergola with vines
- Native plants, but not exclusively
- Vegetables and fruit trees, often in front yard
- Herbaceous or mixed border
- Incorporation of local materials

Prairie

From the late 1800s and into the twentieth century, garden practitioners and residential architects in the Midwest, mainly based in Illinois, began to develop a uniquely American design style: both the houses (designed by architects like Louis Sullivan, Frank Lloyd Wright, and Walter Burley Griffin) and the landscapes that surrounded them are characterized by the horizontal lines of the Great Plains. Frank Lloyd Wright was a charter member of the Chicago Arts and Crafts Society, and his sympathy for that philosophy was reflected in his Prairie work, particularly in the shared emphasis on local materials and fine craftsmanship.

Prairie-style houses typically have two stories and very strong horizontal lines. The roof is low-pitched with widely overhanging eaves. Massive (not tapered) porch columns support the roof. A common offshoot of Prairie-style architecture with Arts and Crafts highlights is the American Foursquare, found in cities across the country. Foursquares are boxy, two-and-a-half-story residences, usually with a front dormer in a hipped roof. The roof is low-pitched with overhanging eaves, and there is a porch.

The Prairie-style landscape gardeners, as they called themselves, included Jens Jensen, Ossian Cole Simonds, and Wilhelm Miller. Miller (1915) defined his approach:

> The prairie style of landscape gardening is an American mode of design based on the practical needs of the mid-western people and characterized by preservation of typical western scenery, by restoration of local color, and by repetition of the horizontal line of land or sky which is the strongest feature of prairie scenery.

Like other Craftsman-era design styles, this garden style sought to combine local resources, including plants and stone (Miller's "local color"), to create a simple yet elegant functional cultivated landscape. Miller emphasized repetition throughout the garden and encouraged the use of plants native to the midwestern prairies, especially those that were "stratified in branch or flower"; for example, the plant might have a horizontal branching pattern (dogwood) or flat flower form (milkweed). Houses should be framed "with haws and crabs" (hawthorns and crabapples) and then a wide lawn, surrounded by more prairie trees and shrubs. If a resident had little or no available space for an extensive landscape, Miller suggested at least planting a prairie rose (*Rosa arkansana*) by the front door to demonstrate a commitment to the movement.

1

Essential Elements of Prairie-style Landscapes
· Horizontal lines
· Native plants
· Repetition of plants and materials
· Conservation of existing features

3

2

4

1. A bungalow in Nashville, Tennessee.

2. American Foursquare, Stony Point, New York.

3. Little bluestem grass (*Schizachyrium scoparium*) and orange coneflower (*Rudbeckia fulgida*), both natives, combine in a reproduction Prairie-style urn.

4. Prairie-style house, Chicago, Illinois.

Colonial Revival

Even as the Craftsman philosophy was inspiring garden design, several alternative landscape approaches were being implemented across the country, again inextricably linked to the architecture of the house. A renewed interest in colonial practices, spurred by the Philadelphia Centennial Exposition, reached a crescendo at the turn of the century, when colonial gardens, old-fashioned gardens, and grandmothers' gardens all were the subject of many magazine articles; and the style of architecture we now call Colonial Revival became prevalent in the new suburbs.

Most Colonial Revival houses had two stories, the exception, in the West, being Spanish Colonial Revival houses, which like the early missions were single-level. Houses in the Colonial Revival style display strong symmetry of all elements, with the door in the center of the façade and windows evenly spaced. The entryway usually includes a decorated crown over the door and fanlights and sidelights surrounding the door. Porches have multiple columns. Houses in this style were best landscaped with "the good old-fashioned plants": "Frame the entrance with clumps of lilacs, or more formally with round bushes of box. Use vines . . . to soften a hard line, to accentuate the beauty of a chimney, to make a porch part of the house, to lend color and texture to a wall" (Greely 1922).

Essential Elements of Colonial Revival Landscapes

- Symmetry
- Balance and a central axis
- Geometric beds
- Picket fence
- Old-fashioned flowers

Featured Designer:
Grace Tabor (1873–1973)

A small sampling of Grace Tabor's garden books.

GRACE TABOR DESIGNED LANDSCAPES for middle-class homes, and in her many books and articles, she combined gardening advice with creative and functional designs for the interested homeowner. Her topics were eclectic, everything from advice for the rank beginner, to how to use bulbs and shrubbery effectively, from appreciation for old-fashioned garden practices to comprehensive landscape design. Tabor (1913) championed native plants ("I have made it a rule not to use exotics when native growth that would serve as well was obtainable") and helped to popularize residential landscape design in the formative years of the twentieth century: "The entire grounds about a suburban dwelling constitute its garden [; it] is these in their entirety that are to be furnished with a design—that is, that are to be planned and made orderly and beautiful. And they must be considered as a unit in order to accomplish this with the best results."

1. Colonial Revival house.

2. An inviting arbor entry in the Colonial Revival style.

3. This strongly symmetrical design would suit a Colonial Revival house (Kellaway 1915).

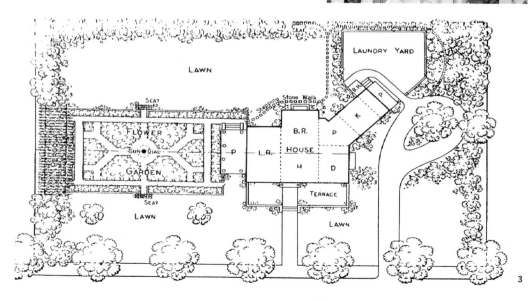

SCALE OF FEET.

0   10   20   30   40   50

STREET

Landscape Design

Approaches to landscape design in general were varied (not to say eclectic) at this time, with many vocal and enthusiastic practitioners throughout the country. The field of landscape architecture was defining itself, and the popularization of gardening and landscape design was demonstrated in many books and periodicals, including *Garden Magazine*, *House Beautiful*, and *Country Life in America*. A vanguard of primarily female authors, including Neltje Blanchan (Mrs. Frank Nelson Doubleday), Grace Tabor, Louisa Yeoman (Mrs. Francis King), and Alice Morse Earle, described their personal experiences with gardening in a plethora of books. In addition to new styles or approaches to the landscape, some thematic gardens were in vogue, including the grandmother's garden, Japanese gardens, Italian gardens, and, with the advent of World War I, victory gardens.

Flower gardens

In the early twentieth century gardeners were becoming more and more interested in ornamental plants and most particularly in flower gardens. Savvy gardeners learned how to plan gardens based on color combinations or on seasonal interest. Striking partnerships of perennials with shrubs formed the basis for the mixed border so ably promoted by Gertrude Jekyll. Attention to foliage colors and textures was *haute decor.*

Although herbaceous perennials had been central to garden design for a century, in the early 1900s they took on a new significance. Plant breeding in many genera offered gardeners a whole new palette of plants from which to choose their garden stars. *Anemone*, *Astilbe*, *Iris*, and by the 1920s, *Hemerocallis*, were among the genera that benefited from scientific innovation during this time. Indeed, gardens devoted to a single genus were sometimes touted, and collector's gardens (filled with roses, dahlias, peonies) were common. Similarly, for those whose love extended more broadly to families of plants, lovers of the newly popular ornamental grasses used their yard as a canvas to mix grasses and sedges in with colorful annuals and shrubs. Even in the earliest years of the new century, the literature spoke of gardens that would appeal to contemporary "plant nerds":

> It is a delightful task to collect plants for their own sakes, without any reference to their relation with the surrounding scenery. But collections should be arranged on spots specially set apart for them, where they will not injure the main picture formed by the general environment of the house and the encircling landscape (Van Rensselaer 1903).

American gardeners arguably began their love affair with the perennial border during this time. Following the English precedent, borders, five to eight feet wide, were fashioned along pathways or along a property line. An alternative was to construct formal geometric beds in the ancient style, bordered by gravel paths and filled with bright and fragrant flowers. Designers arranged perennials by height, color, and season of bloom. They added annuals to extend the season of color and flowering shrubs to provide structure. Sometimes these gardens were set apart, separated from the surrounding landscape by a hedge or a white wooden trellis. Suggested edgings for the flowerbed or border included boxwood hedging, glass bottles, and shells. The eminent Louise Beebe Wilder (1919) preferred something else: "For the garden laying not too great a claim to magnificence, I think no edging is prettier than large irregular stones sunk part way in the earth."

Trees and shrubs

By the turn of the twentieth century, the Arts and Crafts philosophy that a house ought to be tied to the landscape by means of plantings at its foundation was making inroads; but photographic evidence tells us that a now-typical foundation planting of shrubs was not a common practice until after World War I. This isn't to suggest that writers from the early twentieth century lacked enthusiasm for trees and shrubs; in fact, they frequently described their virtues in the residential landscape, as screens and hedges featuring fall color, fragrance, winter interest, unique foliage, flowers, and fruit. "Every yard ought to have its quota of shrubs. They give it a charm which nothing else in the plant-line can supply" (Rexford 1912). Shrubs were sometimes in a shrubbery by themselves, but

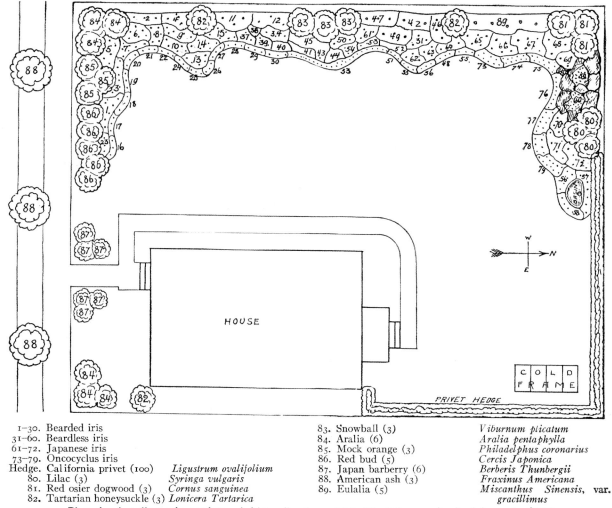

1–30. Bearded iris	83. Snowball (3)	*Viburnum plicatum*
31–60. Beardless iris	84. Aralia (6)	*Aralia pentaphylla*
61–72. Japanese iris	85. Mock orange (3)	*Philadelphus coronarius*
73–79. Oncocyclus iris	86. Red bud (5)	*Cercis Japonica*
Hedge. California privet (100) *Ligustrum ovalifolium*	87. Japan barberry (6)	*Berberis Thunbergii*
80. Lilac (3) *Syringa vulgaris*	88. American ash (3)	*Fraxinus Americana*
81. Red osier dogwood (3) *Cornus sanguinea*	89. Eulalia (5)	*Miscanthus Sinensis*, var. *gracillimus*
82. Tartarian honeysuckle (3) *Lonicera Tartarica*		

Plan 4. A collector's garden. A big collection of iris like this may be had for only $100

"A collector's garden," this time for irises (*Garden Magazine* 1907).

'Indian Chief' (1929) was an exciting new tall bearded iris, back in the day.

dramatic bulbous plants were often interspersed among them, for floral and multiseason interest. Our featured designer argued the point persuasively:

> There is no reason . . . for not putting summer bulbs against shrubbery in a shrubbery border, just as hardy bulbs—such as lilies—are so often, and with such delightful effect, planted. [D]ahlias may make a border by themselves almost as effective as shrubs [; c]annas, towering above so many of the garden's occupants, are well suited to light up the foliage of shrubbery groups; gladioli and tigridia, though not so tall, may occupy similar positions (Tabor 1917).

In particular, broadleaved evergreens were a treasured component of the eclectic landscapes of this era: "[T]he most precious quality in broad-leaved evergreens is a certain *mystic charm* which has nothing at all to do with showy flowers or berries. It resides in the foliage . . . I venture to call it the 'classic' effect" (Miller 1917).

Rhododendron in bloom.

Kitchen gardens

World War I and fears of a possible food shortage motivated many people to cultivate their own food, and garden clubs across the country urged their members to install kitchen gardens. Besides, if further inducement were necessary, "The care of the space usually given to raising grass which must be cut at least once a week to keep it in good shape will not take up any more time actually if vegetables take the place of grass, than this weekly running about it with the lawnmower" (Tabor 1913). It should be noted here that an herb garden as a separate garden was *not* typical of this or any earlier period; the notion of herb gardens as specialty gardens came later, in the 1930s.

So, a kitchen garden remained a feature of the landscape. Recommendations to site it "within convenient reach of the house" and in such a way as to be ornamental were frequent—say, a gate over-arched with roses leading to it, or "a grass path down the centre, spanned at the cross-paths [perhaps] by an arch of Scarlet Runner beans [would give] a deal of satisfaction to the eye" (Duncan 1918). A kitchen garden, with its rows upon rows, was by its nature formal, and with geometric shapes for the vegetable beds—squares and rectangles—it appeared even more so. Because of this, some writers urged their readers to use a hedge, fence, or trelliswork to screen this garden from the rest of the property, particularly if the latter was more wild and naturalistic. And yet . . .

> A properly kept vegetable garden is in its way as beautiful as a flower garden, and by treating it decoratively and letting it have here and there a few clumps of flowers, it can be made a very charming spot indeed. It will be in conformity with the Craftsman spirit that so essential a part of the home as the vegetable garden need not be hidden (Burnett 1910).

The old-fashioned or grandmother's garden

The "grandmother's garden" touted in the last quarter of the nineteenth century now became even more popular; in part a reaction to the annual hauling in and out of bedding schemes and newfangled subtropicals, such a garden featured plants of the past and emphasized fragrance and

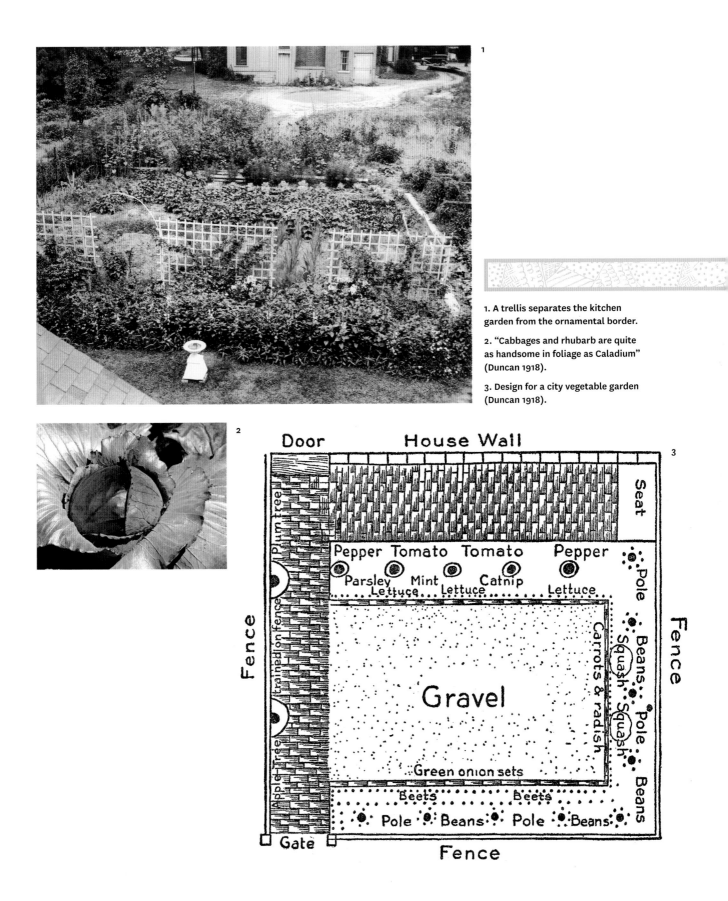

1. A trellis separates the kitchen garden from the ornamental border.

2. "Cabbages and rhubarb are quite as handsome in foliage as Caladium" (Duncan 1918).

3. Design for a city vegetable garden (Duncan 1918).

Door   House Wall

Plum Tree

Seat

Pepper   Tomato   Tomato   Pepper

Parsley   Mint   Catnip

Lettuce   Lettuce   Lettuce

Fence

Trained on fence

Pole

Gravel

Carrots & radish

Beans

Squash

Squash

Pole

Fence

Beans

Apple Tree

Green onion sets

Beets   Beets

Gate   Pole   Beans   Pole   Beans   Beans

Fence

1. An old-fashioned garden makes the front cover (*Garden Magazine* 1919).

2. Roses, peonies, and other "dear delights," including a sundial, capture the manner, if not the matter, of days gone by.

sentimental associations. Writing about the old-fashioned flowers, Maurice Maeterlinck (1905) exclaimed,

> I love above all the simplest, the commonest, the oldest and the most antiquated; those which have a long human past behind them, a large array of kind and consoling actions; those which have lived with us for hundreds of years and which form part of ourselves, since they reflect something of their grace and their joy of life in the soul of our ancestors.

Alice Morse Earle (1901) extolled the old-fashioned garden, and in 1919 *Garden Magazine* devoted its December issue to the style, to which Grace Tabor, our design maven for this era, contributed an insightful piece. In it, she reminded readers not to impose their contemporary attitudes on the garden practices of the past (always good advice!):

> The old-fashioned garden is *not an actual entity* but rather *the embodiment of a set of principles* [, and] the charm of these old gardens remaining to us [is] their manner rather than their matter. Catch the manner, and the flowers of today will furnish the matter quite as well as did the flowers of a century ago.

Tabor reminded readers that gardens of earlier years had order and were functional and practical. Formed mainly to sustain the household, they were not haphazard; there was in them a "neatness and exactness that characterized the times." In the same issue, Louise Beebe Wilder (1919) recommended some of the old-timey plants that she felt deserved to be cultivated in contemporary gardens. Her "dear delights" included hollyhocks, primroses, cowslips, foxgloves, sweet violets, waterlilies, sweet woodruff, and honeysuckle.

A final note: "In the old gardens, instead of being sharp and conspicuous, the colors of the accessories merge and supplement each other so perfectly as to be unnoticed" (Fox 1929).

3

The lily pool

Water features were common landscape elements in gardens large and small—perhaps particularly indispensable in the latter: "Water in a landscape is as a mirror to a room—the feature that doubles and enhances all its charms" (Blanchan 1909). Where they did not naturally exist, small ponds were carefully dug and lined with concrete. Although plastic preformed shapes or liners were not available, design concerns over hiding or camouflaging the artificial edge were the same then as now. Experts recommended lining the top of the pool with stratified rocks, of the flagstone type, which were broken into irregular pieces and layered so that some of them would slightly overhang the pool edge; the presence of moss or lichens on the rocks improved the effect, especially for an informal pool. Another important consideration was the water supply. Often the expense of laying pipes to the site was avoided by simply using the garden hose; today, one might even consider harvesting rainwater to fill an ornamental pool.

3. "A lily pool in a little garden" (Spencer 1922).

4. A much larger lily pool is the formal focal point of this plan (*Fruit, Garden and Home* 1924).

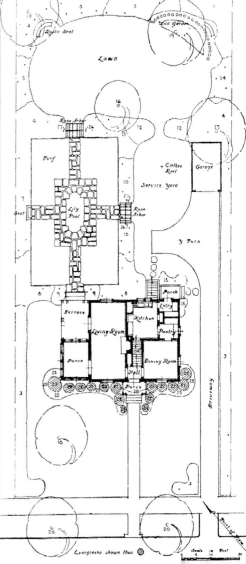

4

Stone lantern and water basin embellish a Japanese garden scene.

The Japanese garden

Gardens influenced by Japanese landscape design were frequent, primarily as accompaniments to the Craftsman architectural style. The stimulus for this interest was the popularity of the Ho-o-den pavilion at the 1893 Columbian Exhibition in Chicago. West Coast garden designers were especially drawn to this stylistic approach, in which, as with other landscape elements of this era, a harmonious composition of the overall landscape was of the utmost importance; California architects Greene and Greene utilized Japanese details in the garden of the famous David B. Gamble house in Pasadena.

Eugene O. Murmann (1914) designed a Japanese tea garden that he explained would fit "cozily" on a corner lot, and indeed the Japanese garden was particularly suited to small spaces. Florence Dixon (1910) described its other unique attributes, some of which echoed the appeal of the grandmother's garden:

> The Japanese garden . . . furnishes a new note for those seeking original treatment of their places. It has a beauty which grows upon acquaintance, and there is no kind of garden which has about it a richer amount of sentiment and tradition than the Japanese. Every hill, tree, rock, and flower has its own special meaning and place in the picture, and although the religious significance which attaches to these things must of necessity be lost, the charm of the symbolism still remains.

The Japanese garden emulates the natural landscape with simplicity and subtlety. Water typically is the dominant feature, around which the others are grouped; a small bridge to cross a pond or stream is a traditional element often included. If no water is available, a Japanese garden of the *karesansui* type might instead emphasize a dry streambed. Specimen trees are incorporated for their evergreen habit or a picturesque shape. Flowers are usually not featured, although potted chrysanthemums or peonies or a clump of iris is sometimes included. Ferns and mosses may be used for verdant enhancement of the setting.

In the Japanese tradition, stones may have symbolic importance and are carefully placed at irregular intervals. William Verbeck (1903), who was born and raised in Japan, knew firsthand the importance of stone in the Japanese garden:

> Indeed the perfect type of the flat garden is nothing but an archipelago of rocks in a sea of white pebbles. The stones must be the foundation; the rest are mere accessories. Speaking stones are what is wanted—stones that suggest moods and passions—for the Japanese recognize that there are sermons in stones. Each stone has its name and relative place in the composition. There is the Guardian Stone in the center, and opposite it the Belleview Stone. Across the cascade is the Moonshade Stone, and so on in orbits [are the] Throne Stone, Worshipping Stone, Snail Stone, Idle Stone.

Other accessories for a Japanese garden might be pergolas, stone lanterns, symbolic statuary (cranes or deer are favorite subjects), or even a teahouse.

Essential Elements of Japanese Gardens
- Water feature
- Interesting small trees and shrubs
- Stones and rocks, strategically placed
- Pots of chrysanthemums and peonies

Landscape Features

Paths and driveways

When cars entered the scene, landscape plans had to address settings for their access and storage. For driveways, the first question was how much traffic it would have to withstand. "If there is but little travel, a gravel drive will be satisfactory [but] if there is more driving, or there is not a good quality of gravel in the neighborhood, a macadam drive should be made" (Kellaway 1915). At the time, a macadam road was constructed by cementing layers of small stones into a durable surface with stone dust and water; and by 1910, petroleum-based asphalt was a popular U.S. road pavement. As for driveway design, the ellipsis was a common form, where there was enough room; and for its placement, "the elliptical turn is attractive and practical either directly in front of the house or at the end" (Cridland 1916).

Walkways from the front door to the street, not to mention additional paths for accessibility throughout the property, were another consideration. The thorny question of whether to curve the path (or not) was still before the garden court, and advocates of each type of construction defended their views. Grace Tabor (1916) has the floor: "Walks and driveways should always be direct—as direct as the line that a tired man or a lazy man or a hurried man, coming into the house or driving to the stable, would naturally follow." But according to Eben Rexford (1912), "A straight path is never a graceful one. A curving path will make you a few more steps, but so much will be gained by it, in beauty." Mrs. Schuyler Van Rensselaer (1903) proposed a compromise: "A happy mean between the two extremes of mathematical rigidity and irrational irregularity is what we want in an approach—a line which is direct enough to seem sensible and yet curved enough to give grace and variety."

Materials for paths, drives, and walkways were as diverse as the various regions could supply; common from coast to coast were cement, brick, flagstone, macadam, slate, and gravel. "For main walks that are much used, cement and stone flagging are good materials because they are durable, and they keep down weeds" (Bailey 1903). But our featured designer had a different opinion: "The

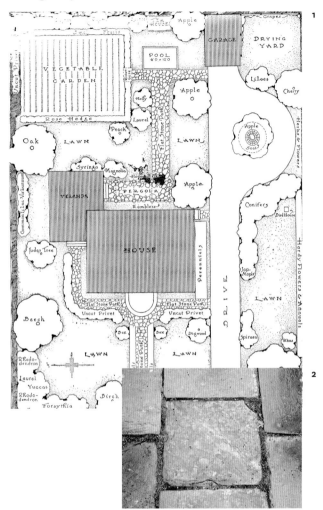

1. A "flat stone path" features in this design (Rose 1920).

2. A flagstone path.

material *par excellence* for interior walks is brick, laid on a bed of sand, this on a bed of cinders. The old-time natural flag stones are next in choice to the bricks, while gravel, properly laid, always makes a walk little inferior to any" (Tabor 1913).

Clearly flagstone was a popular material for residential paths. "Flagstone walks, made with flags of North River blue stone or Indiana limestone, are the most serviceable of all walks. . . . It is customary to lay flags cut in single blocks of various lengths to the full width of the walk" (Cridland 1916). Flagstones found around properties of this era might be thicker than those that are currently available.

Fences and hedges

Fences were as diverse as the properties they enclosed. Rustic wood fences continued to be popular, as were fences made of lattice; those of wire were often utilized as a less costly enclosure solution. Pickets were particularly prized for the Colonial Revival landscape. Concrete walls and copings provided a demarcation of private and public property; a dry stone retaining wall was preferable to an unmowable slope if it was "found advisable to construct the garden on more than one level" (Cridland 1916). The philosophy of the day was that "gateways and fences [should] fit into the harmony of the home and blend with the planting of trees, shrubs or hedge" (Riley 1915).

Hedges have never gone out of fashion completely in American garden history. During this period, they typically were used for one of two purposes, either to mark the property boundary or to screen an unsightly view. Also short hedges, perhaps of boxwood or santolina, were important to the Colonial Revival gardener as borders for geometric flowerbeds.

1. Advertisement for "fence" and "fencing" (*Garden Magazine* 1908).

2. Lattice fence and gate with stone wall (Kellaway 1915).

3. Rustic gate, c. 1910.

1

2

152

A low hedge marks the property line but still permits the
family a clear view of the street, c. 1910.

1. "House proud": a dry-laid stone retaining wall (and Chinese-Chippendale porch railing), c. 1910.

2. Wood fence with "moon" top (Butterfield 1914).

3. Craftsman-style board fences: "The half-open fence with lattice top is just the thing on which to train creepers" (Rogers 1911).

Seating

Wood, whether "in rustic" or painted (white or green, usually), was more often seen than metal, with the primitiveness of its styling increasing in proportion to its distance from the house. Classic Lutyens wood benches, with clean lines, provided a sense of formality; rustic benches, of course, did the opposite. Battens were sometimes attached to the legs of chairs and benches, to prevent damage to grass or gravel. Stone was out of favor as a material; with the Romantic period over, things were more grounded, simple and sensible. "Stone seats have the drawback that they retain moisture after rain, and therefore are not always in a condition for use" (Rogers 1911). Wicker furniture continued its run on porches, sunrooms, and terraces; the design of wicker and other woven furniture too could convey either formality or informality, depending on the setting.

Wicker—indoors (*Garden Magazine* 1910).

WANAMAKER'S Reed Furniture
Fairly Breathes Rest and Comfort

A wooden bench "more suited for a woodland walk, or the wilder parts of the garden, than for a position within view of the house" (Rogers 1911).

GARDEN FURNITURE

Send for catalogue showing a great variety of benches, chairs, tables, etc., in rustic and painted.

We have a Special Offer for October

NORTH SHORE FERNERIES CO.
Beverly, Mass.

Painted garden furniture (*Garden Magazine* 1915).

Settee 106. Price $11.00

Andrew Jackson Chair 32. Price $4.00

Table 199. Price $9.00

Andrew Jackson Rocker 33. Price $4.75

TRADE
OLD HICKORY
CHAIR CO
MARTINSVILLE IND
MARK
Trade Mark burned in wood

The Old Hickory Chair Co.
404 South Cherry St.
Martinsville, Indiana

Chairs woven with strips of hickory (*Garden Magazine* 1912).

1. If the pergola is at a distance from the house, more rustic materials might be used successfully (Bailey 1903).

2. Both Tabor and Blanchan would have disliked this improperly introduced pergola. Unadilla Silo Company, c. 1920.

3. A "private residence pergola," California, 1917.

3

Garden accessories

Pergolas were all the rage in this period. Grace Tabor (1913) defined and opined: "Pergola, be it noted, means nothing more nor less than 'vine arbor' . . . . Only attached to the dwelling, not merely against it but leading from it, may such pergolas be properly introduced." Opinions were mixed, however, on their usefulness and appropriateness to the landscape. Neltje Blanchan (1909) was particularly sharp on the point:

> Quite suddenly and violently . . . have Americans taken to pergolas: every type of house and garden in this broad land now boasts one. Many are meaningless, leading from no place in particular to no place in particular; opening up no vista through leafy arches toward a beautiful view; sheltering no cozy breakfast or tea table; inviting no one to rest awhile on comfortable, shady seats; growing no especially beautiful vines . . . extending no architectural lines that end too abruptly; tying no building to the surrounding garden or landscape—having, in short no well-thought reason for their existence.

From Blanchan's words, it is possible to deduce how such a structure was appropriately sited and used: to open up a vista or lead to a wonderful view, or to provide shelter for seating or dining. The pergola should complement the architecture of the house and, when attached to the house, should be constructed of materials similar to those used on the house or its porch.

Of course, in addition to the elaborate pergolas, simple trellises continued, as they had for decades, to support vines in many landscape situations. Vines were exceptionally functional, and writers often recommended them as the very first plants to grace a new residential landscape. In addition to being decorative, they could bring nearly instant shade to a porch or piazza, perfume the air with a beguiling fragrance, or provide multiseason color. They were chief contributors to the design philosophy of the era: that the house and grounds should be connected in such a way that one did not know where one ended and the other began.

1

A RESIDENCE AT OLDSMAR. FLORIDA.

2

1. A pergola "should look when built as if it belonged to the place and not appear as if dropped by a passing wind without relation to the house or lawn" (Kellaway 1915). Unadilla Silo Company, c. 1920.

2. Simple trellis in front of a Florida home, c. 1915.

3. Wisteria on iron support (*Garden Magazine* 1912).

4. A trellis meant to be attached to the house. Unadilla Silo Company,
c. 1920.

5. Freestanding trellis. Unadilla Silo Company, c. 1920.

1. Prairie-style planting in an urn that is a permanent fixture of the landscape.

2. "An excellent receptacle for tender shrubs." Unadilla Silo Company, c. 1925.

But, "of all the various methods of ornamenting the small garden, or large either, there is none more simple, charming or artistically correct than the use of stone urns and pots for flowers or small trees" (Savage 1916). Sense underlay this sensibility: "It has been found practical to grow flowers in pots . . . where every drop of water has to be carefully hoarded, for a potted plant absorbs all the water it receives and none is wasted" (Fox 1929). Urns and vases occupied positions of distinction in many gardens of this era. Sometimes they simply provided a practical means to display a tender plant, which might then easily be brought indoors; more often, they were themselves the focal points and were constructed in classic designs to enhance the garden scene. Urns and vases were made of traditional terracotta or other earthenware, both glazed and unglazed. Large pots of stone and iron were permanent features of some landscapes. Containers made of concrete and finished to look like stone could also be found. "Pompeian stone" was a composite material made to look like limestone. Wooden tree boxes were decorated in contemporary motifs.

Gazing globes frequently adorned the eclectic gardens of the early twentieth century. The very nature of the globe made it more than a static garden ornament: the sky and the flowers and the trees were reflected in its mirror surface, adding another dimension to the garden scene. Some writers reported that the gazing globe could also be positioned to reflect the persons entering the garden so that the occupants could be on alert—a new twist on a centuries-old concern.

Another way to assure the garden was not static was to welcome wildlife. "The bird-bath is not merely a fad, but a humanitarian feature. There is a spirit of bird conservation sweeping over the country, and the bird-bath in the small garden does its share of the work" (Savage 1916). Magazines of the period featured advertisements for these, as well as sheltered food houses, suet baskets, trees and shrubs to attract birds, and special houses for martins and bluebirds. This remains a contemporary pursuit: gardeners have tried avidly to attract wildlife, mainly birds, to gardens for more than a century, now.

Finally, for Colonial Revival settings, sundials held their position in the landscape. Alice Morse Earle (1902) gave them voice, quoting the concluding couplet from a poem by Austin Dobson, which appeared on sundials in both England and America: "I am a Shade—a Shadowe too, art thou. / I mark the Time. Saye! Gossip! Dost thou soe?" She wrote of the "charm and sentiment" of these primitive clocks, these garden gods, insisting that (although they were no longer essential, as they were to colonial-era gardeners) they remained important. C. Courtenay Savage (1916) agreed, and added some advice about placement: "There is something decidedly formal about the sundial; perhaps it is the majesty of time that has endowed it with its dignity, but to be a real ornament a sundial needs space, and should not be placed in close proximity to luxurious displays of vegetation."

3. "Graystone is the garden pottery of Weller Ware" (*Better Homes and Gardens* 1928).

4. "A Sundial placed on a decorative pedestal at a focal point in your garden will add a touch of Old World charm." Erkins Studios, New York, c. 1925.

5. "Gaze into the future and you will see the past," c. 1910.

▶ NEXT SPREAD In this c. 1915 garden, terracotta pots, including some that have been painted white, hold ferns, rex begonias, and other floral treasures.

An URN or a bird-bath of beautiful Graystone will add a fresh element of beauty to your garden, yet seem to have lived years there. Its mellow gray blends at once with sky and leaves. Graystone is the garden pottery of Weller Ware. It is often pure Greek in effect. Its appearance suggests great price. Yet it is never expensive. Place an urn or a vase near a flight of steps or a low wall. Arrange an urn of vines where a hard place in the garden precludes planting. There are pedestals for sun-dials, child figures, footed jars. Weller Ware offers also a rich variety of colored art pottery and distinctive kitchen ware. Paula Morgan, authority on garden and home decoration, will give free advice regarding any decorative need. Write her in care of The Weller Potteries, Zanesville, Ohio.

WELLER ☍ WARE

3

SUNDIALS

604—Height 37"
Top 12½"
GREY TERRA COTTA
$15.00

C-50
Height 35"
Top 11"
POMPEIAN STONE
$25.00

"O"—10¾" Diam.
Bronze Verde Finish $10.00

No. 4—12¾" in Diam.
BRASS - $16.50
10½" in Diam.
BRASS - $13.50

"H" ARMILLARY
SUNDIAL
12" Diameter
$25.00

4

5

1

Case Studies

1914 house, Stony Point, New York

Stony Point is a small town in the Lower Hudson Valley, just north of New York City on the west side of the Hudson River. Denise Adams's house there was built in 1914 of local materials, including trees felled and cured on the property. The exterior is river rock on the first floor with stucco above; the interior features many details representative of the Craftsman style—oak floors, quarter-sawn oak woodwork, a sleeping porch, a chamfered ceiling in the dining room. The roof is terracotta tile, a material not often seen in this section of the country. Utility connections are on the street (south) side of the house, which is sited to face the river to the east. The house sits on nearly an acre, of which about one-third is a steep slope.

The inspiration for the Stony Point design was an article that began with these words: "A Craftsman house should be surrounded by grounds that embody the Craftsman principles of utility, economy of effort and beauty" (Burnett 1910). The article outlined appropriate design characteristics for four Craftsman dwellings, each with a

different seasonally interesting landscape. One in particular, the "Early Summer Craftsman Garden," provided many artistic details for the Stony Point residence, including the borders that enclose the new curving bluestone path from the front of the house to the street. Flanking this path are five-foot-wide flower borders featuring heirloom iris and other plants from the grandmother's garden. "Hardy herbaceous plants," Burnett continued, "are the best ones for a Craftsman garden because they mean the smallest amount of trouble, and because they are likely to survive the largest amount of neglect." Cosmos, nasturtium, and other annuals, used as fillers, complete these borders.

The "Late Summer Garden" from the same article provided inspiration for the atypical placement of the kitchen garden, between the house and the street. The kitchen garden consists of four rectangular raised vegetable beds, with a birdbath in the center, as a focal point. A small orchard of three heirloom apple and plum trees stands to the west, on the other side of the main drive. Along the perimeter fence are seven highbush blueberries, backed by a line of ornamental grasses. The ground under the fruit trees is planted with *Vinca minor* and the "dear delight" of sweet woodruff (*Galium odoratum*), following the advice

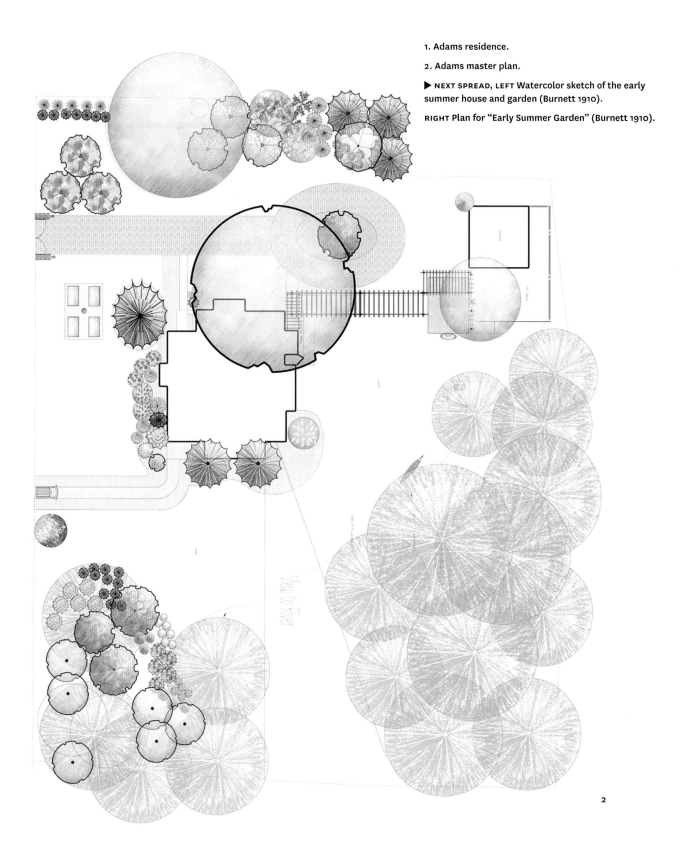

1. Adams residence.

2. Adams master plan.

▶ NEXT SPREAD, LEFT Watercolor sketch of the early summer house and garden (Burnett 1910).

RIGHT Plan for "Early Summer Garden" (Burnett 1910).

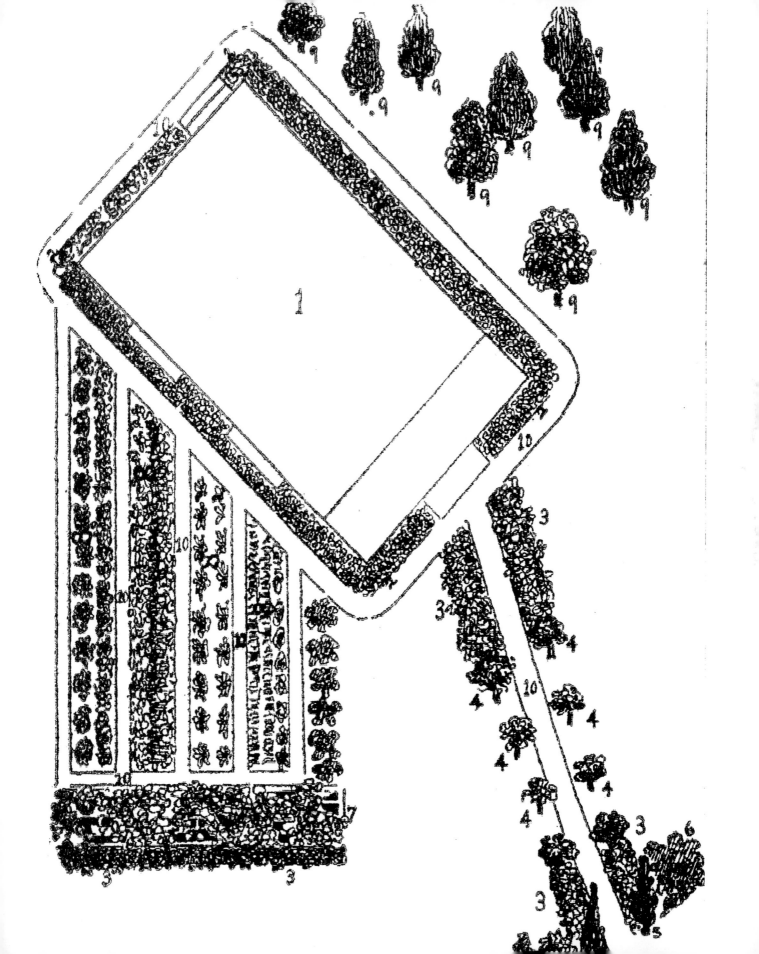

1. A recycled antique millstone is ready for many more years of service.

2. The Stony Point driveway is beautifully obscured each autumn by the leaf fall from the Japanese maple (*Acer palmatum*) and other deciduous trees.

2

1

of Wilhelm Miller (1917), who cautioned, "Wherever man leaves a bare spot nature attempts to cover it, though she may be able to do so only with plants we call 'weeds.'"

This house was built when automobiles were just becoming a part of the American landscape. The driveway still loops in front of a small detached garage, making an ellipse around a venerable Japanese maple, but the original gravel was replaced with concrete brick pavers with an antique appearance—a surface that was as evocative of the past, while demanding less maintenance. These pavers were set in sand to provide good drainage for the driveway, while a soldier course (edge) was mortared in to provide stability.

A pergola will lead from the kitchen door to a new outdoor terrace. Simple in design, it will repeat the square columns found on the main porch and in the front fence of the property. Continuing the Craftsman penchant for functional beauty, the pergola will feature grapes native to the New York region, interspersed with roses. The terrace, which will be used for dining and entertaining, will be constructed of brick and millstones, an accent once chosen by Ellen Biddle Shipman, another prominent designer of the era, for an outdoor dining room; the millstones emphasize the prominence of the round river rocks in the architecture of the house, while the brick warmly echoes the roof

tiles. Antique millstones are heavy and hard to come by. Thankfully, reproductions also are available. A stone barbecue grill, believed to be original to the property, will be dismantled and moved to the dining terrace.

Grace Tabor often recommended *Rhododendron vaseyi*, *R. periclymenoides*, and other native azaleas for shrubberies. The Stony Point property already included several mature specimens of *R. catawbiense*; to these were added, following the removal of invasive species along the west fence (including poison ivy), several antique varieties ('Boule de Neige', 'Cadis', 'Caroline', 'Dexter's Champagne', 'Dexter's Peppermint'). Another shrubbery was added on the street side of the house to screen the utility boxes, inspired again by Tabor. This planting includes such shrubby period favorites as forsythias, weigelas, and Van Houtte's spirea. Another shrub grouping near the road screens the main porch from the street and includes many native shrubs, including summersweet (*Clethra alnifolia*), underplanted with a variety of spring- and summer-blooming bulbs.

A year-round "borrowed" view of the Hudson River was to be the dominant water feature in this landscape. But many invasive Norway maples (*Acer platanoides*) profusely populated the hillside, blocking the view except in the winter; these were removed, ground on location

3

4

3. Kitchen garden at Stony Point, backed by an old yew, cloud-pruned in the Japanese style.

4. Kitchen garden detail.

to feed the hillside, and replaced with native species, strategically planted so as to frame a view of the Hudson River—and shut out the brightly colored roof of the county highway garage at the bottom of the hill. The crest of the hill, the transition area between level ground and slope, is a fertile area for many shrub species, both broadleaved and deciduous. In some future spring, the hill will be a sea of blue and yellow, following the planting of Virginia bluebells (*Mertensia virginica*) and daffodils. "These two effect—daffodils and bluebells—we can reproduce literally" (Miller 1917).

One last piece of inspirational advice from our prescient featured designer, who urged her readers to embrace the vagaries of their site, including an extreme change in grade such as that found at Stony Point:

> If creation has whimsically tilted the ground appropriated to your use at ever so steep an angle, that angle should not only be accepted as a motif but it should be emphasized. Go farther than toleration—or resignation. Seize upon the extravagance of a site always and make it the feature of the place; develop the plan of both house and grounds not merely to fit the situation but to *require* it (Tabor 1913).

The river view, before (top) and after.

PLANT LISTS

PAGE 1 OF 9

* Please check for possibility of invasiveness in your locale.

** Plant is from the period but not necessarily listed in extant resources for the region.

NEW ENGLAND

Trees

Abies balsamea
balsam fir

Abies concolor
white fir

Cercis canadensis
redbud

Cornus florida
dogwood

Juniperus virginiana
eastern red cedar

Picea abies
Norway spruce

Picea pungens 'Koster'
Koster blue spruce

Pinus strobus
white pine

Syringa reticulata
tree lilac

Tsuga canadensis
hemlock

Shrubs

Berberis thunbergii*
Japanese barberry

Deutzia gracilis
slender deutzia

Deutzia 'Pride of Rochester'
double-flowered deutzia

Forsythia suspensa
golden bells

Hamamelis virginiana
witch hazel

Hydrangea paniculata 'Grandiflora'
peegee hydrangea

Kerria japonica 'Pleniflora'
double-flowered Japanese rose

Philadelphus coronarius
mock orange

Rhododendron catawbiense
Catawba rhododendron

Rhus typhina
staghorn sumac

Spiraea japonica 'Anthony Waterer'
dwarf red spirea

Spiraea prunifolia
bridal wreath

Spiraea ×vanhouttei
Van Houtte's spirea

Symphoricarpos albus
snowberry

Syringa vulgaris
lilac

Viburnum opulus
highbush cranberry

Perennials and biennials

Achillea ptarmica 'The Pearl'
double white milfoil

Aquilegia chrysantha
golden-spurred columbine

Aurinia saxatilis
golden alyssum

Campanula medium
Canterbury bells

Coreopsis lanceolata
lance-leaf coreopsis

Gypsophila paniculata
baby's breath

Hibiscus 'Crimson Eye'
hibiscus

Leucanthemum ×superbum
Shasta daisy

Lobelia cardinalis
cardinal flower

Papaver nudicaule
Iceland poppy

Papaver orientale
oriental poppy

Stokesia laevis
Stokes' aster

Annuals

Amaranthus tricolor
Joseph's coat

Arctotis grandis
South African daisy

Calendula officinalis
pot marigold

Callistephus chinensis
China aster

Centaurea cyanus
bachelor's buttons

Chrysanthemum
winter pink

Cosmos bipinnatus
cosmos

Gomphrena globosa
globe amaranth

Lobelia erinus 'Crystal Palace'
blue lobelia

Petunia ×atkinsiana
petunia

Rhodanthe chlorocephala subsp. *rosea*
pink paper daisy

Solenostemon scutellarioides
coleus

Tropaeolum majus
nasturtium

Viola grandiflora
pansy

Roses

Rosa 'Margaret Dickson'

Rosa 'Mme. Norbert Levavasseur'

PLANT LISTS

* Please check for possibility of invasiveness in your locale.

** Plant is from the period but not necessarily listed in extant resources for the region.

Rosa rugosa
rugosa rose

Rosa 'Soleil d'Or'

Rosa wichuraiana
memorial rose

Vines

Aristolochia macrophylla
Dutchman's pipe

Clematis terniflora
sweet autumn clematis

Lathyrus odoratus
sweet pea

Lonicera sempervirens
trumpet honeysuckle

Parthenocissus quinquefolia
Virginia creeper

Wisteria sinensis*
Chinese wisteria

Bulbs

Canna 'Florence Vaughan'
canna

Crocus 'King of the Blues'
crocus

Dahlia
dahlia

   'Bishop of Llandaff'**

   'Jersey's Beauty'**

Galanthus nivalis
snowdrop

Galtonia candicans
summer hyacinth

Hyacinthus orientalis
hyacinth

   'Gipsy Queen'**

   'Madame Sophie'**

Lilium auratum
gold-band lily

Lilium speciosum 'Rubrum'
crimson banded lily

Narcissus
daffodil

   'Avalanche'**

   'Carlton'**

Tulipa
tulip

   'Dillenburg'**

   'Generaal de Wet'**

MIDDLE ATLANTIC

Trees

Acer palmatum
Japanese maple

Aesculus hippocastanum
horse chestnut

Cornus florida
dogwood

Fagus sylvatica
European beech

Morus alba 'Pendula'
weeping mulberry

Picea abies
Norway spruce

Picea pungens f. *glauca*
Colorado blue spruce

Populus nigra 'Italica'
Lombardy poplar

Prunus cerasifera 'Pissardii'
purple-leaf plum

Thuja occidentalis
arborvitae

Shrubs

Berberis thunbergii*
Japanese barberry

Chaenomeles speciosa
Japanese quince

Clethra alnifolia
summersweet

Hibiscus syriacus
rose of Sharon

Hydrangea paniculata 'Grandiflora'
peegee hydrangea

Ligustrum ovalifolium*
California privet

Philadelphus coronarius
mock orange

Rhododendron
rhododendron

Spiraea japonica 'Anthony Waterer'
dwarf red spirea

Spiraea ×*vanhouttei*
Van Houtte's spirea

Perennials and biennials

Alcea rosea
hollyhock

Anemone ×*hybrida* 'Whirlwind'
Japanese anemone

Anthemis tinctoria
golden chamomile

Arabis alpina
rock cress

Bellis perennis
English daisy

Campanula carpatica
Carpathian bellflower

Campanula persicifolia 'Alba'
white peach-leaved bellflower

Convallaria majalis
lily-of-the-valley

Dianthus barbatus
sweet William

Digitalis grandiflora
great-flowered foxglove

Gypsophila paniculata
baby's breath

Iberis sempervirens
candytuft

Lychnis chalcedonica
Maltese cross

Paeonia
peony

   'Golden Dawn'**

   'Sarah Bernhardt'**

Papaver orientale
oriental poppy

Platycodon grandiflorus
balloon flower

Rudbeckia laciniata 'Hortensia'
golden glow

Scabiosa caucasica
pincushion flower

Sedum spectabile
showy sedum

Yucca filamentosa
Adam's needle

Annuals

Callistephus chinensis
China aster

Consolida ambigua
larkspur

Coreopsis tinctoria
bright eyes

Gomphrena globosa
globe amaranth

Impatiens balsamina
balsam

Mirabilis jalapa
four o'clock

Phlox drummondii
annual phlox

Salpiglossis sinuata
painted tongue

Viola grandiflora
pansy

Viola tricolor
Johnny-jump-up

Roses

Rosa 'Dorothy Perkins'

Rosa 'Frau Karl Druschki'

Rosa 'Margaret Dickson'

Rosa 'Mme. Norbert Levavasseur'

Rosa 'Turner's Crimson Rambler'

Vines

Aristolochia macrophylla
Dutchman's pipe

Clematis terniflora
sweet autumn clematis

Parthenocissus quinquefolia
Virginia creeper

Parthenocissus tricuspidata
Boston ivy

*Wisteria sinensis**
Chinese wisteria

Bulbs

Anemone coronaria
windflower

Canna indica
Indian shot

Crocus
crocus

Dahlia
dahlia

   'Bishop of Llandaff'**

   'Jersey's Beauty'**

Gladiolus
sword lily

Hyacinthus orientalis
hyacinth

   'Gipsy Queen'**

   'Madame Sophie'**

Lilium lancifolium
tiger lily

   'Flore Pleno'
   double tiger lily

Narcissus
daffodil

   'Avalanche'**

   'Carlton'**

Tulipa
tulip

   'Dillenburg'**

   'Generaal de Wet'**

Trees

Acer saccharinum
silver maple

Catalpa speciosa
northern catalpa

Cedrus deodora
Deodar cedar

Cycas revoluta
sago palm

Ficus elastica
Indian rubber tree

Firmiana simplex
Chinese parasol tree

Juniperus communis 'Hibernica'
Irish juniper

Lagerstroemia indica
crepe myrtle

Magnolia grandiflora
southern magnolia

*Melia azedarach**
chinaberry

Phoenix canariensis
Canary Island date palm

Picea abies
Norway spruce

Picea pungens f. *glauca*
Colorado blue spruce

Poncirus trifoliata
trifoliate orange

PLANT LISTS

* Please check for possibility of invasiveness in your locale.

** Plant is from the period but not necessarily listed in extant resources for the region.

Sabal palmetto
cabbage palmetto

Thuja occidentalis
arborvitae

Shrubs

Calycanthus floridus
Carolina allspice

Cinnamomum camphora
camphor tree

Hydrangea macrophylla 'Thomas Hogg'
mophead hydrangea

Hydrangea paniculata 'Grandiflora'
peegee hydrangea

Jasminum sambac 'Grand Duke'
Arabian jasmine

Ligustrum ovalifolium*
California privet

Nerium oleander
oleander

Rhododendron
rhododendron

Robinia hispida
rose acacia

Spiraea ×vanhouttei
Van Houtte's spirea

Trachelospermum jasminoides
confederate jasmine

Viburnum opulus 'Roseum'
snowball

Perennials and biennials

Acorus calamus
sweet flag

Adiantum pedatum
maidenhair fern

Aquilegia canadensis
Canadian columbine

Arundo donax 'Versicolor'
striped reed

Asclepias tuberosa
butterfly milkweed

Asparagus sprengeri
feather fern

Aster novae-angliae
New England aster

Bambusa metake
bamboo

Baptisia australis
false indigo

Begonia
begonia

Chrysanthemum
winter pink

Convallaria majalis
lily-of-the-valley

Cortaderia selloana*
pampas grass

Dicentra eximia
fringed bleeding heart

Hibiscus moscheutos
rosemallow

Iris cristata
crested iris

Matteuccia struthiopteris
ostrich fern

Miscanthus sinensis 'Zebrinus'
zebra grass

Monarda didyma
beebalm

Osmunda cinnamomea
cinnamon fern

Paeonia
peony

  'Golden Dawn'**

  'Sarah Bernhardt'**

Phlox paniculata
perennial phlox

Tradescantia virginiana
spiderwort

Yucca filamentosa
Adam's needle

Annuals

Ageratum houstonianum
flossflower

Callistephus chinensis
China aster

Cosmos bipinnatus
cosmos

Dianthus chinensis
China pink

Heliotropium arborescens
cherry pie

Impatiens walleriana
sultan's balsam

Lobularia maritima
sweet alyssum

Pelargonium
geranium

Petunia ×atkinsiana
petunia

Salvia splendens
scarlet sage

Solenostemon scutellarioides
coleus

Verbena ×hybrida
verbena

Viola grandiflora
pansy

Viola tricolor
Johnny-jump-up

Roses

Rosa 'Clotilde Soupert'

Rosa 'Dorothy Perkins'

Rosa 'Duchesse de Brabant'

Rosa 'Frau Karl Druschki'

Rosa 'Maman Cochet'

Rosa 'Mme. Norbert Levavasseur'

Rosa 'Reine Marie Henriette'

Rosa 'Turner's Crimson Rambler'

Vines

Antigonon leptopus
coral vine

Bignonia capreolata
crossvine

Clematis terniflora
sweet autumn clematis

Gelsemium sempervirens
Carolina jasmine

Hedera helix*
English ivy

Lonicera flava
yellow trumpet honeysuckle

Vinca major*
creeping periwinkle

Wisteria frutescens
American wisteria

Bulbs

Alocasia macrorrhizos
giant taro

Caladium bicolor
angel wings

Canna indica
Indian shot

Colocasia esculenta
elephant ears

Crinum
swamp lily

Crocus
crocus

Dahlia
dahlia

   'Bishop of Llandaff'**

   'Jersey's Beauty'**

Gladiolus
sword lily

Hedychium
ginger lily

Hyacinthus orientalis
hyacinth

Lilium lancifolium
tiger lily

Narcissus
daffodil

   'Thalia'**

   'Trevithian'**

Polianthes tuberosa 'Flore Pleno'
double tuberose

Zantedeschia aethiopica
calla lily

Trees

Abies balsamea
balsam fir

Betula pendula 'Laciniata'
cut-leaf weeping birch

Catalpa speciosa
northern catalpa

Picea abies
Norway spruce

Sorbus aucuparia
European mountain ash

Thuja occidentalis
arborvitae

Tilia americana
basswood

Shrubs

Calycanthus floridus
Carolina allspice

Chionanthus virginicus
fringe tree

Hibiscus syriacus
rose of Sharon

Hydrangea paniculata 'Grandiflora'
peegee hydrangea

Rhododendron
rhododendron

Spiraea ×vanhouttei
Van Houtte's spirea

Spiraea japonica 'Anthony Waterer'
dwarf red spirea

Syringa vulgaris
lilac

Viburnum opulus 'Roseum'
snowball

Viburnum plicatum
Japanese snowball

Weigela florida
weigela

Perennials and biennials

Achillea ptarmica 'The Pearl'
double white milfoil

Alcea rosea
hollyhock

Antirrhinum majus
snapdragon

Cyperus alternifolius
umbrella plant

Dianthus barbatus
sweet William

Dicentra spectabilis
bleeding heart

Iris 'Honorabile'
miniature tall bearded iris

Leucanthemum ×superbum
Shasta daisy

Lychnis chalcedonica
Maltese cross

Paeonia officinalis 'Rubra Plena'
double red peony

Papaver orientale
oriental poppy

Platycodon grandiflorus
balloon flower

Rudbeckia laciniata 'Hortensia'
golden glow

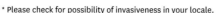

PLANT LISTS

* Please check for possibility of invasiveness in your locale.

** Plant is from the period but not necessarily listed in extant resources for the region.

Tanacetum parthenium 'Flore Pleno'
double feverfew

Annuals

Ageratum houstonianum
flossflower

Callistephus chinensis
China aster

Celosia argentea var. *plumosa*
feathered cockscomb

Centaurea cyanus
bachelor's buttons

Heliotropium arborescens
cherry pie

Impatiens balsamina
balsam

Lobularia maritima
sweet alyssum

Phlox drummondii
annual phlox

Salvia splendens
scarlet sage

Solenostemon scutellarioides
coleus

Roses

Rosa 'American Beauty'

Rosa arkansana**
prairie rose

Rosa 'Frau Karl Druschki'

Rosa 'Gruss an Teplitz'

Rosa 'Marshall P. Wilder'

Rosa 'Mrs. John Laing'

Vines

Clematis 'Jackmanii'
Jackman's clematis

Clematis terniflora
sweet autumn clematis

Lathyrus latifolius
everlasting pea

Parthenocissus tricuspidata
Boston ivy

Wisteria sinensis*
Chinese wisteria

Bulbs

Canna indica
Indian shot

Colocasia esculenta
elephant ears

Dahlia
dahlia

   'Bishop of Llandaff'**

   'Jersey's Beauty'**

Gladiolus
sword lily

Hyacinthus orientalis
hyacinth

Lilium auratum
gold-band lily

Lilium lancifolium 'Flore Pleno'
double tiger lily

Polianthes tuberosa
tuberose

Tulipa
tulip

   'Dillenburg'**

   'Generaal de Wet'**

Zantedeschia aethiopica
calla lily

CENTRAL STATES & GREAT PLAINS

Trees

Acer negundo
box elder

Acer saccharinum
silver maple

Acer saccharum
sugar maple

Catalpa bungei
umbrella catalpa

Cornus florida
dogwood

Crataegus laevigata
English hawthorn

Fraxinus americana
white ash

Juniperus virginiana
eastern red cedar

Picea abies
Norway spruce

Picea pungens f. *glauca*
Colorado blue spruce

Platanus occidentalis
sycamore

Thuja occidentalis
arborvitae

Shrubs

Berberis thunbergii*
Japanese barberry

Calycanthus floridus
Carolina allspice

Cotinus coggygria
purple smoke tree

Deutzia gracilis
slender deutzia

Hibiscus syriacus
rose of Sharon

Hydrangea paniculata 'Grandiflora'
peegee hydrangea

Spiraea ×vanhouttei
Van Houtte's spirea

Spiraea japonica 'Anthony Waterer'
dwarf red spirea

Syringa vulgaris
lilac

Viburnum opulus 'Roseum'
snowball

Perennials and biennials

Alcea rosea
hollyhock

Antirrhinum majus
snapdragon

Bellis perennis
English daisy

Convallaria majalis
lily-of-the-valley

Coreopsis lanceolata
lance-leaf coreopsis

Delphinium formosum
showy larkspur

Dianthus barbatus
sweet William

Dianthus plumarius
grass pink

Digitalis purpurea
foxglove

Gypsophila paniculata
baby's breath

Hemerocallis lilioasphodelus
lemon lily

Iris germanica
German bearded iris

Paeonia 'Festiva Maxima'
peony

Papaver orientale
oriental poppy

Phlox paniculata
perennial phlox

Stokesia laevis
Stokes' aster

Tanacetum parthenium 'Aureum'
golden feather

Annuals

Ageratum houstonianum
flossflower

Amaranthus caudatus
love-lies-bleeding

Centaurea cyanus
bachelor's buttons

Consolida ambigua
larkspur

Impatiens balsamina
balsam

Phlox drummondii
annual phlox

Salvia splendens
scarlet sage

Solenostemon scutellarioides
coleus

Verbena ×*hybrida*
verbena

Viola grandiflora
pansy

Viola tricolor
Johnny-jump-up

Roses

Rosa 'Mme. Norbert Levavasseur'

Rosa 'Sweetheart'

Rosa 'Tausendschön'
thousand beauties rose

Rosa 'Turner's Crimson Rambler'

Rosa 'White Dorothy'

Vines

Anredera cordifolia
Madeira vine

Campsis radicans
trumpet creeper

Clematis 'Jackmanii'
Jackman's clematis

*Ipomoea quamoclit**
cypress vine

Lablab purpureus
hyacinth bean

Parthenocissus quinquefolia
Virginia creeper

Parthenocissus tricuspidata
Boston ivy

Bulbs

Canna 'Roi Humbert'
King Humbert canna

Colocasia esculenta
elephant ears

Dahlia
dahlia

'Bishop of Llandaff'**

'Little Beeswings'**

Gladiolus
sword lily

Polianthes tuberosa
tuberose

Zantedeschia aethiopica
calla lily

FAR WEST & MOUNTAIN STATES

Trees

Araucaria heterophylla
Norfolk Island pine

Catalpa speciosa
northern catalpa

Cedrus deodora
Deodar cedar

Cercis canadensis
redbud

Chamaecyparis lawsoniana
Lawson's cypress

Chilopsis linearis
flowering willow

Cryptomeria japonica
Japanese cedar

*Eucalyptus globulus**
blue gum

Firmiana simplex
Chinese parasol tree

*Grevillea robusta**
silky oak

PLANT LISTS

* Please check for possibility of invasiveness in your locale.

** Plant is from the period but not necessarily listed in extant resources for the region.

Lagerstroemia indica
crepe myrtle

Laurus nobilis
sweet bay

Magnolia grandiflora
southern magnolia

Melia azedarach*
chinaberry

'Umbraculiformis'
umbrella tree

Phoenix canariensis
Canary Island date palm

Platanus occidentalis
sycamore

Platycladus orientalis
Chinese arborvitae

Quercus agrifolia
California live oak

Schinus molle
Peruvian peppertree

Sequoia sempervirens
coast redwood

Washingtonia robusta
California fan palm

Shrubs

Camellia japonica
camellia

Cercis canadensis
redbud

Deutzia crenata
deutzia

Euonymus japonicus 'Aurea'
Japanese spindle tree

Hibiscus syriacus
rose of Sharon

Hydrangea macrophylla
mophead hydrangea

Hypericum moserianum
gold flowers

Lantana camara*
lantana

Ligustrum ovalifolium*
California privet

Philadelphus coronarius
mock orange

Pittosporum tobira
pittosporum

Plumbago auriculata
Cape leadwort

Spiraea japonica 'Anthony Waterer'
dwarf red spirea

Spiraea ×vanhouttei
Van Houtte's spirea

Syringa vulgaris
lilac

Viburnum opulus 'Roseum'
snowball

Viburnum tinus
laurustinus

Perennials and biennials

Alcea rosea
hollyhock

Antirrhinum majus
snapdragon

Bellis perennis
English daisy

Campanula medium
Canterbury bells

Chrysanthemum
winter pink

Coreopsis lanceolata
lance-leaf coreopsis

Cortaderia selloana*
pampas grass

Dianthus barbatus
sweet William

Dianthus caryophyllus
carnation

Digitalis purpurea
foxglove

Erysimum cheiri
wallflower

Gaillardia ×grandiflora
blanket flower

Gypsophila paniculata
baby's breath

Leucanthemum ×superbum
Shasta daisy

Miscanthus sinensis*
Japanese silver grass

'Variegatus'
variegated Japanese silver grass

'Zebrinus'
zebra grass

Papaver nudicaule
Iceland poppy

Papaver orientale
oriental poppy

Pelargonium
geranium

Tanacetum parthenium
feverfew

Annuals

Celosia argentea var. *cristata*
crested cockscomb

Centaurea cyanus
bachelor's buttons

Consolida ambigua
larkspur

Cosmos bipinnatus
cosmos

Impatiens balsamina
balsam

Lobularia maritima
sweet alyssum

Matthiola incana
gillyflower

Phlox drummondii
annual phlox

Portulaca grandiflora
moss pink

Salpiglossis sinuata
painted tongue

Salvia splendens
scarlet sage

Scabiosa atropurpurea
mourning bride

Tagetes erecta
African marigold

Verbena ×hybrida
verbena

Viola grandiflora
pansy

Viola tricolor
Johnny-jump-up

Roses

Rosa banksiae
Lady Banks' rose

Rosa 'Bridesmaid'

Rosa 'Catherine Mermet'

Rosa 'Frau Karl Druschki'

Rosa 'Gruss an Teplitz'

Rosa 'Magna Charta'

Rosa 'Mme. Norbert Levavasseur'

Vines

*Cardiospermum helicacabum**
balloon vine

Clematis terniflora
sweet autumn clematis

*Hedera helix**
English ivy

Humulus japonicus
Japanese hops

*Ipomoea quamoclit**
cypress vine

Lathyrus odoratus
sweet pea

Parthenocissus quinquefolia
Virginia creeper

Parthenocissus tricuspidata
Boston ivy

Bulbs

Agapanthus africanus
blue African lily

Canna indica
Indian shot

Colocasia esculenta
elephant ears

Crinum
swamp lily

Dahlia
dahlia

   'Bishop of Llandaff'**

   'Little Beeswings'**

Gladiolus
sword lily

Hyacinthus orientalis
hyacinth

Lilium auratum
gold-band lily

Lilium lancifolium
tiger lily

Lilium speciosum
Japanese lily

   'Album'
   white Japanese lily

   'Rubrum'
   crimson banded lily

Narcissus
daffodil

   'Thalia'**

   'Trevithian'**

Polianthes tuberosa
tuberose

Tulipa
tulip

   'Dillenburg'**

   'Generaal de Wet'**

6

Landscapes
for Modern Homes
(1930–1960)

1930 — J. I. Rodale establishes a publishing house that becomes a leading U.S. voice for organic gardening and healthful living.

1932 — **All-America Selections award program begins.**

1941–45 — World War II spurs a revival of victory gardens.

1958 — *Bacillus thuringiensis* (Bt), a Japanese beetle deterrent, becomes commercially available.

1930

1940

1950

1960

1931 First plant patent awarded, to Henry F. Bosenberg for a climbing rose.

1933 **The Herb Society of America is founded in Boston.**

1943 The pesticide DDT is widely used during and after World War II.

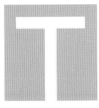he years between 1930 and 1960 were tumultuous in the United States. The era opened in the Great Depression that followed the stock market crash of 1929 and ended with ever-increasing prosperity; in the interim, World War II embroiled the nation. Following the war, the U.S. government encouraged homeownership as never before, with low-interest mortgages through the Veteran's Administration and other incentives. Housing construction boomed, and the rate of homeownership rose dramatically, from 43.6 percent in 1940 to 61.9 percent by 1960. It is fair to say that making a "nest" in the United States was never more fashionable or affordable. Along with homeownership came the responsibilities of designing and maintaining a landscape. This chapter will discuss the many options available to homeowners as they attempted to make their houses into homes and design their American gardens.

Architecture Styles

The American ranch house had been developing since the early 1800s, primarily in California. It was a simple style, originally influenced by Spanish design and often featuring adobe as the building material. Houses were typically one story and included an attached garage and picture window. Sunset Magazine Editors and Cliff May (1946) popularized the style, which was particularly suited to indoor-outdoor living, in *Sunset Western Ranch Houses*. According to May, a Los Angeles architect, ranch houses were "fitted to the site," built of local materials, and always included a patio. The idea was simple: to extend living space to the outdoors. Homeowners were counseled to consider their living requirements and challenged to "think outside the box": how could they satisfy these requirements in outdoor rooms, not just in California, but across the country? Patios (and terraces, porches, and breezeways) meant that recreation, dining, cooking, and socializing could take place out of doors. In the years following World War II, the ranch became ubiquitous all over the country (witness the case studies in this chapter), thanks to its functional design and relatively inexpensive cost.

Featured Designer:
Thomas D. Church (1902–1978)

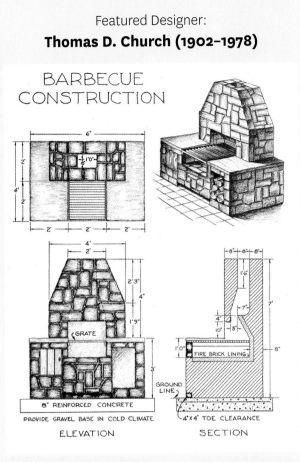

Whatever you called it, the grill or barbecue had arrived (Morris 1946).

THE LANDSCAPE PERSPECTIVE of this time continued to follow the Arts and Crafts ideal of making garden rooms as an extension of the house, and no one provided more insight for this concept than California designer Thomas D. Church. His seminal book, *Gardens Are For People* (1955), illustrated dozens of design ideas for the homeowner in almost any income bracket. Church favored strong geometric lines and popularized the outdoor dining room complete with a cooking facility and the concept of a deck, calling it a detached porch. Above all, he taught how to combine beauty with practicality and how to convey a sense of one's own personality to one's landscape.

1

Another prominent style in middle-class neighborhoods, particularly during the 1940s, was the Cape Cod, a one-story form of Colonial Revival architecture. These houses were inspired by the early wooden houses common in New England and usually were simple in detail except for a Georgian- or Federal-style doorway. Colonial Revival houses featuring a second-story overhang were also popular during this time.

Essential Elements of Modern Landscapes

- Distinct garden rooms
- Foundation plantings
- Shade trees
- Patio or terrace
- Barbecue grill
- Perennial border
- Areas for family activities

Landscape Design

Designing the landscape as a series of garden rooms was an effective strategy for both large estates and smaller properties in the new suburban communities being built. Middle-class homeowners received extra reassurance, as needed: "Good landscape design for the home is a simple, comprehensible art, as easily understood as a folk song" (Carhart 1935). And many emerging publications provided point-by-point considerations for designing a landscape that would be functional for the entire family, from adults to children to pets.

Combining this functionality with simplicity was the key philosophy. In general, the front yard was a more formal area, meant to be seen from the street, while the backyard was the place where the family activities took place: relaxation, dining, or recreation. The front yard was open to view and the backyard frequently would be screened so that activities such as sunbathing could take place. Citing the popularity of the picture window and

2   3

also garage doors at the front of the house, some designers suggested that a harmonious garden of shrubs and flowers would be well placed in the front of the house. Such a garden served a double purpose: it could be viewed from the picture window and would help to draw attention away from the garage doors.

A catalog cover from Peter Henderson Co. for 1946 captures many of the desirable aspects of a home landscape: a shady area for repose, colorful and beautiful flowerbeds, and a vegetable garden with produce for the table. Only hinted at in the image is a terrace with a barbecue, a feature that became nearly ubiquitous in newly developing suburbs (best exemplified by Levittown, New Jersey).

Indeed, that premier incarnation of an "outdoor room"—a dining terrace with outdoor barbecue grill—complemented many landscapes of the period. Usually the dining terrace was conveniently adjacent to the kitchen; some were accessed from a living room door, though that situation was not as practical. Concrete, flagstones, or bricks were common surfaces, and do-it-yourself publications supplied diagrams for building a grill from brick or stone. Often a short hedge or low wall provided enclosure

and some privacy; further screening could be had from a trellis with vines. Plants in containers helped connect the dining terrace to the rest of the natural landscape, and of course, the space was furnished with a table and chairs.

Big-city dwellers dug in and cultivated landscapes in more cramped quarters, and it was suddenly, after decades of experiment, all the fashion to make gardens on roofs. Large ornamental trees and shrubs in heavy containers were not the norm in these urban aeries; rather, the rooftop terraces of high-rise buildings were enhanced by discrete placement of planter boxes filled with colorful annuals and a pergola or trelliswork covered with many vines, creating vertical gardens in sympathy with the skyscrapers around them.

1. Cape Cod.

2. "Everything for the Garden 1946."

3. "A Continental idea," the pergola covered with annual creepers, moves to the rooftop (Matschat 1934).

Flower gardens

If the plethora of published articles concerning the topic is any indication, then making and tending flower gardens were *very* popular activities between 1930 and 1960. Garden styles of previous eras (including the grandmother's garden and perennial borders) prevailed, but with a modern consciousness to take up new plants offered by a flourishing nursery industry. Dooryard gardens and even foundation plantings might have featured both annuals and herbaceous perennials. Writers recommended that flower borders adhere to a landscape plan and not be scattered about; formal flower gardens at entries or under a picture window were recommended. Cut flower gardens also were fashionable.

KEY

31–32 meadow rue *(Thalictrum flavum* subsp. *glaucum)*	**44** Shasta daisy *(Leucanthemum* ×*superbum* 'Alaska')
33–35 regal lily *(Lilium regale)*	**46–48** wood lily *(Lilium philadelphicum)*
36–37 hardy leadwort *(Ceratostigma plumbaginoides)* and sundrops *(Oenothera fruticosa* 'Youngii'), mixed	**54–55** sneezeweed *(Helenium autumnale)*
38 chrysanthemums	**57, 59–61, 63–64** bee larkspur *(Delphinium* Belladonna Group)
39–42, 49–53, 56, 58 asters	**62** speedwell *(Veronica spicata* 'Blue Champion')
43, 45 sea statice *(Limonium gerberi)*	

1. A 1960 plan for a border with two seasons of interest (WaysideGardens.com).

2. A 1938 garden scene, featuring irregular stone paving, an arbor seat, and mixed beds of annuals and perennials.

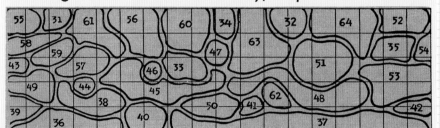

Planting Plan for the June-July; Sept.-Oct. Garden

1

2

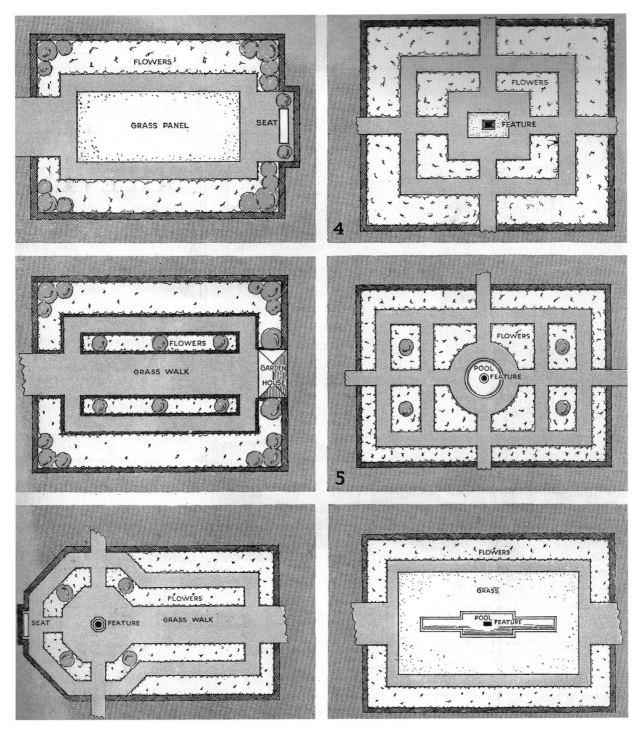

Six formal garden designs for landscapes of any size (*Better Homes and Gardens* April 1931). All Rights Reserved.

Kitchen gardens

Kitchen gardens were a frequent part of residential landscapes, especially during the war years. Gardeners cultivated rows of various vegetables and fruits in square or rectangular beds usually located in the backyard. There were even rooftop victory gardens. Not only did victory gardens make gardeners feel patriotic, but they provided additional—and fresh—produce for the families at home during a time when much of the commercially produced fruits and vegetables were shipped overseas to the troops. "This year several millions of gardeners, in deadly earnest, are preparing to set about growing their own vegetables. This huge scale digging for victory is going to be 'double digging,' . . . digging to help along the war effort and at the same time digging to help oneself" (Rockwell 1943).

Victory gardens had psychological benefits as well, as reported by Helen Van Pelt Wilson (1943):

> Remember that if a vegetable garden all on your own is hard work, it is work of the rewarding kind. Being busy outdoors kept me from feeling lonely and useless with my husband away and my country at war. And I never had better health in my life than after a summer of vegetable gardening which averaged more than 40 hours a week.

Even after the war years, vegetable gardening was a popular activity in suburbia. Many landscape designs included a small kitchen garden and also indicated the placement of several fruit trees. Herbs in separate gardens, rather than mixed with fruits and vegetables, also became popular during this time.

As gardeners have appreciated for centuries, vegetables (here, the purple foliage of beets) can be as decorative as flowers.

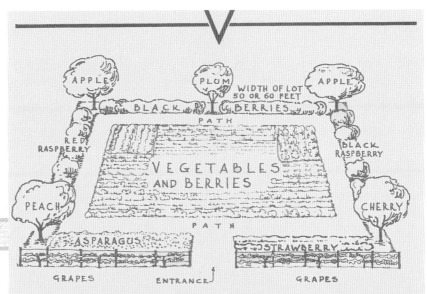

WIDTH OF LOT
50 OR 60 FEET

APPLE · PLUM · APPLE

BLACK · · BERRIES

PATH

RED
RASPBERRY

BLACK
RASPBERRY

VEGETABLES
AND BERRIES

PEACH · CHERRY

PATH

ASPARAGUS · STRAWBERRY

GRAPES · ENTRANCE · GRAPES

The above suggested arrangement is especially suitable for a back yard where space
is limited. It demonstrates how you can get double duty from your ground through
"two-story" gardening — fruit trees above and berries and vegetables below.

THE SMALL YARD VICTORY GARDEN

1. A forward-thinking, "two-story" plan for a "Small Yard Victory Garden" (Stark Brothers Nursery 1943).

2. Vegetables are planted in long rows within a brick-edged garden; at left, wisteria climbs a ladder-style trellis, c. 1945.

Foundation plantings

By 1930, foundation plantings were a staple of the American residential landscape, the essential backbone of front yards. Leonard H. Johnson (1927) reminded his readers that the design of their foundation plantings was but another facet of landscape design, "the art of tastefully arranging plants so as to imitate Nature and yet preserve utility." The goal, to connect the house to its natural surroundings, was a legacy from the earlier Arts and Crafts movement. Before committing to the plants of a foundation planting, one should consider several questions, according to Johnson:

- What is the architectural style of the house?
- Will the plants be in a shaded or an exposed location?
- Is the soil adapted to the kind of plants preferred?
- Is the planting's effect to be year-round or seasonal?
- What is the height of the foundation (i.e., distance between the ground and the bottom of the first-floor windows)?
- Are there any undesirable features of the house to be concealed?
- Is the house located in a smoky district?

Fortunately, that final question, concerning air pollution, is now less urgent; but in earlier years, a plant's ability to thrive in the midst of a smoky environment was a standard of quality for urban environments. A final consideration for a successful foundation planting was the willingness of the homeowner to remove or drastically prune plants that outgrew their situation; it was, of course, best then and still to plant wisely in the first place, being aware of the ultimate mature sizes of all the plants.

Early foundation plantings were often combinations of deciduous and evergreen shrubs and small trees, designed for beautiful as well as practical effect. Vines were used to cover transitions and provide more vertical interest. Plants that should not be used in a period foundation planting include Colorado blue spruce, variegated weigela, peegee hydrangea, and purple-leaf plum—any plant, in other words, that would draw the eye away from the total composition.

Foundation planting (D. Hill Nursery 1935).

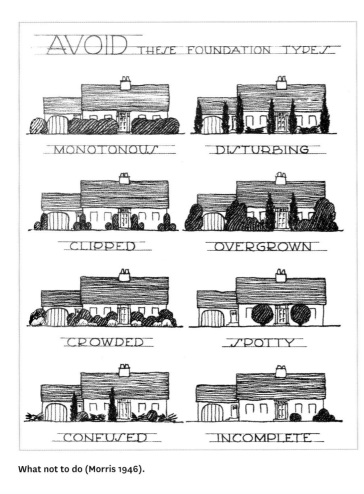

What not to do (Morris 1946).

Foundation planting (Johnson 1927).

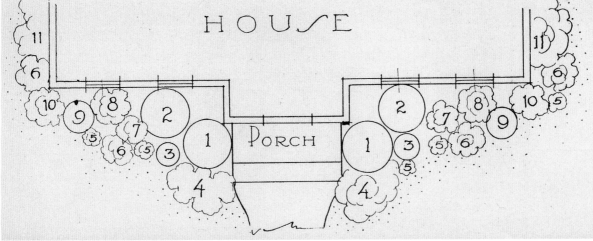

"An effective planting" of deciduous and evergreen shrubs (Johnson 1927).

Utility areas

Landscape designers typically included utility areas, such as the place for trash containers, in their renderings, often near the kitchen door; likewise, a play area for the children was within view of a kitchen window, so that adequate supervision could be provided. One important feature of these earlier landscapes is coming back into fashion (what with increased concerns about energy consumption and associated costs), and that is the drying yard, an area for the outdoor drying of clothes using a clothesline. Some municipalities are currently struggling with the appearance of clotheslines (and fluttering unmentionables), considering them an objectionable view from the street, but surely no one would object to such an economical feature, if properly screened! A drying yard was an ordinary part of the landscape during the first half of the twentieth century, and many of that era's considerations for the location of a drying yard are still pertinent (Morris 1946):

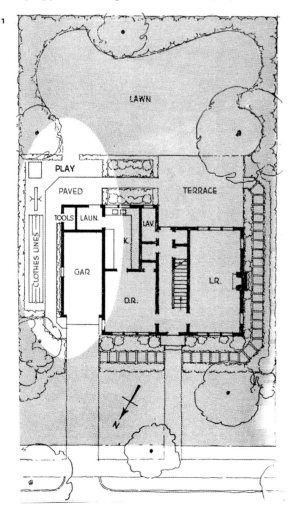

- Laundry is heavy, *therefore* the drying yard should be as close as possible to the laundry room.
- Sunshine and air circulation are requisite elements, *therefore* the drying yard must be in an open, airy location, and lines should be a minimum of eighteen inches apart.
- Plants should not be near the clotheslines, *therefore* approximately four feet of space should exist between outer lines and any plantings or hedges.
- All lines should be easily reached from an all-weather ground surface, *therefore* the drying yard should be graveled or surfaced in some manner.
- Clotheslines are out of place in any livable garden, for they are usually unattractive and often personal in appearance when used, *therefore* the drying yard should be screened from the livable garden and, if possible, traffic from the laundry room to drying yard should not be through the garden.

1. Landscape design with play and utility areas (Robinson 1950).

2. Different colors and shapes of stone form a mosaic paving perfectly suited to this c. 1945 California ranch.

Landscape Features

Paths and driveways

Materials for paths and walks were many and varied in these years. In the most successful cases, a particular choice was made because it was in keeping with a certain residential architecture style. For example, paths of brick or gravel were especially suitable for the Cape Cods and other Colonial Revival homes being built during this period. The brick was laid in traditional patterns of running bond, herringbone, and basketweave, as well as in combination with flagstone for designs, both rectilinear and circular, with more artistic flair. Sometimes a wooden border of two-by-fours defined the brick path, or the bricks were laid within a band of concrete.

Writers recommended concrete for walks but cautioned that its cold, institutional appearance, which was tolerated in driveways, should be softened somehow.

One ploy was to break up large pieces of concrete into faux steppingstones, or "crazy paving." Some homeowners utilized concrete blocks for walks but laid them in patterns similar to those used for brick, particularly basketweave, for interest. Others dulled sharp edges with herbaceous perennial plantings, such as candytuft.

Flagstone walks continued in fashion; the stone, often a local bluestone-type, was cut into squares or rectangles and laid in a regular or irregular pattern. Designers also combined pebbles with brick or stone to create mosaic pavements. Any irregular pattern invited the cultivation of small plants between the stones—something that could tolerate being walked on, such as moss phlox.

Common sense dictated whether paths should be straight or curved; one sage advised, "As surely as you make a curved walk without a reason, someone will take a beeline to his objective and wear holes in the lawn as he goes" (Coffey 1943).

2

Above. A typical arrangement of brick and pebble

Below. Cross section

PEBBLES

ADOBE

BRICK

SAND

GRAVEL

SUBSOIL

2

1. Mosaic paving for a patio or terrace (Kiler 1939).

2. Concrete blocks laid as pavement in the basketweave pattern (Bell 1953).

3. Concrete crazy paving (Wills's Cigarettes cards, "Garden Hints," 1938). George Arents Collection, The New York Public Library, Astor, Lenox and Tilden Foundations.

3

WILLS'S CIGARETTES

CONCRETE CRAZY PAVING

Fences and hedges

Fences were used for privacy, enclosure, and ornamentation in the landscape. Designers wrote that an additional attribute for the fence or hedge should be "individuality." One way of achieving individuality was by training fruit trees on a fence, or as fences themselves. Although no one could call it low maintenance, an espalier always adds a sophisticated touch, not to mention a harvest of delicious fruit; a perennial border might be located in front of the fruit tree fence to hide its "legs." One fence design that conveyed a sense of lightness and yet was substantial was constructed with a combination of masonry posts with lattice in between; the lattice could be diagonal, horizontal, or vertical. The new ranch houses seemed to call for a rail fence to simulate an informal effect, but without question, picket fences and board fences continued in abundance.

1. "Fruit trees trained as a fence" (Findlay 1934).

2. A pear tree espaliered along a post fence.

3. Alternating-height pickets enclose a 1940s California cottage.

Fruit trees trained as a fence.

Seating

Selecting outdoor seating was just as important as selecting a couch and recliner for the "family room" (a concept introduced by *Better Homes and Gardens* in the 1950s). Appearance and practicality were paramount. Materials ranged from iron and lighter metals to wood, bamboo, and willow. Some seating demanded brightly colored chintz-covered cushions. Furniture for the yard could be heavy and destined for a permanent location. Furniture for the terrace or patio had to be movable for ease of entertaining and cleaning; heavier pieces were often wheeled. From comfortable, adjustable lounge chairs for relaxing under a shade tree to more formal seats for entertaining on the patio, homeowners had many choices from which to furnish their landscapes.

4. Bentwood patio furniture could be used with or without a cushion (Knight 1934).

▶ NEXT SPREAD, 5. Comfortable, portable metal chairs, 1950.

6. Adirondack-style wood bench, 1944.

7. The seating should suit the setting (Aul 1945b).

4

5

6

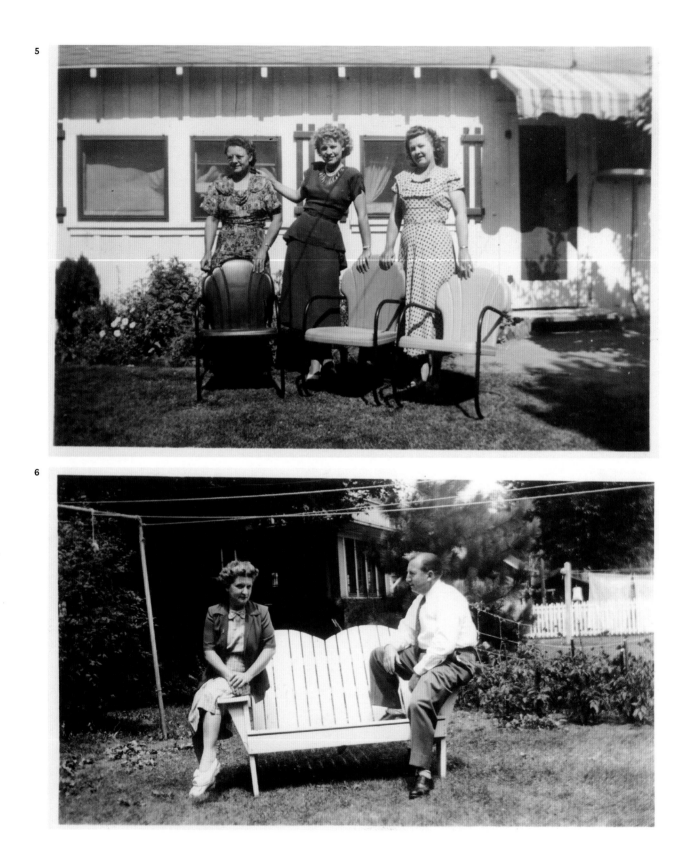

IN DOOR-YARD

BY THE GATE

RUSTIC FOR THE ROCK GARDEN

AT END OF PATH

MOVABLE TYPES ON TERRACE

Garden accessories

The "area for family activities," that essential element of modern landscapes, was especially crowded: the idea that backyards were for family recreation changed how gardens were used and accessorized and created a desire for amenities for children in the landscape. Not just lily pools and other ornamental water features but wading pools, basic swing sets, seesaws, and sand boxes began to appear regularly beside the clotheslines, barbecues, and continuing themes of birdbaths, sundials, gazing globes, and simple terracotta pots. Victory gardens were turned back into lawns; badminton nets were hung, and croquet posts dotted the landscape. For a splash of color, umbrellas shaded many an overexposed patio or terrace. And where they could not, vines stepped in. Vines, bringing not only cooling shade but color and scent, continued to be an integral part of the landscape and so did support for them, in the form of pergolas, arches, and trellises; simple geometric trelliswork was still the main outdoor ornamental feature in many residential settings. And in 1957, the first plastic pink flamingo came to roost in an American lawn—a herald of geese to come!

1

2

1. Bring on the plastic: wood trelliswork required maintenance in the form of painting, c. 1950.

2. Hoping for vines: extensive trelliswork all but covers this house and yard, Taft, California, 1940.

3. A whirligig, a birdhouse, a rose arch, and three fan trellises.

4. Pergolas and arches may not be whimsical, but they are and remain functional and beautiful in a residential setting (Aul 1945a).

3

PERGOLAS AND ARCHES IN *THE HOME GARDEN*
DESIGNED & DRAWN BY HENRY B. AUL

PERGOLA OVER PATH TO TOOL HOUSE

ROSE ARCH

SHED ROOF PERGOLA OVER TERRACE

4

Case Studies

1940s Spanish-style ranch

Charm Logan and Jim Crandall stumbled upon this property when visiting the area and fell in love with the character of the old California ranch house and the landscape of contrasts from majestic native oaks, to citrus orchards, to upland semiarid native habitat. Remodels over the years had covered much of the house's traditional features, but Charm and Jim were able to see past this and are now bringing it back to its former beauty.

Charm and Jim enjoy entertaining and desired a landscape that would welcome them and their guests into a serene and lush sanctuary. A circular drive under huge old Peruvian peppertrees (*Schinus molle*) leads up to the house. We recommend that the area under these trees remain clear and covered only with natural leaf mulch; a planting of spring ephemerals would be a nice addition. The entryway to the ranch itself is a large circular plaza, perfect for accommodating many guests for drinks or dinner beneath the stars. A large planting bed, filled with mature camellias and one enormous California live oak (*Quercus agrifolia*), dominates the center-front of the house, and lovely low seat walls of stone surround the beds closer to the house. Near the midway point of the curved wall is a set of steps that lead down a slope to the swimming pool.

The constructed landscape around the house is in need of renovation. The form of the entry plaza will stay the same, as will the existing seat wall, which is a perfect place for Spanish-style urns or large terracotta pots to be placed and planted with annuals and perennials. But the plaza should be resurfaced, since the existing tiles are in poor condition. And the large existing water feature, which interrupts valuable outdoor entertaining space, will be removed. Perhaps matching tile can be found from a salvage company, but if not, if there are issues with the new surface matching, we will create a round tile mosaic to act as a focal point or "welcome mat" at the entry.

During the 1940s, when this house was built, California residents became more conscious of the need to conserve water and began to cultivate more drought-tolerant plants in their landscapes. We chose plants for this

1. The tiled entrance marker is a wonderful historic piece.

2. Peruvian peppertrees line the drive.

3. Logan-Crandall residence.

4. House entry detail, with planned addition and steps to pool leading off to the left.

4

design primarily from this palette of Southern California natives. The majority of the thirsty camellias in the front bed will be removed to open up the view, and new plantings in a dooryard garden on the right will lead the eye to the front door. These low-growing, drought-tolerant vines and shrubs will enhance the space and provide a verdant connection between the natural and built landscape. California lilac and other specimen shrubs will be placed throughout the upper portion of the slope leading to the pool, not only providing color but sweetly fragrant as well. Under these will be low evergreen shrubs and herbaceous natives. The planned addition will have a large picture window on the end, so care must be taken to preserve and frame the view.

A terrace, another calling card of the era, will be added on the east end of the house, outside the French doors of the master bedroom, extending that space into the outdoors. Even though this is the front of the house, the area is secluded and private; the existing trees provide a wonderful overhead canopy, and abundant plantings, including a coral vine (*Antigonon leptopus*) climbing up a trellis, will enclose the terrace on all three sides. The fruits of the hollyleaf cherry and creeping snowberry (*Symphoricarpos mollis*) create multiseason interest. Though not envisioned as a dining area, there is room to enjoy morning coffee at a small table with chairs, or to settle back in some rustic willow or cane furniture, cushioned for comfort. The floor will be paved with mellow terracotta tiles, and the focal point, a smaller, tiled water feature, will add to the cloister patio atmosphere.

1. Spanish decorative tiles enhance the terracotta paving at the entry steps.

2. The swimming pool is sited to take full advantage of an exceptional territorial view.

3. Master bedroom terrace detail.

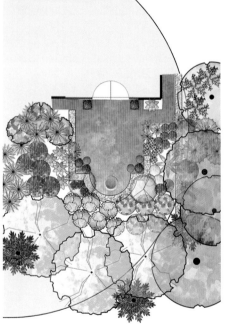

1950s eastern ranch

When the homeowners, both keen gardeners, purchased this 1955 brick ranch in 2010, the only "garden" feature was a severely pruned foundation planting. Their first reaction? "We need to get rid of this Fifties landscape!" We hope you'll agree that our proposed design demonstrates there is more to a Fifties landscape than foundation plantings.

The house is in a quiet older suburb, where most houses have a large area of lawn, a single mature tree, and a similarly uniform and overclipped foundation planting. The owners wanted to change that by adding a seating area in front and plantings with more interest than a lawn. We decided to use the strong geometric lines and "outdoor room" concept of Thomas Church, combined with informal flowerbeds. This front patio, now the outdoor living room, continues the thought started by the existing porch, connecting strongly to it and providing low screening to the street and higher (although not too high) screening to block the driveway view.

1950s eastern ranch.

Ranch master plan.

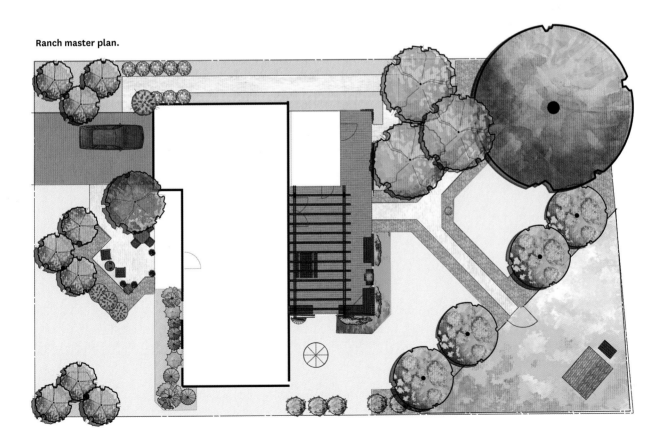

The flowerbeds feature a variety of plants that will ensure multiseason interest, including dwarf red spirea, period bulbs, and perennials available in the 1950s ('Hyperion' daylilies, 'Souvenir de Madame Gaudichau' irises, 'Beauty of Livermere' oriental poppies). Viburnums, mugo pine, and other evergreens were chosen for their year-round presence along the front of the house, with the intention that they will be maintained in their natural form/habit, more correctly in keeping with foundation plantings recommendations for the period. Careful initial selection means foundation plantings won't outgrow their space too quickly, tempting someone to prune specimens into meatballs or boxes.

At back, the outdoor "family room" is a wood deck with a vine-covered lattice ceiling. In-and-out wooden screens on two sides create privacy and enclosure while framing a view to the garden beyond. A built-in barbecue adds another essential element of period character. Furnishings will be arranged in conversational groupings and will have clean-cut lines for that streamlined modern look. The owners entertain family and friends and like to use outdoor spaces in an informal way; they have groups of a dozen or so people over for meals and prefer casual seating on such a dining terrace to a more formal dining table and chairs.

The rest of the backyard is a series of garden rooms. Again, we selected plants for multiseason interest with attention to fall color and winter form. Herbs will be planted in narrow beds under the espaliered trees near the deck. A border of fruiting shrubs ends at a vegetable and cutting garden; adjacent is a small shed for potting and storing tools, a rain barrel to collect from the shed roof, and compost bins along the side. A fence around the edible garden room is bordered with bramble fruits. A shady seating area will provide a quiet place to rest after a long workday.

The overall landscape design is a combination of layout, furnishings, and structures from the period. The intent of the garden areas is twofold: to eliminate lawn and to create a pleasant place for leisure. The plantings are more extensive than the typical homeowner of the period might have had, but if the ranch was owned by avid gardeners like this couple, we like to think they may have been similar.

1

4

1. Front entry detail: "Such a garden served a double purpose: it could be viewed from the picture window and would help to draw attention away from the garage doors."

2. Shade garden detail.

3 & 4. *Lilium* 'Black Beauty' (1957) and *Narcissus* 'Dreamlight' (1934). Photos courtesy of Old House Gardens–Heirloom Bulbs, Ann Arbor, Michigan.

3

2

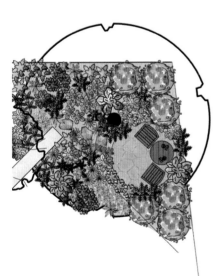

PLANT LISTS

* Please check for possibility of invasiveness in your locale.

As time progressed, the ever-expanding mail-order nursery and seed industries ensured that many plants were offered on a national basis, and it is safe to assume that homeowners could order and receive (from somewhere) almost any plant they knew would thrive on their property. Thus, though we continue in this chapter to choose plants from dated nursery catalogs in each region, the following plant lists could be considered in accumulation for your modern landscape needs.

Narcissus nodded on the front cover of many a modern "garden book" catalog.

Bulbs

Few extant general nursery catalogs for this period included named varieties of common bulbs, although clearly they were cultivated across the country.

The following selections of *Crocus*, *Narcissus*, and *Tulipa* would be great accompaniments to any U.S. landscape from this era; we have added parenthetical dates of introduction to help guide your choice.

Crocus chrysanthus
snow crocus

'Blue Pearl' (1950)

'Cream Beauty' (1943)

'Snow Bunting' (1939)

Narcissus
daffodil

'Baby Moon' (1958)

'Dreamlight' (1934)

'Erlicheer' (1934)

'Horn of Plenty' (1947)

'Jack Snipe' (1951)

'Salome' (1958)

'Sweetness' (1940)

Tulipa
tulip

'Angelique' (1959)

'Apeldoorn' (1951)

'China Pink' (1944)

'Maytime' (1942)

'Mrs. John T. Scheepers' (1930)

'Queen of Night' (1944)

NEW ENGLAND & MIDDLE ATLANTIC

Trees

Acer palmatum 'Atropurpureum'
purple Japanese maple

Acer saccharum
sugar maple

Chamaecyparis pisifera 'Plumosa'
Sawara cypress

  'Plumosa Aurea'
  golden Sawara cypress

Cornus florida
dogwood

  'Rubra'
  red-flowering dogwood

Crataegus laevigata
English hawthorn

  'Paul's Scarlet'
  double red hawthorn

Juniperus virginiana
eastern red cedar

Malus ioensis 'Plena'
Bechtel prairie crabapple

Picea abies
Norway spruce

Picea glauca
white spruce

Picea pungens f. *glauca*
Colorado blue spruce

Prunus cerasifera 'Pissardii'
purple-leaf plum

Sorbus aucuparia
European mountain ash

Thuja occidentalis
arborvitae

  'Fastigiata'

  'Globosa'

Shrubs

Berberis thunbergii*
Japanese barberry

Calycanthus floridus
Carolina allspice

Deutzia ×lemoinei
Lemoine's deutzia

Hydrangea paniculata 'Grandiflora'
peegee hydrangea

Juniperus ×pfitzeriana
Pfitzer juniper

Kolkwitzia amabilis
beautybush

Philadelphus coronarius
mock orange

Spiraea japonica 'Anthony Waterer'
dwarf red spirea

Spiraea ×vanhouttei
Van Houtte's spirea

Syringa vulgaris
lilac

  'Alba'
  white lilac

  'Charles X'

  'Marie Legraye'

  'President Grevy'

Viburnum ×burkwoodii
fragrant viburnum

Viburnum plicatum f. *tomentosum*
doublefile viburnum

Weigela florida
weigela

Perennials and biennials

Alcea rosea
hollyhock

Anchusa azurea 'Dropmore'
alkanet

Anemone ×hybrida
Japanese anemone

  'Honorine Jobert'

  'Queen Charlotte'

Campanula medium 'Calycanthemum'
cups and saucers

Caryopteris incana
blue spirea

Dianthus plumarius
grass pink

Geum quellyon
avens

  'Lady Stratheden'

  'Mrs. J. Bradshaw'

Gypsophila paniculata 'Bristol Fairy'
baby's breath

Hemerocallis
daylily

  'Cinnabar'

  'Hyperion'

Heuchera sanguinea
coral bells

Iberis sempervirens
candytuft

Lychnis chalcedonica
Maltese cross

Papaver orientale
oriental poppy

Phlox
perennial phlox

  'Brigadier'

  'Bright Eyes'

  'Fairy's Petticoat'

  'Widar'

Primula veris
cowslip

Tanacetum coccineum
painted daisy

Annuals

Ageratum houstonianum
flossflower

Calendula officinalis
pot marigold

  'Radio'

PLANT LISTS

* Please check for possibility of invasiveness in your locale.

Callistephus chinensis
China aster

  'Crego'

Consolida ambigua
larkspur

Cosmos bipinnatus
cosmos

Lobularia maritima
sweet alyssum

  'Carpet of Snow'

Matthiola incana
gillyflower

Mirabilis jalapa
four o'clock

Petunia ×atkinsiana
petunia

  Balcony Mix

  'Giants of California'

Portulaca grandiflora
moss rose

Tagetes erecta
African marigold

Tagetes patula
French marigold

Tropaeolum majus
'Golden Gleam'
nasturtium

Zinnia 'Purple Prince'
zinnia

Roses

Rosa 'Dr. W. Van Fleet'

Rosa 'Prince Camille de Rohan'

Rosa rugosa
rugosa rose

  'Alba'

  'F. J. Grootendorst'

  'Hansa'

Rosa setigera
prairie rose

Vines

Aristolochia macrophylla
Dutchman's pipe

Campsis ×tagliabuana
'Madame Galen'
hybrid trumpet creeper

Campsis radicans
trumpet creeper

*Cardiospermum helicacabum**
balloon vine

Clematis 'Jackmanii'
Jackman's clematis

Clematis terniflora
sweet autumn clematis

Lathyrus odoratus
sweet pea

  'America'

  'Black Knight'

  'Senator'

Parthenocissus tricuspidata
Boston ivy

Phaseolus coccineus
scarlet runner bean

*Wisteria sinensis**
Chinese wisteria

  'Alba'

Bulbs

Canna
canna

  'City of Portland'

  'Richard Wallace'

  'Roi Humbert'

  'Wyoming'

  'Yellow Humbert'

Galanthus elwesii
greater snowdrop

Lilium auratum
gold-band lily

Lilium speciosum 'Album'
white Japanese lily

Trees

Cedrus deodora
Deodar cedar

Ginkgo biloba
ginkgo

Ilex opaca
American holly

Ilex vomitoria
yaupon

Lagerstroemia indica
crepe myrtle

Liriodendron tulipifera
tulip tree

Magnolia grandiflora
southern magnolia

Magnolia ×soulangeana
saucer magnolia

Photinia serrulata
Chinese photinia

Platycladus orientalis
'Conspicua'
golden Chinese arborvitae

Trachycarpus fortunei
windmill palm

Shrubs

Abelia ×grandiflora
glossy abelia

Aucuba japonica
gold dust tree

Buxus sempervirens
boxwood

Camellia japonica
camellia

  'Otome' ('Pink Perfection')

  'Prof. Charles S. Sargent'

Chaenomeles japonica
Japanese quince

Deutzia crenata
deutzia

Gardenia jasminoides
Cape jasmine

Ligustrum ibota
Japanese privet

Michelia figo
banana shrub

Nandina domestica
heavenly bamboo

Pittosporum tobira
Japanese pittosporum

Prunus laurocerasus
cherry laurel

Punica granatum
pomegranate

Rhododendron indicum
Chinese azalea

Spiraea ×billardii
Billard's spirea

Perennials and biennials

Alcea rosea
hollyhock

Antirrhinum majus
snapdragon

Bellis perennis
English daisy

Campanula medium
Canterbury bells

Cortaderia selloana*
pampas grass

Dianthus barbatus
sweet William

Digitalis purpurea
foxglove

Hemerocallis 'Hyperion'
daylily

Leucanthemum ×superbum 'Alaska'
Shasta daisy

Phlox
perennial phlox

   'Brigadier'

   'Bright Eyes'

   'Fairy's Petticoat'

   'Widar'

Sedum album
white sedum

Tanacetum coccineum
painted daisy

Annuals

Callistephus chinensis
China aster

   'Crego'

Catharanthus roseus
Madagascar periwinkle

Coix lacryma-jobi
Job's tears

Consolida ambigua
larkspur

Cosmos bipinnatus
cosmos

Lobularia maritima
sweet alyssum

Petunia ×atkinsiana
petunia

   Balcony Mix

Portulaca grandiflora
moss rose

Salvia splendens
scarlet sage

Tagetes patula
French marigold

Tropaeolum majus
nasturtium

Verbena ×hybrida
verbena

Viola tricolor
Johnny-jump-up

Roses

Rosa 'American Beauty'

Rosa 'Paul Neyron'

Rosa rugosa
rugosa rose

   'Alba'

   'F. J. Grootendorst'

   'Hansa'

Rosa 'Turner's Crimson Rambler'

Vines

Antigonon leptopus
coral vine

Campsis radicans
trumpet creeper

Gelsemium sempervirens
Carolina jasmine

Hedera helix*
English ivy

Lablab purpureus
hyacinth bean

Lathyrus odoratus
sweet pea

   'America'

   'Black Knight'

   'Senator'

Momordica balsamina
balsam apple

Tropaeolum peregrinum
canary creeper

Wisteria sinensis*
Chinese wisteria

   'Alba'

Bulbs

Caladium bicolor
angel wings

Canna
canna

   'Richard Wallace'

PLANT LISTS

* Please check for possibility of invasiveness in your locale.

Canna continued
  'Roi Humbert'

  'Wyoming'

  'Yellow Humbert'

Colocasia esculenta
elephant ears

Crocosmia crocosmiiflora
montbretia

Hippeastrum ×johnsonii
St. Joseph lily

Lilium auratum
gold-band lily

Polianthes tuberosa
tuberose

Zephyranthes atamasca
rain lily

GREAT LAKES CENTRAL STATES & GREAT PLAINS

Trees

Abies balsamea
balsam fir

Abies concolor
white fir

Acer saccharinum 'Laciniatum Wieri'
Wier's cutleaf maple

Acer saccharum
sugar maple

Catalpa bungei
umbrella catalpa

Cercis canadensis
redbud

Chamaecyparis pisifera 'Plumosa'
Sawara cypress

Crataegus laevigata
English hawthorn

Malus ioensis 'Plena'
Bechtel prairie crabapple

Picea abies
Norway spruce

Picea pungens
Colorado spruce

Pinus mugo
mugo pine

Prunus cerasifera 'Pissardii'
purple-leaf plum

Quercus palustris
pin oak

Salix babylonica
weeping willow

Sorbus aucuparia
European mountain ash

Ulmus glabra 'Camperdownii'
Camperdown elm

Shrubs

Deutzia 'Pride of Rochester'
double-flowered deutzia

Euonymus alatus*
burning bush

Forsythia ×intermedia
golden bell

Juniperus ×pfitzeriana
Pfitzer juniper

Lonicera tatarica*
shrub honeysuckle

Spiraea japonica 'Anthony Waterer'
dwarf red spirea

Spiraea prunifolia
bridal wreath

Symphoricarpos albus
snowberry

Syringa vulgaris
lilac

  'Charles X'

  'Marie Legraye'

  'President Grevy'

Viburnum plicatum f. *tomentosum*
doublefile viburnum

Viburnum trilobum
cranberrybush

Weigela florida
weigela

Perennials and biennials

Achillea ptarmica 'The Pearl'
double white milfoil

Anchusa azurea 'Dropmore'
alkanet

Anthemis ×hybrida 'Kelwayi'
hardy marguerite

Aurinia saxatilis
madwort

Coreopsis lanceolata
lance-leaf coreopsis

Delphinium Belladonna Group
perennial larkspur

Dianthus plumarius
grass pink

Digitalis purpurea
foxglove

Eryngium amethystinum
sea holly

Gaillardia ×grandiflora
blanket flower

Gypsophila paniculata 'Bristol Fairy'
baby's breath

Hemerocallis 'Hyperion'
daylily

Iris
iris

  'Lohengrin'

  'Madame Chéreau'

  'Souvenir de Madame Gaudichau'

Limonium gerberi
sea statice

Paeonia
peony

  'Edulis Superbus'

  'Festiva Maxima'

Papaver orientale
oriental poppy

  'Beauty of Livermere'

Phlox
perennial phlox

  'Rheinlander'

  'Ryndstrom'

Rudbeckia laciniata 'Hortensia'
golden glow

Tanacetum coccineum
painted daisy

Tanacetum parthenium
feverfew

Yucca filamentosa
Adam's needle

Annuals

Ageratum houstonianum
flossflower

Callistephus chinensis
China aster

  'Crego'

Centaurea cyanus
bachelor's buttons

Cosmos bipinnatus
cosmos

Eschscholzia californica
California poppy

Helichrysum bracteatum
strawflower

Lobularia maritima
sweet alyssum

Matthiola incana
gillyflower

Mirabilis jalapa
four o'clock

Petunia ×atkinsiana
petunia

Salvia splendens
scarlet sage

Zinnia elegans
zinnia

Roses

Rosa 'American Beauty'

Rosa 'Mme. Norbert Levavasseur'

Rosa rugosa
rugosa rose

  'Alba'

  'F. J. Grootendorst'

  'Hansa'

Rosa setigera
prairie rose

Vines

Clematis
clematis

  'Henryi'

  'Jackmanii'
  Jackman's clematis

  'Ramona'

terniflora
sweet autumn clematis

Lathyrus latifolius
everlasting pea

Parthenocissus quinquefolia
Virginia creeper

*Wisteria sinensis**
Chinese wisteria

  'Alba'

Bulbs

Canna
canna

  'City of Portland'

  'Richard Wallace'

  'Roi Humbert'

  'Wyoming'

Galanthus elwesii
greater snowdrop

Lilium auratum
gold-band lily

Lilium regale
regal lily

FAR WEST & MOUNTAIN STATES

Trees

Acer palmatum
Japanese maple

*Albizia julibrissin**
mimosa

Chamaecyparis obtusa
Hinoki cypress

Cupressus macrocarpa
Monterey cypress

*Eucalyptus globulus**
blue gum

Ficus elastica
India rubber tree

Ginkgo biloba
ginkgo

Jacaranda mimosifolia
blue jacaranda

Juniperus virginiana 'Canaertii'
pyramidal red cedar

Lagerstroemia indica
crepe myrtle

Laurus nobilis
sweet bay

Liquidambar styraciflua
sweetgum

Magnolia grandiflora
southern magnolia

Magnolia ×soulangeana
saucer magnolia

Picea pungens f. *glauca*
Colorado blue spruce

Prunus ilicifolia
hollyleaf cherry

Quercus agrifolia
California live oak

PLANT LISTS

* Please check for possibility of invasiveness in your locale.

Salix babylonica
weeping willow

Schinus molle
Peruvian peppertree

Taxus baccata
English yew

  'Fastigiata'
  Irish yew

Shrubs

Abelia ×grandiflora
glossy abelia

Aucuba japonica
gold dust tree

Berberis thunbergii*
Japanese barberry

Buxus sempervirens
boxwood

Camellia japonica
camellia

  'Alba Plena'

  'Otome' ('Pink Perfection')

Ceanothus cyaneus
California lilac

Chaenomeles speciosa
Japanese quince

Cotoneaster microphyllus
little-leaf cotoneaster

Erythrina crista-galli
coral tree

Hydrangea arborescens 'Hills of Snow'
snowball

Kerria japonica 'Pleniflora'
double-flowered Japanese rose

Myrtus communis
sweet myrtle

  'Variegatus'

Nerium oleander
oleander

Pittosporum tobira 'Variegata'
variegated pittosporum

Rosmarinus officinalis
rosemary

Spiraea thunbergii
Thunberg's spirea

Spiraea ×vanhouttei
Van Houtte's spirea

Syringa ×persica
Persian lilac

Syringa vulgaris
lilac

  'Charles X'

  'Marie Legraye'

  'President Grevy'

Viburnum carlesii
fragrant viburnum

Perennials and biennials

Achillea millefolium 'Roseum'
red yarrow

Achillea ptarmica 'Boule de Neige'
sneezewort

Anemone ×hybrida
Japanese anemone

  'Honorine Jobert'

  'Queen Charlotte'

  'September Charm'

  'Whirlwind'

Aurinia saxatilis
golden alyssum

Bellis perennis
English daisy

Campanula medium 'Calycanthemum'
cups and saucers

Centranthus ruber
Jupiter's beard

Delphinium ×bellamosum
delphinium

Erysimum cheiri
wallflower

Geum quellyon
avens

  'Lady Stratheden'

  'Mrs. J. Bradshaw'

Gypsophila paniculata 'Bristol Fairy'
baby's breath

Hemerocallis fulva 'Flore Pleno'
Kwanso daylily

Hemerocallis lilioasphodelus
lemon lily

Leucanthemum ×superbum 'Alaska'
Shasta daisy

Lobelia cardinalis
cardinal flower

Nepeta mussinii
catmint

Phlox
perennial phlox

  'Brigadier'

  'Bright Eyes'

  'Fairy's Petticoat'

  'Widar'

Potentilla nepalensis 'Miss Willmott'
cinquefoil

Romneya coulteri
California tree poppy

Annuals

Calendula officinalis
pot marigold

Callistephus chinensis
China aster

　'Crego'

Celosia argentea var. *cristata*
crested cockscomb

Centaurea cyanus
bachelor's buttons

Consolida ambigua
larkspur

Cosmos bipinnatus
cosmos

Lobelia erinus 'Crystal Palace'
blue lobelia

Lobularia maritima 'Carpet of Snow'
sweet alyssum

Matthiola incana
gillyflower

Mirabilis jalapa
four o'clock

Petunia ×*atkinsiana*
petunia

　Balcony Mix

Phlox drummondii
annual phlox

Portulaca grandiflora
moss rose

Tagetes erecta
African marigold

Tagetes patula
French marigold

Roses

Rosa 'Blaze'

Rosa 'Frau Karl Druschki'

Rosa 'Golden Dawn'

Rosa 'Gruss an Teplitz'

Rosa 'Silver Moon'

Vines

Antigonon leptopus
coral vine

Bougainvillea braziliensis
bougainvillea

Clematis 'Jackmanii'
Jackman's clematis

Jasminum officinale f. *affine*
large-flowered jasmine

Lathyrus odoratus
sweet pea

　'America'

　'Black Knight'

　'Senator'

Mandevilla suaveolens
Chile jasmine

Parthenocissus quinquefolia
Virginia creeper

Parthenocissus tricuspidata
Boston ivy

*Wisteria sinensis**
Chinese wisteria

　'Alba'

Bulbs

Canna
canna

　'Richard Wallace'

　'Roi Humbert'

　'Wyoming'

　'Yellow Humbert'

Gladiolus
sword lily

Lilium auratum
gold-band lily

Lilium regale
regal lily

7

Suburban Landscape to Green Revolution
(1960–2000)

1960

1962
Rachel Carson's *Silent Spring* draws attention to the harmful effects of pesticides and pollution on wildlife and the environment.

1970
First Earth Day celebration; Nobel Peace prize is awarded to Norman Borlaug, "Father of the Green Revolution."

1970

1972
DDT is banned; string trimmers hit the market.

1975
Vietnam War ends; Diane Ott Whealy and Kent Whealy found the Seed Savers Exchange.

1980

1980
First U.S. patent issued for a genetically engineered organism.

1992
AmeriFlora, the first international horticultural exposition held in the United States, closes on Columbus Day in Columbus, Ohio.

1990

1994
First transgenetic food (the Flavr Savr tomato) is approved for sale in the United States.

2000

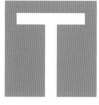

The way people lived changed monumentally in these four decades. This was the time of the space age, of developing computer technology, and of urban sprawl. The housing construction boom that began in the 1940s and '50s continued; houses got larger with each decade, culminating in the McMansions of the late 1990s. Suburban developments offered variations on just a few architectural styles, which gave them a homogenous appearance with few regional differences. Landscaping created some small measure of diversity, but the typical suburban front yard consisted of a lawn area, a shade or ornamental tree or two, and an assortment of shrubs, usually evergreen, as foundation plantings; backyards were larger lawns.

The good news is that by this time, landscape design was a well-established profession; the Associated Landscape Contractors of America and Professional Land Care Association of America were founded in 1961 and 1979, respectively (both have since merged into PLANET, the Professional Landcare Network). Gardening stayed in the top-ten hobbies throughout the period, and the popularity of gardening as recreation grew throughout the 1970s and '80s.

The back-to-the-land movement of the 1960s and '70s, spurred by the consumerism of and separation from nature in urban and suburban life, had an impact on how people thought about their landscapes. For some, the ideals of self-sufficiency and getting in touch with nature influenced how they gardened. Edible landscapes, planting for wildlife, native plantings, organic gardening practices—all were a product of the larger trends in environmentalism and a yearning to return to more simple living. Yet, simultaneously, a large group of people in the growing suburban population desired the perfect lawn, which was achievable only through liberal applications of chemical fertilizers, herbicides, and pesticides. There was an inherent conflict between the quest for that smooth expanse of lawn and concerns about the new horticultural products that were helping people achieve it. The green revolution began when people who realized that many modern technologies were causing harm to the planet decided to act.

The way we received information about plants and gardening practices underwent a radical tranformation, too. *Victory Garden* debuted on PBS in 1975 (and is still on

Featured Designers:
Wolfgang Oehme (1930–2011) and James van Sweden (b. 1935)

Meadow landscape.

THE DESIGN TEAM of Oehme, van Sweden is widely recognized as having pioneered the lawnless New American Garden style of landscape architecture. Taking inspiration from native prairies, they created vistas of sweeping grasses and perennials that were a welcome alternative to the common landscape of lawns and pruned shrubs; in *Bold Romantic Gardens* (1990), they describe the style as "naturalism," an artistically designed landscape that has a naturalized look. Oehme and van Sweden considered foundation plantings "a waste" and recommended placing trees and shrubs away from the house and nearer to the street, allowing the front yard to be used by the homeowners rather than merely be for public viewing. They were also strong proponents of selecting vigorous plants that are right for the site—the happy result being a long-lasting, minimal-upkeep landscape with multiseason interest. This approach to landscape design had wide appeal both aesthetically and practically: the idea of less maintenance was popular in a society whose daily activities were increasingly fast-paced.

today, making it not only the first but also the longest running gardening show on television); soon, morning news programs, both local and national, had regular gardening segments. Martha Stewart began sharing gardening techniques on *Martha Stewart Living* in 1993; *Rebecca's Garden*, another popular television show, first aired in 1996. Home and Garden Television (HGTV), a cable television network focusing on home and garden improvement, launched in 1994; *Gardening by the Yard*, *Surprise Gardener*, and others of its shows were widely viewed in the late 1990s.

The Internet was an increasingly essential source of information (and misinformation) about plants (and where to purchase them), and by the mid-1990s websites, both educational and commercial, by the thousands were available for consumers on all topics of landscape design and horticulture. This new resource was fast, but the ability of virtually anyone to start a website or blog meant that opinion was sometimes confused with fact. Nevertheless, the information age was an overall benefit to gardeners, who would still turn to books and periodicals for in-depth knowledge, not just information.

Live Outside and Love It!

Make Your Outdoor "Living Room" More Enjoyable, Beautiful and Livable

2

1. Typical suburban front yard.

2. 1960 ad for the Stroller, which allowed gardeners to "apply the right pesticide easily, economically and quickly."

3. Rachel Carson's *Silent Spring* (1962) arrived in bookstores just in the nick of time.

1

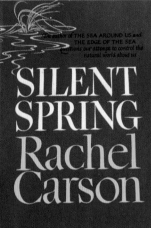

3

Architecture Styles

The American ranch continued to predominate in the early part of this period, but other architectural styles developed as more and more suburban neighborhoods grew from what were once agricultural fields. The split-level house, a multistory modification of the ranch, answered the need for more separation of spaces in the home. One-third to one-half of the structure was a single story, with the balance being two stories. The front-facing garage and family room were often under the two-story portion and sometimes at a lower grade. The exterior was of various materials, often in combination.

The Contemporary house, derived from the earlier International style or American International style, was usually architect-designed and typically one-story. There are two types: the flat-roofed, in combinations of brick, wood, or stone, with little detailing; and the gabled type, with large overhanging eaves and, often, exposed beams reminiscent of the Craftsman and Prairie styles. Contemporary Folk homes include A-frames and geodesic domes.

The Neocolonial house provided even more living space and separation between private and communal areas. While not as popular as the ranch early in this period, it became very popular in the 1970s and beyond. These two-story houses were loose interpretations of English Colonial and the later Colonial Revival; they had the symmetrical façades of their predecessors but not necessarily their regular placement of windows. They were followed by Neo-Tudor, Neo-French, and combinations of these styles. Neo-Tudor houses have dominant front gables with steep roofs and narrow windows, sometimes with diamond-shaped panes; decorative half-timbers were common. Neo-French houses can be recognized by their high-hipped roofs and round-topped, through-the-cornice dormers.

Neo-Mediterranean homes, mostly built after 1970 in the Southwest and California, were inspired by the Spanish Eclectic, Mission, and Italian Renaissance styles. Instead of the heavy clay tiled roofs of those earlier styles, the tiles of Neo-Mediterranean were lighter-weight composites; the stucco walls and round arches of the windows and doors are an identifying feature.

Essential Elements of 1960–2000 Landscapes

· Distinct garden rooms
· Themed gardens
· Naturalistic plantings
· Deck or patio
· Barbecue grill
· Areas for recreation and entertaining

Brick ranch.

1. Split level with Tudor details.

2. Contemporary Folk geodesic dome.

3. American International.

4. Neocolonial.

Landscape Design

The landscapes of this era were a mix of new and old ideas, styles, and materials. At first, they reflected the lifestyle and architecture changes of the 1950s; foundation planting and the obsession with the perfect lawn continued as a staple element of the suburban front yard. Truly modern and postmodern landscape design style was limited to a small, artistic, and trendsetting population; simple or minimalist landscapes never really caught on with the general population.

As suburban sprawl crept across America, the contractor's or builder's package—cookie-cutter landscape designs included in the purchase price of a new home—became the norm. A low-end builder's package for the front yard consisted of a shade tree, five to seven shrubs, and a seeded or sodded lawn; in the backyard, a builder might include a small patio or deck, a privacy fence, and more lawn. Landscape companies often specialized in this type of work. It was easy to manage, and operations were simple and regimented, much like any type of production work. Unfortunately, the resulting landscapes also lacked creativity; homogeneity reigned from coast to coast, except for minor regional differences in plant selection, to do with cultural requirements.

The front porch was nonexistent in suburbia. If people were going to use their outdoor space, it would be in the backyard. Not only did this have an impact on the landscape, it impacted society. The front yard was an innocuous public area presented to the world as it drove or, more rarely now, walked by. The main visual feature of the front landscape was the garage and driveway, and garden books and periodicals jumped in with suggestions for lessening or masking the visual weight of these features. Sunset Editors (1978b) recommended planting beds on both sides of the driveway or creating small planting beds in the center of a double driveway to soften and break up the large expanse of pavement. Another suggestion was to balance the garage door by placing a mass of trees with coarse groundcover on the opposite side of the yard.

Only when environmental and labor-minimizing considerations came to the forefront did landscapes begin to move away from clipped shrubs, annual beds, and manicured lawns. As the new millennium approached, the front yard especially began to change as the negative environmental impact of lawns became known and people realized that reducing lawn size reduced the time (and fossil fuels) required for maintenance. Progressive landscape designers and homeowners chipped away at the lawn in favor of groundcovers and perennial plantings. The trend began in urban and older suburban neighborhoods with smaller lots, where a lawn was an unneeded feature. But though attitudes about it were shifting, the lawn continued to be a mainstay of landscape design throughout this period and beyond.

The backyards of 1960s and '70s were places for gathering of family and friends; if large enough, they would boast multiple areas for entertaining and recreation. Nearly every backyard had a patio or deck, with seating, and often with some sort of overhead structure or canopy. The desire for privacy in the open, adjoining backyards of suburbs called for fences, hedges, or walls: "Neighbors are a wonderful institution, and we'd be the last to abolish 'em. But you often need a fence or two for privacy" (Editor 1960b). Within these mostly rectangular backyard enclaves, the overall layouts were randomly ordered. Designed landscapes tended to be naturalistic rather than formal.

Themed gardens or garden styles were popular. A homeowner could create a landscape using a particular theme as guide in their landscape choices and be fairly certain of success. "Landscape planning works better if you have a unifying idea[;] keep in mind this principle: select a garden style that is compatible with your home's style" (Sunset Editors 1978a). Several books were available on the subject of theme gardens, including very popular works by Barbara Damrosch (1982) and Rosalind Creasy (1982, 1986).

The concept of distinct garden rooms, which had continued strong since 1930, saw a particular resurgence in the 1980s and '90s. Outdoor rooms became more and more like the rooms of the house, with full kitchens, fireplaces, light fixtures, and designer furnishings. As people's affluence increased, the quantities and types of amenities in their garden rooms became more elaborate; witness the transformation of the simple swing set into a full-blown play structure.

1. A builder's package for the front yard.

2. Front yard with minimized lawn area.

1

1. **The New American Garden style of sweeping grasses and perennials.**

2. **Perennial planting.**

3. **Meadow landscape as an alternative to lawn.**

Flower gardens

Annual bedding plants were relied upon as a way to create seasonal color. So many new cultivars came on the market each year, it was difficult for homeowners to keep up; they generally purchased annuals by color rather than cultivar. These "color spots" were used as borders along walkways and foundations, as rings around shade trees and lamp and mailbox posts, and as fillers in the perennial border. The regimented rows and geometric beds of earlier annual plantings gave way to more curvilinear plantings. Annuals filled containers and window boxes as well; only in the latter half of the period did mixed container plantings of annuals, perennials, bulbs, trailing vines, and even shrubs begin to be widely used.

Perennial plantings increased in popularity for a variety of reasons. The activities of breeders and plant explorers during this time meant that more and more plant species and cultivars with appealing characteristic (larger and more abundant flowers, interesting foliage patterns, more compact habits) were available to gardeners. Books touted low-maintenance perennials as more economical than annuals, and every month magazines revealed more wonderful perennials that gardeners needed to try in their gardens. And with the formation of the Perennial Plant Association in 1984 came active promotion of their use by growers, retailers, and designers.

American gardeners were enchanted with the English flower garden. The books of Gertrude Jekyll from the early twentieth century were reprinted multiple times during the 1980s and '90s, and contemporary English landscape designers wrote for and spoke to the American audiences, who so wanted to emulate their style. Penelope Hobhouse, Rosemary Verey, Beth Chatto, Christopher Lloyd, and John Brookes were a few of the more popular designers who wrote for American periodicals and whose books were widely read in the United States.

Gardeners in all regions of the country tried to recreate the gardens of England in their landscapes. Their success, however, was often marginal; the soils and climates of most U.S. regions were very different from those of England, and the labor-intensive nature of this garden type was another limiting factor. Perhaps in response, many garden experts began to tout the idea of selecting plants to fit the conditions of the site. Nicola Ferguson's *Right Plant, Right Place* (initially released in England, interestingly enough) was first distributed in the United States in 1984, and careful plant selection was soon considered an essential first step toward the success of a landscape.

Native plants, too, were prominent in flower gardens. Not only were they well suited to the naturalistic design style, but the perception that they were more environmentally friendly was in keeping with the green movement's ethos. Landscaping with native plants was about creating

2

3

functional ecosystems that duplicated or mimicked those found in nature. Not just flower gardens, but native woodland gardens, bog/wetland gardens, and prairie gardens were planted in residential landscapes, where space would allow. These ecological landscapes, when appropriate for the site and the region, increased biodiversity, improved soils, and recharged the water table.

Prairie Nursery of Wisconsin was one of the first nurseries to specialize in prairie plants; their catalog contained extensive information about how to establish and maintain a prairie landscape. Clever marketers jumped on this desire for prairie gardens, and "Meadow in a Can" was sold in garden centers and gift shops nationwide. Unfortunately, these instant flower gardens gave the home gardener poor results. The seed mixes were unsuitable for all regions; the mixes were not balanced to create a lasting ecosystem; and the broadcast planting method was not an adequate way to establish this type of planting.

> Gardeners nationwide have been lured by the charm of "wildflowers" and "meadow gardens" and commercial suppliers have both recognized and generated a market for seed mixes to create these gardens. In reality, the flower species included in these seed mixes are often neither native nor wild (although they are quite beautiful), and the gardens have many more colorful flowers than do true meadows, which are dominated by grasses (Lyons 1989).

The prairie "look", which so influenced landscape designers such as Oehme and van Sweden and Piet Oudolf created a spillover interest in ornamental grasses, both native and nonnative. Indeed, the popularity of grasses in landscape planting was at an all-time high during the 1980s and '90s. Among their many enduring appeals: the dynamic way they move in the wind, the interest they create in winter landscapes, and their relative ease of cultivation.

Finally, as people became aware of water being a limited resource, they looked for ways to reduce its use in the garden. An alternative to the thirsty landscape of the American lawn and English flower garden was to create a xeriscape, a landscape that used little or no water. Xeriscaping began in the Southwest, where water was limited, but spread to other regions where people wanted, yes, to reduce their water bills, but also to create more sustainable landscapes that did not require irrigation. Xeriscapes too made use of native plants. Cactus and succulents were used in some regions, and tough drought-tolerant shrubs and perennials in others; instead of lawn, the ground surface would consist of these other plant types, or a covering of gravel or mulch.

Kitchen gardens

By the 1960s, kitchen gardens had been relegated to an unused corner of the backyard; rarely was the area for growing vegetables integrated into the overall landscape (except perhaps in the case of cottage gardens). They were considered to be utilitarian, not ornamental. All that changed with Rosalind Creasy's *Edible Landscaping* (1982). Many previous books and articles on home food production using organic methods had been published and read by the gardening public. Creasy, however, brought an aesthetic sensibility to the topic of gardening with edibles. Her combination of sound design principles and creativity inspired people to rethink their uniform suburban landscapes, but not everyone bought in to these ideas.

Municipalities and neighborhood associations, who valued conformity, often fought these and other unconventional landscapes. Still, the idea was planted, and edible plants slipped into many more landscapes.

The nostalgia and lore of herbal associations could be seen in the many publications devoted to the growing and use of herbs. Especially among gardeners who enjoyed the culinary arts, separate herb gardens continued to be laid out in the traditional geometric forms, even when they were incorporated into container and cottage gardens. Another trend in vegetable gardening that had a renaissance at this time was the French intensive method, or square foot gardening. Such planting schemes, which often made use of raised beds, were promoted as a way to produce a lot of food in a small, urban or suburban area.

1. Cottage garden.

2. Edible landscape.

3. Herb garden with the traditional note of a sundial.

Children's gardens

Children's gardens were not new, but the notion of what a children's garden should be had changed by the end of the twentieth century. Earlier gardens were about children working in a healthful outdoor setting, and learning how to garden; gardens of this era were more about instilling an appreciation of nature and stimulating young people to explore and use their imaginations. Often they were extensions of the concept of the backyard for recreation and exercise. A typical suburban backyard had play equipment for children to keep them busy and entertained. Swing sets, sand boxes, and playhouses could be found behind most any home where children lived. More elaborate children's areas might have had a themed garden based on popular children's literature or television characters. These gardens may have developed from the concern that children's busy lives of scheduled activities and pervasive technology needed to be offset somehow by linking them to nature.

1970s sandbox and swing set.

Wildlife gardens

Along with concern for the health of our planet came an increased sense of responsibility for the other creatures with which we shared it. Proponents of wildlife gardening suggested that plant selections in the landscape be made based on their beneficial value to all life, from those on the wing to invisible members of the soil food web. "Environmental awareness and landscaping with native North American plants have grown hand in hand," wrote Jim Wilson (1992). "While there is no end to the ways in which you can express your concern for environmental quality, from political action to composting and recycling, you can also make a real contribution by growing native plants, including species known to attract, feed, and shelter non-intrusive wildlife."

Books, magazine articles, and even videos could be found explaining how to create a specific backyard garden habitat for butterflies or hummingbirds. Bird feeding of all sorts was the number one passive hobby, and as they had been for more than a century, birdbaths, birdhouses, and bird feeders continued to be used for both functional and ornamental purposes. This keen interest in birding continues in the new millennium.

1. Be sure to choose sterile *Buddleia* (butterfly bush) cultivars for your butterfly garden.

2. Birdhouse and birdbath in shade garden.

Landscape Features

Paths and driveways

Paths and driveways were a continuation, both in terms of material and style, of those found in previous periods. Concrete, with its relatively low cost and widespread availability, was the most widely used paving surface, followed by blacktop. New methods for concrete included stamping and dyeing to create the look of other types of surfaces, such as brick and stone. Modular pavers were initially an alternative to brick; later they were made to imitate other paving materials, such as granite setts and stone. Ease of installation, lower cost, and flexibility in creating curves and patterns made modular pavers a popular product for landscapes.

Fences and hedges

The need for privacy in the suburban environment meant that screening between properties was a necessity, and creating outdoor rooms, too, required some treatment of the vertical plane. Garden books recommended that a fence or wall be at least five to six feet high (but it is best to check with your local zoning board concerning possible fence height restrictions). Offset sections of fence and screens were also used to create a less solid privacy. Fences were most commonly made from wood; redwood and cedar were both favored materials. Plastic and fiberglass panels and corrugated metal were also encountered.

Walls were constructed of concrete, brick, concrete and glass blocks, and stone. A modular "stone" introduced in the 1970s was popular with landscape contractors and do-it-yourselfers; it was easy to install and less expensive than brick or stone.

Living walls were also used to create privacy. Mixed shrub borders and single species planting of flowering shrubs were recommended for an informal look. Clipped hedges of boxwood, privet, or yew were used in more formal landscapes. Training vines over structures was another suggested means of creating privacy.

3. Modular paver driveway.

4. Fence styles (Sunset Editors 1978a).

5. Concrete block wall (Kramer 1972).

3

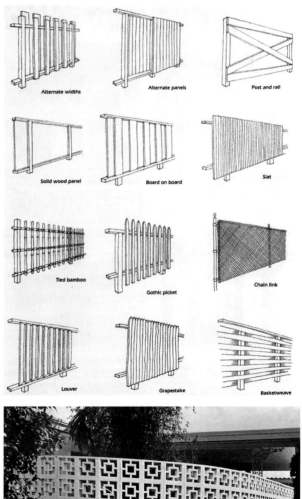

4

5

Decks and patios

Outdoor rooms in the landscape needed durable surfaces for the activities that took place there, such as dining, barbecuing, entertaining, relaxing, or sunbathing. Almost every backyard had a patio or deck to serve this purpose. Whether of brick or concrete, tile or flagstone, carpeting, precast slabs, or patio blocks, "a patio or terrace is almost essential for outdoor areas" (Kramer 1972).

Decks were a common alternative. Unlike patios, they did not require a level surface, so they were ideal in situations where the ground was irregular or sloped—a big advantage. Most were attached to the house, although freestanding decks were used in some landscapes. Small decks for family activities were a common sight in sub-urban backyards; elaborate multilevel decks were used to create large entertaining areas. Planting boxes and built-in benches were features common to all. Decks were typically made of wood; redwood, cedar, and pressure treated lumber were used. Most were stained, but they could also be painted. Later decks were made from manu-factured lumber, which was more durable and required less maintenance.

1. Precast concrete slab patio.

2. Modular paver patio.

3. Small freestanding deck.

Seating

Enjoying one's landscape and entertaining guests required adequate, comfortable seating, and new designs and materials for tables and chairs were available at all price points. Redwood furniture, with simple construction and clean lines, was common in the early part of this era. Teak furniture, especially in the style of the English landscape of the late nineteenth and early twentieth century, became popular in the 1980s and '90s, although newer styles in teak were also available. Canvas chairs in the butterfly and director's styles added shots of color, and vinyl strap chairs were favored for their portability. All-weather wicker, the choice for durability, came in both contemporary and traditional styles. Extruded plastic furniture was mass produced and affordable, in an ever-expanding range of colors and styles.

4

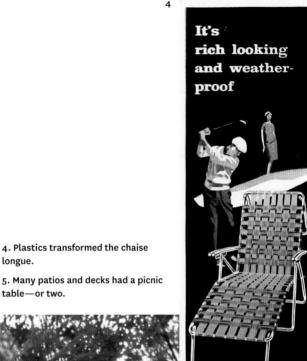

4. Plastics transformed the chaise longue.

5. Many patios and decks had a picnic table—or two.

5

Overhead structures

Overhead structures for shade and shelter were important features in landscapes marked by outdoor rooms. Most popular were those with simple, clean, modern lines, although classical and rustic examples could also be found. Canopies often covered portions of the patio or deck; they could be freestanding or be extensions of the house. Materials were wood, corrugated metal, fiberglass panels, or canvas. Both natural and colorful styles were used, depending on the region and style of the landscape. Retractable canvas awnings and large collapsible umbrellas were also used to create overhead structure.

Periodicals of the day often made reference to the "playhouse" or summer house. These might be the gazebo type with open sides, but many other styles were popular, such as a Japanese teahouse, pavilion, or a canvas cabana. These could be permanent structures in the landscape or lightweight and portable.

1. A gazebo, being enjoyed.

2. Lath overheads filtered sun and wind (Editor 1960b).

1

2

Garden accessories

Lawn ornaments and sculpture ranged from the classical to the whimsical to the ridiculous. Modern sculpture, Asian-influenced pagodas and lanterns, gazing balls, sundials, plastic flamingos—all could be found in American landscapes. Brightly painted wooden cutouts of the bent-over gardener expressed individuality in less sophisticated landscapes. Concrete statuary of all types—a menagerie of animals and religious figures such as St. Francis, Buddha, and the Virgin Mary—provided focal points and flanked driveway entrances. But nothing in the way of lawn ornamentation could approach the popularity of the concrete goose of the 1980s: it seemed there was one standing guard in front of every house in some neighborhoods, and an entire industry was developed to provide wardrobes for these omnipresent ornaments. While there was limited discussion of this sort of garden accessory in books and periodicals, they were part of the popular culture, and advertisements for them could be found at the back of those same magazines.

Swimming pools were prized amenities in the suburban landscape. They began as a luxury item, but by the 1970s few homes in Southern California and Florida did not have a pool, in styles ranging from the classic blue rectangle to what appeared to be natural ponds. The trend spread across the country, spottily, avoiding colder climates where a pool would have limited use. Still, the pool was seen as a status symbol, a must-have for the modern suburban family.

> A swimming pool can do more to increase a family's enjoyment of leisure hours together than almost any other addition to the garden. It provides a pleasant, healthful place for exercising and relaxation. And when properly planned, a swimming pool can enhance the landscape and serve as a center for entertaining (Reader's Digest Editors 1972).

Accessories to do with backyard family recreation continued to change and evolve. In the 1970s, multi-purpose play structures for children arrived. More than just swings and a slide, these structures often had forts, monkey bars, climbing ropes, and more. There were often areas for shuffleboard, hopscotch, and other games; some

3. Buddha statue, flanked by everlasting topiary and destined for the garden.

4. Concrete Japanese lantern.

5. Dressed concrete goose.

even had a track for riding bikes. Backyards rivaled public playgrounds in some cases; in fact, it was suggested that the concern for safety might be the reason the backyard developed into the family play yard—and that adults might also enjoy using some of the elements (Reader's Digest Editors 1972). Later, all kinds of premade play structures, many of extruded plastic, from Little Tikes Company and others, hit the market. From playhouses complete with kitchen appliances to pirate ships, there were play sets for every taste.

Recreation for older children and adults was also part of the landscape. Spas and hot tubs were all the rage in the 1960s and '70s. The hot tub—basically a wooden barrel with heated water—came first. Then, in 1968, Roy Jacuzzi invented the jets that changed the experience, and recommendations for incorporating spas (the subsequent fiberglass and acrylic tubs) into the landscape came fast and furious. Croquet ruled as a lawn game in the 1960s, perfect for even the roughest grass in rectangular backyards from coast to coast, and although most properties did not accommodate regulation sports fields and courts, modified versions were common features in suburbia. Badminton and volleyball nets were still strung across a stretch of lawn. Basketball hoops were mounted on garages or on poles so driveways could be used as courts. Goals for soccer, football, field hockey, and lacrosse jockeyed for space in many a backyard. And let's not forget the trampoline.

While not necessarily what we think of as "garden accessories," these all had a great, not to say looming presence in many landscapes of the period. There was some discussion on how to integrate or camouflage these special areas, but for the most part they were just there.

1. 1990s play structure.

2. Driveway basketball hoop.

3. Behind that traditional trelliswork screen? A soccer goal and a trampoline.

Case Studies

1960s split level, Great Lakes

Emmy Regnier and Kent Harrison moved into their 1962 split level home in 1997. Their young family and busy careers left them with no time or inclination to enhance the landscape at that time. Now that their children have become more independent, they decided they would like to work on the landscape. The front yard is not very large, but the backyard is quite deep and slopes down to an undeveloped wooded parcel with wet soils most of the year.

Emmy and Kent are both educators and research scientists specializing in weed ecology. Emmy is interested in the urban agriculture movement and wanted an edible front landscape, one that is productive and functional as well as ornamental, so as not to upset their neighbors. Taking inspiration from Rosalind Creasy, we designed an edible front garden that contains agronomic rows of plants in the center, surrounded by a variety of edible plants—

apples, pears, currants, gooseberries, blueberries—selected for ornamental characteristics.

The front yard also needed a more welcoming entry, with better access from the street. We redesigned the steps up from the driveway, which is at a lower grade, and added a brick paver walkway through the front garden to the door. A low wall separates a small courtyard area in front of the house from the rest of the front yard. The courtyard continues with the brick pavers from the new path and adds a bench and a small table with chairs under a lath overhead. The existing *Magnolia virginiana* in the southwest corner of the courtyard will remain, underplanted with *Galium odoratum*, and be echoed by a second magnolia, for balance. Bold, colorful herbaceous plantings along the edge of the wall will soften the space and give it a cottage garden feel. Containers placed on the patio add to this and will provide seasonal color, perhaps filled with a succession of annual color spots. A path leads to the side yard, where the garden utility areas are located. These include a potting bench, compost bins, and a small tool

Regnier-Harrison residence.

shed. This location allows easy access to the front garden, but keeps the area hidden from view in case it is messy.

In the backyard, Emmy and Kent wanted to reduce or eliminate the lawn area and the need for weekly mowing during the growing season. They wanted a "wild" garden in the sense that it would not look cultivated or require much maintenance. They also enjoy watching the wildlife in their yard and so wanted a backyard habitat that was welcoming to the various creatures in the area. To satisfy all these hopes, and with a nod to our featured design team of Oehme, van Sweden, the backyard design is mostly a naturalistic meadow of native plants with a curvilinear path mown through to provide a place to wander and explore the yard. Plants like black-berried aronia, downy serviceberry, and persimmon, selected for the backyard, have wildlife value, providing food or shelter or both.

The design takes into account the varied conditions across the site: the upper area is drier with some sunny and shady areas; the center yard is gently sloping with sun; and the lower area is shady and wet near the property line. To create privacy, inkberry holly, candleberry, and other mixed native shrubs of varying heights are placed along the perimeter. The large white wands of the bottlebrush buckeye will highlight the summer scene. The borrowed view of the woodlot will help create the feeling that the property is a natural setting rather than a suburban neighborhood. A bench at the bottom of the property provides a place for rest and meditation.

Near the house is a concrete terrace with a stone retaining wall. A bird feeding area was placed near this terrace, so they could watch the birds from the kitchen eating area. A butterfly garden, located at the east side of the terrace, adds both living drama and color, with butterfly milkweed, cardinal flower, and the yellow and red of Canadian columbine, among other attractants.

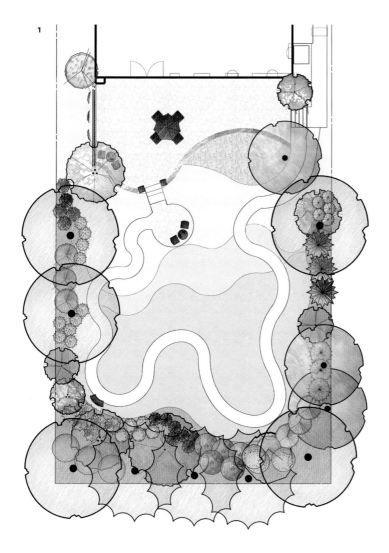

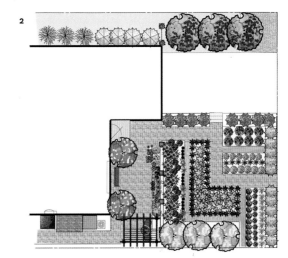

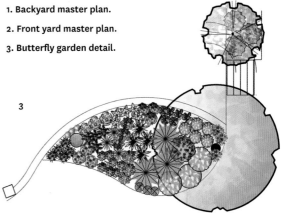

1. Backyard master plan.

2. Front yard master plan.

3. Butterfly garden detail.

* Please check for possibility of invasiveness in your locale.

By the close of the twentieth century, most ornamental plants were available to anyone anywhere in the country, whether from a local nursery or garden center, or tracked down on the Internet and shipped. We have chosen the listed plants for this chapter, therefore, without regard to regions and from several mail-order catalogs including Wayside Gardens (1960); Van Bourgondien's (1974); and Burpee's (1978). As always, choose plants for your landscape based on the environmental conditions at your site.

Trees

Aesculus ×carnea 'Briotii'
red horse chestnut

Aesculus parviflora
bottlebrush buckeye

Amelanchier arborea
downy serviceberry

Aronia melanocarpa
black-berried aronia

Cercidiphyllum japonicum
katsura tree

Cornus florida
dogwood

Diospyros virginiana
persimmon

Ginkgo biloba
ginkgo

Gleditsia triacanthos var. *inermis*
thornless honey locust

  'Moraine'

  'Sunburst'

Magnolia liliiflora 'Nigra'
lily magnolia

Magnolia ×loebneri 'Merrill'
Loebner's magnolia

Magnolia ×soulangeana
saucer magnolia

Malus
flowering crabapple

  'Crimson Brilliant'

  'Katherine'

  'Red Jade'

Robinia pseudoacacia
black locust

  'Fastigiata'

  'Frisia'

Shrubs

Berberis thunbergii 'Crimson Pygmy'
dwarf red barberry

Buddleia*
butterfly bush

Buxus microphylla var. *koreana*
Korean boxwood

Euonymus alatus 'Compactus'*
dwarf burning bush

Hibiscus syriacus 'Blue Bird'
rose of Sharon

Hypericum patulum 'Sungold'
St. John's wort

Ilex glabra
inkberry holly

Ligustrum 'Vicaryi'
golden privet

Morella pensylvanica
candleberry

Rhododendron Exbury Hybrids
Exbury azaleas

Rhus aromatica
fragrant sumac

Salix purpurea 'Nana'
dwarf blue arctic willow

Viburnum ×carlcephalum
fragrant snowball

Viburnum opulus 'Nanum'
hedge viburnum

Perennials and biennials

Within each listed genus or species, there are many other cultivars that could just as easily represent this floriferous era. We invite you to expand this research and ask your families and neighbors for suggestions as to the best cultivars to represent the final decades of the twentieth century.

PLANT LISTS

* Please check for possibility of invasiveness in your locale.

Achillea 'Coronation Gold'
yarrow

Aquilegia canadensis
Canadian columbine

Aquilegia McKana Hybrids
columbine

Artemisia ludoviciana var. *albula*
silver king

Artemisia schmidtiana 'Nana'
silver mound

Asclepias tuberosa
butterfly milkweed

Astilbe chinensis 'Superba'
Chinese astilbe

Coreopsis verticillata 'Moonbeam'
tickseed

Delphinium King Arthur Series
Pacific hybrid delphinium

Dianthus plumarius
grass pink

  'Essex Witch'

  'Her Majesty'

Festuca glauca 'Elijah Blue'
blue fescue

Galium odoratum
sweet woodruff

Helleborus ×*hybridus*
hellebore

Hemerocallis 'Stella de Oro'
daylily

Heuchera 'Chocolate Ruffles'
coral bells

Heuchera micrantha 'Palace Purple'
coral bells

Iris sibirica
Siberian iris

  'Butter and Sugar'

  'Flight of Butterflies'

  'Little White'

Hosta
hosta

  'Ginko Craig'

  'Golden Tiara'

  'Honeybells'

  'Sum and Substance'

Leucanthemum ×*superbum*
Shasta daisy

  'Aglaia'

  'Mount Shasta'

  'Wirral Pride'

Lobelia cardinalis
cardinal flower

Miscanthus sinensis*
Japanese silver grass

  'Morning Light'

  'Yaku Jima'

Perovskia atriplicifolia
Russian sage

Rudbeckia fulgida
orange coneflower

  var. *sullivantii* 'Goldsturm'

Annuals

Catharanthus roseus
Madagascar periwinkle

Dianthus chinensis
China pink

Dimorphotheca sinuata
South African daisy

Gomphrena globosa
globe amaranth

Helianthus annuus
sunflower

  'Sungold'

  'Teddy Bear'

Limonium sinuatum 'Mixed Art Shades'
statice

Lobularia maritima
sweet alyssum

Petunia ×*atkinsiana*
petunia

  Grandiflora

  Multiflora

Verbena ×*hybrida*
verbena

  'Amethyst'

  'Blaze'

Zinnia
zinnia

  'Cut and Come Again'

  'Persian Carpet'

  'Thumbelina'

Roses

Rosa 'Chrysler Imperial'

Rosa 'Garden Party'

Rosa 'New Dawn'

Rosa 'Peace'

Rosa rugosa 'Fru Dagmar Hastrup'
rugosa rose

Rosa 'Sarabande'

Rosa 'The Fairy'

Vines

Clematis
clematis

  'Crimson Star'

  'Nelly Moser'

  tangutica
  golden clematis

Euonymus fortunei var. *vegetus*
evergreen bittersweet

Hedera helix*
English ivy

Hydrangea petiolaris var. *anomala*
climbing hydrangea

Pachysandra terminalis
Japanese spurge

*Vinca minor**
periwinkle

Wisteria floribunda 'Royal Purple'
Japanese wisteria

Bulbs

The following selections would be great accompaniments to any landscape designed to recall the 1960–2000 era. Again, we hope the parenthetical dates of introduction provided will help guide you in your selection.

Allium
ornamental garlic

'Firmament' (1993)

'Globemaster' (1971)

'Purple Sensation' (1963)

Crocus
crocus

biflorus 'Miss Vain' (1962)

chrysanthus 'Romance' (1973)
snow crocus

Lilium
lily

'Black Dragon Strain'

'Citronella Strain'

'Connecticut Yankee'

Lilium regale
regal lily

Narcissus
daffodil

'Bravoure' (1974)

'Chit Chat' (1975)

'Falconet' (1979)

'Jetfire' (1966)

'Las Vegas' (1981)

'Sailboat' (1980)

'Stratosphere' (1968)

Tulipa
tulip

'Abba' (1978)

'Ballerina' (1980)

'Cashmir' (1969)

'China Town' (1988)

'Golden Parade' (1963)

'Happy Family' (1985)

humilis 'Persian Pearl' (1975)

BIBLIOGRAPHY

Introduction and Chapter 1

Adams, Denise Wiles. 2004. *Restoring American Gardens: An Encyclopedia of Heirloom Ornamental Plants, 1640–1940*. Portland, Ore.: Timber Press.

von Baeyer, Edwinna. 2007. *Down the Garden Path: A Guide for Researching the History of a Garden or Landscape*. Ottawa: EvB Communications.

Birnbaum, Charles A., and Robin Karson. 2000. *Pioneers of American Landscape Design*. New York: McGraw-Hill.

Birnbaum, Charles A., and Stephanie S. Foell. 2009. *Shaping the American Landscape: New Profiles from the Pioneers of American Landscape Design Project*. Charlottesville: University of Virginia Press.

Booth, Norman K., and James E. Hiss. 1991. *Residential Landscape Architecture*. Upper Saddle River, N.J.: Prentice-Hall.

Breck, Joseph. 1858. *The Flower-Garden*. New York: A. O. Moore.

Copeland, Robert M. 1867. *Country Life*. New York: Orange Judd.

Favretti, Rudy, and Joy Favretti. 1990. *For Every House a Garden*. Hanover, N.H.: University Press of New England.

Harris, Cyril M., ed. 1993. *Dictionary of Architecture and Construction*. New York: McGraw-Hill.

Hill, May Brawley. 1995. *Grandmother's Garden*. New York: Harry N. Abrams.

Lockwood, Alice. 1931. *Gardens of Colony and State*. 2 vols. New York: Charles Scribner's Sons.

McAlester, Virginia, and Lee McAlester. 1984. *A Field Guide to American Houses*. New York: Alfred A. Knopf.

National Park Service. *Guidelines for the Treatment of Cultural Landscapes*. nps.gov/tps/standards/four-treatments/landscape-guidelines/index.htm

O'Malley, Therese, and Marc Treib, eds. 1995. *Regional Garden Design in the United States*. Washington, D.C.: Dumbarton Oaks.

Otis, Denise. 2002. *Grounds for Pleasure: Four Centuries of the American Garden*. New York: Harry N. Abrams.

Pregill, Philip, and Nancy Volkman. 1999. *Landscapes in History*, 2d ed. New York: John Wiley and Sons.

Robinette, Gary O. 1972. *Plants, People, and Environmental Quality*. Washington, D.C.: U.S. Department of the Interior.

Tucker, David M. 1993. *Kitchen Gardening in America*. Ames: Iowa State University Press.

Chapter 2. Landscapes of the Colonial Period and New Republic (1620–1820)

Ash, Thomas. 1682. *Carolina; or a Description of the Present State of that Country*. London: W. C.

Ashe, Thomas. 1808. *Travels in America, Performed in 1806*. London: William Sawyer.

Barber, John Warner. 1839. *Historical Collections*. Worcester, Mass.: Dorr, Howland.

Blanchan, Neltje. 1909. *The American Flower Garden*. Garden City, N.Y.: Doubleday, Page.

Bradford, William. 1654. Some observations. In *William Bradford, The Collected Verse*, Michael Runyan, ed., 1974. St. Paul, Minn.: John Colet Press.

A Citizen of Virginia. 1826. *A Treatise on Gardening*.

Cobbett, William. 1821. *The American Gardener, or a Treatise on the Situation, Soil, Fencing and Laying-out of Gardens*. London: C. Clement.

Denton, Daniel. 1670. *A Brief Description of New-York*. London: Printed for John Hancock. Reprint 1845. New York: William Gowan.

Dwight, Timothy. 1821. *Travels in New-England and New-York*. New Haven: Timothy Dwight.

Earle, Alice Morse. 1901. *Old Time Gardens*. New York: Macmillan.

Favretti, Rudy F., and Gordon P. DeWolf. 1972. *Colonial Gardens*. Barre, Mass.: Barre Publishers.

Gardiner, John, and David Hepburn. 1826. *The American Gardener*. 3d ed. Washington: William Cooper.

Green, Roland. 1828. *A Treatise on the Cultivation of Ornamental Flowers*. Boston: Russell and Thorburn.

Hedrick, U. P. 1950. *A History of Horticulture in America to 1860*. Reprint 1988. Portland, Ore.: Timber Press.

Hill, May Brawley. 1995. *Grandmother's Garden*. New York: Harry N. Abrams.

Israel, Barbara. 1999. *Antique Garden Ornament*. New York: Harry N. Abrams.

Johnson, Edward. 1654. *A History of New-England*. London: Printed for Nath. Brooke.

Josselyn, John. 1672. *New England Rarities Discovered*. London: G. Widdowes. Reprint 1865 with notes. Boston: William Veazie.

Leighton, Ann. 1986a. *Early American Gardens "For Meate or Medicine."* Amherst: University of Massachusetts Press.

———. 1986b. *American Gardens in the Eighteenth Century "For Use and Delight."* Amherst: University of Massachusetts Press.

Lockwood, Alice. 1931. *Gardens of Colony and State*. 2 vols. New York: Charles Scribner's Sons.

Maccubbin, Robert P., and Peter Martin, eds. 1984. *British and American Gardens in the Eighteenth Century*. Williamsburg, Va.: Colonial Williamsburg Foundation.

Martin, Peter. 2001. *The Pleasure Gardens of Virginia*. Charlottesville: University of Virginia Press.

Meager, Leonard. 1670. *The English Gardener*. London: Printed for P. Parker.

M'Mahon, Bernard. 1806. *The American Gardener's Calendar*. Reprint nd. Philadelphia: B. Graves.

An Old Gardener. 1822. *The Practical American Gardener*. Baltimore: Fielding Lucas, Jr.

Parkinson, John. 1629. *Paradisi in sole, paradisus terrestris*. London: Humphrey Lownes and Robert Young. Facsimile 1991. Dover Publications.

Prentis, Joseph. 1992. *Monthly Kalender and Garden Book*. Chillicothe, Ill.: American Botanist.

Sarudy, Barbara. 1998. *Gardens and Gardening in the Chesapeake, 1700–1805*. Baltimore: Johns Hopkins University Press.

Slade, Daniel Denison. 1895. *The Evolution of Horticulture in New England*. New York: Putnam's Sons.

Squibb, Robert. 1787. *The Gardener's Calendar for South-Carolina, Georgia, and North-Carolina*. Charleston, S.C. Reprint 1980. Athens: University of Georgia Press.

Sutcliff, Robert. 1811. *Travels in Some Parts of North America in the Years 1804, 1805, and 1806*. York: C. Peacock.

Webster, Nancy V., and Clarissa F. Dillon, eds. 1996. *Margaret Morris, Burlington, N.J., 1804 Gardening Memorandum*. Chillicothe, Ill.: American Botanist.

Wood, William. 1634. *New England Prospect*. Reprint 1898. Boston: E. M. Boynton.

Plant lists

E. Davies, *Boston Gazette*, 1719

Thomas Arnott, *South Carolina Gazette*, Charleston, S.C., 1754

J. Townley, *Boston Evening-Post* (seed list), 1760

John Watson, *South Carolina Gazette*, Charleston, S.C., 1765

William Prince, Flushing, N.Y., 1771, 1790, 1799, 1818, 1820

Bartram Nursery, Philadelphia, Pa., 1783, 1792, 1807

Peter Crowells, Charleston, S.C., 1786

Minton Collins, Richmond, Va., 1792, 1793

Goldthwaite and Moore, Philadelphia, Pa., 1796

George French, *The Virginia Herald*, Fredericksburg, Va., 1799

Bernard M'Mahon, Philadelphia, Pa., 1804

John Bryant, *Charleston Times*, Charleston, S.C., 1808

William Booth, Baltimore, Md., 1810

D and C Landreth, Philadelphia, Pa., 1811

Robert Squibb, *Charleston Courier*, Charleston, S.C., 1812

James Bloodgood and Co., Flushing, N.Y., 1819

Chapter 3. Landscapes of the Early to Mid-Nineteenth Century (1820–1860)

A. D. G. 1855. Hints to beginners in ornamental planting. *The Horticulturist* 5 ns (12):543–547.

An Amateur. 1850. A few words on rustic arbours. *The Horticulturist* 4(7):320–321.

The American Rose Culturist. 1855. New York: C. M. Saxton.

Barry, Peter, ed. 1853. Garden furniture. *The Horticulturist* 3(8):355–359.

Beecher, Henry W. 1859. *Plain and Pleasant Talk about Fruits, Flowers and Farming*. New York: Derby and Jackson.

Breck, Joseph. 1858. *The Flower-Garden*. New York: A. O. Moore.

Buel, Hon. J. 1837. The garden. *Magazine of Horticulture* 3(3):84–89.

Buist, Robert. 1839. *The American Flower Garden Directory*. Philadelphia: E. L. Carey and A. Hart.

———. 1854. *The Rose Manual*. Philadelphia: A. Hart and Lippincott, Grambo.

Cothran, James. 2003. *Gardens and Historic Plants of the Antebellum South*. Columbia: University of South Carolina Press.

D. W. L. 1857. Landscape gardening. *New England Farmer* 9(4):170–171.

Douglas, Lake, and Jeannette Hardy. 2001. *Gardens of New Orleans: Exquisite Excess*. San Francisco: Chronicle Books.

Downing, A. J. 1836. Remarks on the different styles of architecture and on the employment of vases in garden scenery. *The American Gardener's Magazine* 2(8):281–286.

———. 1837. Notices on the state and progress of Horticulture in the United States. *Magazine of Horticulture* 3(1):1–10.

———. 1841. *A Treatise on the Theory and Practice of Landscape Gardening, Adapted to North America*. New York: Wiley and Putnam.

———. 1842. *Cottage Residences*. New York: Wiley and Putnam.

———. 1846. A chapter on lawns. *The Horticulturist* 1(5):201–204.

———. 1850a. *The Architecture of Country Houses*. New York: D. Appleton. Facsimile 1969. Dover Publications.

———. 1850b. How to arrange country places. *The Horticulturist* 4(9):392–396.

Doyle, Martin. 1835. *The Flower Garden*. New York: Moore and Payne, Clinton Hall.

Durand, L. 1857. Grounds for farm houses. *The Horticulturist* 7(5):225–226.

Editor. 1850. Notes on gardens and nurseries. *Magazine of Horticulture* 16(9):406–417.

Editor. 1856. A trip to Cuba and the Southern States, 9. *The Horticulturist* 8(2):70–72.

Editor. 1856a. A house to live in. *New England Farmer* 8(1):17–18

———. 1856b. A village or farm cottage. *New England Farmer* 8(4):176–177.

———. 1857. A small cottage. *New England Farmer* 9(5): 208.

Elder, Walter. 1850. *The Cottage Garden of America*. Philadelphia: Moss and Brother.

Fessenden, Thomas G. 1857. *The Complete Farmer and Rural Economist*. New York: C. M. Saxton.

Heaver, W. 1851. Rough notes on gardens in the vicinity of Cincinnati. *Western Horticultural Review* 1:21–23.

Hooper, Edward James. 1839. *The Practical Farmer, Gardener and Housewife.* Cincinnati: Geo. Conclin.

Hovey, Charles M., ed. 1841. Residence of A. J. Downing, botanical gardens and nurseries, Newburgh, New York. *Magazine of Horticulture* 7(11): 403, 409.

Kenrick, William. 1841. *The New American Orchardist.* Boston: Otis, Broaders.

Kern, G. M. 1855. *Practical Landscape Gardening.* Cincinnati: Moore, Wilstach, Keys.

Langhart, Nick. 1999. *Antique Homes Guide to Styles.* Douglas, Mass.: Antique Homes Magazine.

Lelievre, Jacques-Felix. 1838. *New Louisiana Gardener.* Trans. Sally Kittredge Reeves. Reprint 2001. Baton Rouge: Louisiana State University.

Leuchars, R. B. 1850. Notes on gardens and gardening in the neighborhood of Boston. *Magazine of Horticulture* 16(2):47–60.

Munn, B. 1854. On the employment of statuary in the decoration of gardens and pleasure grounds. *The Horticulturist* 4 ns (5): 208–210.

Paulsen, J. W. 1846. Plants in bloom, in the garden of C. L. Bell, Esq., in the vicinity of New Orleans, in November, 1845. *Magazine of Horticulture* 12(1):22–24.

Prince, William. 1828. *A Short Treatise on Horticulture.* New York: T. and J. Swords.

R. 1856. Ornamental gardening. *New England Farmer* 7(4):188–189.

R. B. L. 1853. On laying out and planting villa residences. *Magazine of Horticulture* 19(2):56–60.

Rion, Mary C. 1860. *The Ladies' Southern Florist.* Facsimile 2000. Columbia: University of South Carolina.

"S." 1859. Hints for landscape gardening. *The Horticulturist* 4(9):448–449.

Saunders, William. 1855. Designs for improving country residences. *The Horticulturist* 5 n.s. (9):403–405.

Sayers, Edward. 1837. The farm house garden. *The Horticultural Register* 3(10):362.

——. 1838. *The American Flower Garden Companion.* Boston: Weeks, Jordan.

Sylvanus. 1851. Random notes on southern horticulture. *The Horticulturist* 6(5):220–224.

Teschemacher, James Englebert. 1835. On artificial rockwork. *The Horticultural Register* 1:457–458.

Thomas, J. J. 1848. Grouping flowers. *The Horticulturist* 1(3):120–122.

——. 1858. *Illustrated Annual Register of Rural Affairs 1855-6-7,* vol. 1. Albany, N.Y.: Luther Tucker and Son.

W. D. B. 1856. Ornamental gardening. *New England Farmer* 8(4):166.

Warder, John A. 1858. *Hedges and Evergreens.* New York: A. O. Moore.

Wells, Samuel R. 1858. *The Garden: A Pocket Manual of Practical Horticulture.* New York: Fowler and Wells.

Plant lists

William Prince, Flushing, N.Y., 1822, 1826, 1829, 1831, 1841, 1844, 1854, 1857, 1860

D. Landreth and Sons, Philadelphia, Pa., 1826, 1828, 1847

Owens and Leckie, *The Virginian,* Lynchburg, Va., 1826

Albany Nursery, Albany, N.Y., 1827, 1830, 1839

G. Thorburn and Son, New York, N.Y., 1827

William Kenrick, Boston, Mass., 1832, 1835

Brighton Nursery, Boston, Mass., 1833, 1841

Hovey and Co., Boston, Mass., 1834, 1835, 1836, 1839, 1844, 1845, 1847, 1852, 1859

Thomas Hogg, New York, N.Y., 1834

S. C. Parkhurst, Cincinnati, Ohio, 1835

George C. Barrett, Boston, Mass., 1836

Joseph Breck, Boston, Mass., 1838, 1845, 1851

Spring Garden Nursery, Cincinnati, Ohio, 1843

Robert Buist, Philadelphia, Pa., 1844, 1857, 1859, 1860

Winter and Co., Flushing, N.Y., 1844

Cleveland Nursery, Cleveland, Ohio, 1845

Lake Erie Nursery, Cleveland, Ohio, 1846

McIntosh and Co., Cleveland, Ohio, 1846

A. H. Lazell, Columbus, Ohio, 1848

Ellwanger and Barry, Rochester, N.Y., 1848, 1860

Southern Nurseries, Washington, Miss., 1851

Denmark Nursery, Iowa, 1853

Joseph Rennie, Richmond, Va., 1853

Saco Nurseries, Saco, Maine, 1853

Thomas Lindley, Fayetteville, N.C., 1854

Pomaria Nurseries, Pomaria, S.C., 1856

Old Colony Nurseries, Plymouth, Mass., 1857

Alton Nursery, Alton, Ill., 1858

P. J. Berckmans, Augusta, Ga., 1858, 1859

Persimmon Grove Nursery, Princeton, Ill., 1858

Staunton Nurseries, Staunton, Va., 1858

Vineland Nurseries, Langdon Station, Ala., 1858

Bloomington Nursery, Bloomington, Ill., 1859

Hopewell Nursery, Fredericksburg, Va., 1859

Columbus Nursery, Columbus, Ohio, 1860

St. Louis Nursery, St. Louis, Mo., 1860

Thomas Affleck, Brenham, Tex., 1860

Chapter 4. American Victorian Landscapes (1860–1900)

Mrs. A. G. W. 1886. Flower bed edgings. *Vick's Monthly Magazine* 9(8):250.

Anon. 1888. An open letter on planting a small place in the suburbs. *The American Garden* 9(4):153.

Arms, Walter F. 1881. *Caldwell's Illustrated Historical Atlas of Adams County, Ohio*. Reprint nd. Newark, Ohio: J. A. Caldwell.

Arnold, C. M. 1882. Wild gardens. *Vick's Monthly Magazine* 5(4):101–102.

Bailey, L. H. 1891. *Annals of Horticulture in North America for the Year 1890*. New York: Orange Judd.

Blauvelt, Isaac. 1878. Garden on the house top. *Vick's Monthly Magazine* 1(1):22.

Boardman, Samuel. 1860. Rustic adornments for gardens and waysides. *The Gardener's Monthly* 2(4):112–113.

Buckeye Woman. 1882. New use for barrels. *Vick's Monthly Magazine* 5(5):149.

Butz, Paul. 1886. *Illustrated Catalogue of Plants and Trees*. New Castle, Penn.: Paul Butz and Sons.

Caldwell, J. A. 1873. *Caldwell's Atlas of Wayne Co. and of the City of Wooster, Ohio*. Sunbury, Ohio: J. A. Caldwell. Reprint 1974. Knightstown, Ind.: The Bookmark.

Colby, Fred M. 1884. The gardens of our grandmothers. *The Ladies Floral Cabinet* 12(7):222–223.

De Loup, Maximilian. 1889. Grounds of a suburban residence. *The American Garden* 10(3):92–94.

Editor. 1878a. Making and beautifying roads. *Vick's Monthly Magazine* 1(1):6.

——. 1878b. Improving home grounds. *Vick's Monthly Magazine* 1(2):35–38.

——. 1879. Town and suburban gardens. *Vick's Monthly Magazine* 2(10):291–295.

——. 1880a. Progress and improvement. *Vick's Monthly Magazine* 3(2):33–36.

——. 1880b. Sub-tropical beds. *Vick's Monthly Magazine* 3(4):113.

——. 1880c. Laying out a front yard. *Vick's Monthly Magazine* 3(7):211–212.

——. 1881. Carpet bedding. *Vick's Monthly Magazine* 4(4):120–122.

——. 1883a. Herbaceous perennials. *Vick's Monthly Magazine* 6(4):114–115.

——. 1883b. Shrubs and perennials. *Vick's Monthly Magazine* 6(2):38.

——. 1885. Ornamental hedge. *Vick's Monthly Magazine* 8(2):51.

Editor. 1894. How to beautify our home grounds. *American Gardening* 15(14):157–158.

Elder, Walter. 1861. The kitchen-garden. *The Gardener's Monthly* 3(10):302–304.

Eliot, Charles. 1891. Two studies for house plantings. *Garden and Forest* 4(165):184–185.

Elliott, F. R. 1881. *Hand Book of Practical Landscape Gardening*. New York: D. M. Dewey.

Everts, L. H. 1875. *Combination Atlas Map of Fairfield County, Ohio*. Philadelphia: L. H. Everts. Reprint 1967. Detroit: Gale Research.

Henderson, Charles. 1901. *Henderson's Picturesque Gardens and Ornamental Gardening Illustrated*. New York: Peter Henderson.

Hints for May. 1863. Flower-garden and pleasure-ground. *The Gardener's Monthly* 5(5):129–130.

Hoopes, Joshua. 1872. How to plant a rural home. *The Horticulturist* 27(6):164–167.

J. B. 1881. The herbaceous border. *Vick's Monthly Magazine* 4(10):314.

J. F. S. 1860. Questions and answers. *The Gardener's Monthly* 2(3):89.

Long, Elias. 1893. *Ornamental Gardening for Americans*. New York: Orange Judd.

MacPherson, J. 1885. A well kept garden. *Vick's Monthly Magazine* 8(8):231.

Parkman, Francis. 1871. *The Book of Roses*. Boston: J. E. Tilton.

Parsons, Samuel. 1869. *Parsons on the Rose*. New York: Orange Judd.

——. 1891. *Landscape Gardening*. New York: G. P. Putnam's Sons.

R. S. B. 1894. Home ground arrangements. *American Gardening* 15(12):212.

Sanders, Edgar. 1877. The kitchen garden. *Illustrated Annual Register of Rural Affairs* 2:84–91.

Sargent, Charles S. 1895. Old-fashioned gardens. *Garden and Forest* 8 (July): 281–282.

Scott, Frank J. 1870. *The Art of Beautifying Suburban Home Grounds of Small Extent*. New York: D. Appleton.

Simonds, O. C. 1893. Ornamentation of tennis and other play grounds. *American Gardening* 14(6):334–336.

Thomas, J. J. 1877. *Rural Affairs*, vol. 2. Albany, N.Y.: Luther Tucker and Son.

——. 1878. *Rural Affairs*, vol. 8. Albany, N.Y.: Luther Tucker and Son.

——. 1881. *Rural Affairs*, vol. 9. Albany, N.Y.: Luther Tucker and Son.

Treat, Mary. 1891. How to make a wild garden. *Garden and Forest* 4(165):188–189.

Vaux, Calvert. 1867. *Villas and Cottages*. New York: Harper and Brothers.

Weidenmann, Jacob. 1870. *Beautifying Country Homes*. Reprint 1978 as *Victorian Landscape Gardening*. Watkins Glen, N.Y.: American Life Foundation.

Woodward, George. 1867. *Cottages and Farmhouses*. New York: American News Company.

Plant lists

Old Colony Nurseries, Plymouth, Mass., 1861

P. J. Berckmans, Augusta, Ga., 1861, 1873

Ellwanger and Barry, Rochester, N.Y., 1862, 1867, 1875, 1882

Hovey and Co., Boston, Mass., 1862, 1863, 1866, 1873, 1875, 1888

E. Y. Teas and Bros. Richmond, Ind., 1866, 1872, 1873

R. Buist, Philadelphia, Pa., 1866

Bloomington Nursery, Bloomington, Ill., 1867, 1868, 1872, 1873, 1875, 1883, 1886

Theodore Wendel, Boston, Mass., 1867

B. Truett and Son, Nashville, Tenn., 1868

D. Landreth and Sons, Philadelphia, Pa., 1868, 1879, 1889

Denmark Nursery, Denmark, Iowa, 1868

B. K. Bliss and Son, New York, N.Y., 1869

Brookfield Nursery, Brookfield, Mo., 1869

Joseph Breck, Boston, Mass., 1869, 1871, 1875, 1878, 1881, 1894

Atlanta Nurseries, Atlanta, Ga., 1870

J. S. Downer and Son, Fairview, Ky., 1870

Moon Mahlon, Morrisville, Pa., 1870

Washburn and Co., Boston, Mass., 1870

Benjamin Wells, Boston, Mass., 1871

C. B. Denson, Pittsboro, N.C., 1871

Sunnyside Nurseries, Clinton, Iowa, 1871

Briggs and Bros., Rochester, N.Y., 1873

R. J. Trumbull, Oakland, Calif., 1873

Miller and Sievers, San Francisco, Calif., 1874

Storrs and Harrison Co., Painesville, Ohio, 1874, 1894, 1896

Manning Nurseries, Reading, Mass., 1875, 1887, 1889

Plant Seed Co., St. Louis, Mo., 1875, 1884

Henry A. Dreer, Philadelphia, Pa., 1876

Henry Michel, St. Louis, Mo., 1876

Columbus Nursery, Columbus, Ohio, 1877

Edward Gillett, Southwick, Mass., 1879, 1880, 1883, 1886, 1890

Santa Rosa Nursery, Santa Rosa, Calif., 1880

Arnold Puetz, Jacksonville, Fla., 1881

James Vick, Rochester, N.Y., 1881

Langdon Nurseries, Mobile, Ala., 1881

Willis Nursery, Ottawa, Kans., 1885

D. M. Moore, Ogden, Utah, 1887

Exeter and Geneva Nurseries, Geneva, Neb., 1888

George Thompson and Sons, Louisville, Ky., 1888

Mission Valley Nurseries, Victoria County, Tex., 1888, 1898

Pearfield, Nursery, Frelsburg, Tex., 1888

A. F. Boardman, Auburn, Calif., 1889

C. E. Allen, Brattleboro, Vt., 1889

Theodosia Burr Shepherd, Ventura, Calif., 1891

H. H. Berger, San Francisco, Calif., 1892

American Exotic Nurseries, Seven Oaks, Fla., 1894

California Nursery Co., Niles, Calif., 1894

Ellis Brothers, Keene, N.H., 1894

A. Blanc, Philadelphia, Pa., c. 1895

Fancher Creek Nursery, Fresno, Calif., c. 1895

Ullathorne Seed Co., Memphis, Tenn., 1895

Rosedale Nurseries, Brenham, Tex., 1898

Chapter 5. Eclectic Landscapes (1900–1930)

Angier, Belle S. 1906. *The Garden Book of California*. San Francisco: Paul Elder.

Bailey, L. H., ed. 1903. *How to Make a Flower Garden*. New York: Doubleday, Page.

———. 1908. *Garden Making*. New York: Macmillan.

Bennett, Ida D. 1903. *The Flower Garden*. New York: McClure, Phillips.

Blanchan, Neltje. 1909. *The American Flower Garden*. Garden City, N.Y.: Doubleday, Page.

Braunton, Ernest. 1915. *The Garden Beautiful in California*. Los Angeles: Times-Mirror Press.

Burnett, Vivian. 1910. Craftsman gardens for craftsman homes. *The Craftsman* 18(1):46–58.

Butterfield, W. H. 1914. *Making Walls, Fences and Hedges*. New York: McBride, Nast. Reprint 2003. Davenport, Iowa: Gustav's Library.

Byne, Arthur, and Mildred Stapley Byne. 1928. *Spanish Gardens and Patios*. Philadelphia: J. B. Lippincott. Reprint 2008. Atglen, Pa.: Schiffer.

Conrad, Henry S. 1906. The making of a water garden. *The Garden* (March): 78–81.

Cridland, Robert B. 1916. *Practical Landscape Gardening*. New York: A. T. De La Mare.

Dixon, Florence. 1910. Japanese effects for small gardens. *The Craftsman* (Sept.): 632–638.

Duncan, Frances. 1911. Suburban gardening. *The Century* 81(113):910–918.

——. 1918. *Home Vegetables and Small Fruits*. New York: Charles Scribner's Sons.

Earle, Alice Morse. 1901. *Old Time Gardens*. New York: Macmillan.

——. 1902. *Sun-Dials and Roses of Yesterday*. New York: Macmillan.

Ely, Helena Rutherford. 1903. *A Woman's Hardy Garden*. New York: Macmillan.

Fox, Helen Morgenthau. 1929. *Patio Gardens*. New York: Macmillan.

Greely, Rose. 1922. Planting around the city house. *House Beautiful* 52(2):128–129, 160.

Hamblin, Stephen F. 1916. Making the best of it, part 4: what will grow under lawn trees. *Garden Magazine* (June): 295–296.

Jensen, Jens. 1906. Ideal edging plants for walks and flower beds. *Garden Magazine* (April): 136–138.

Kellaway, Herbert J. 1915. *How to Lay Out Suburban Home Grounds*. New York: John Wiley and Sons.

King, Mrs. Francis. 1915. *The Well-Considered Garden*. New York: Charles Scribner's Sons.

——. 1921. *The Little Garden*. Boston: Atlantic Monthly Press.

Lounsberry, Alice. 1910. *Gardens Near the Sea*. New York: Frederick A. Stokes.

Maeterlinck, Maurice. 1905. *Old Fashioned Flowers and Other Out-of-door Studies*. New York: Dodd, Mead.

McLaren, John. 1908. *Gardening in California: Landscape and Flower*. San Francisco: A. M. Robertson.

Miller, Wilhelm. 1915. *The Prairie Spirit in Landscape Gardening*. Reprint 2002. Amherst: University of Massachusetts Press.

——. 1917. *What England Can Teach Us About Gardening*. Garden City, N.Y.: Doubleday, Page.

Murmann, Eugene O. 1914. *California Gardens*. Los Angeles: Eugene O. Murmann. Reprint 2008 as *California Gardens of the Arts and Crafts Period*. Atglen, Pa.: Schiffer Publishing.

Northend, Mary H. 1916. *Garden Ornaments*. New York: Duffield.

Ramsey, Leonidas W., and Charles H. Lawrence. 1930. *Garden Pools*. New York: Macmillan.

Rexford, Eben E. 1912. *Amateur Gardencraft*. Philadelphia: J. P. Lippincott.

Ries, Victor H. 1928. Planting the lily pool. *Better Homes and Gardens* 6(9):7–9.

Riley, Phil M. 1915. Garden entrance and the home. *Garden Magazine* 22(2):36–37.

Rogers, W. S. 1911. *Garden Planning*. New York: Doubleday, Page.

Rose, Jim. 1920. A landscape plan for a complete place. *Garden Magazine* 31(5):311.

Savage, C. Courtenay. 1916. Pottery, statuary and garden ornaments. *Garden Magazine* (January): 201–202.

Shelton, Louise. 1916. *Beautiful Gardens in America*. New York: Charles Scribner's Sons.

Spencer, J. B. 1922. A lily pool in a little garden. *Garden Magazine* 35(4):243–244.

Steele, Fletcher. 1924. *Design in the Little Garden*. Boston: Atlantic Monthly Press.

Swett, Naomi, and Adolph Meyer. 1928. Landscaping plans and upkeep. *House and Garden* 53(6):80, 150, 158.

Tabor, Grace. 1912. *Making the Grounds Attractive with Shrubbery*. New York: McBride, Nast.

——. 1913. *Suburban Gardens*. New York: Outing. Reprint 2003. Davenport, Iowa: Gustav's Library.

——. 1916. *The Landscape Gardening Book*. New York: Robert M. McBride.

——. 1917. *Making a Garden to Bloom This Year*. New York: McBride, Nast.

——. 1919. The dear old-fashioned garden. *Garden Magazine* 30(5):171–172.

Thoms, Craig. 1928. Gardening on the rim of the prairie. *Better Homes and Gardens* 6(9): 25, 56–57.

Van Rensselaer, Mrs. Schuyler. 1903. *Art Out-of-Doors.* New York: Charles Scribner's Sons.

Verbeck, William. 1903. A Japanese garden in an American yard. In *How to Make a Flower Garden*, L. H. Bailey, ed. New York: Doubleday, Page.

Waugh, Frank A. 1928. *Book of Landscape Gardening.* New York: Orange Judd.

Wickson, E. J. 1915. *California Garden-Flowers, Shrubs, Trees and Vines*. San Francisco: Pacific Rural Press.

Wilder, Louise Beebe. 1919. Old time flowers to use in modern gardens. *Garden Magazine* 30(5):173–177.

Plant lists

Call's Nursery, Perry, Ohio, 1901

R. B. Dunning, Bangor, Maine, 1901

Highlands Nursery, Kawana, N.C., 1903

A. G. Tillinghast, LaConner, Wash., 1904

J. E. Jackson, Gainesville, Ga., 1904

Royal Palm Nurseries, Oneco, Fla., 1904

Hooker, Wyman, and Co., Rochester, N.Y., c. 1905

Rice Bros. Geneva, N.Y., c. 1905

Wagner Park, Sidney, Ohio, 1905

P. J. Berckmans, Augusta, Ga., 1906

Biltmore Nursery, Biltmore, N.C., 1907

Cox Seed Co., San Francisco, Calif., 1907

John Lewis Childs, Floral Park, N.Y., 1907, 1910, 1914

Valdesian Nurseries, Bostic, N.C., 1907

W. A. Yates, Brenham, Tex., c. 1907

Ashby Nursery, Berkeley, Calif., 1908

Griswold Seed Co., Lincoln, Neb., 1908

Henry A. Dreer, Philadelphia, Pa., 1908, 1925

J. M. Thorburn, New York, N.Y., 1908

Storrs and Harrison Co., Painesville, Ohio, 1908, 1925

J. W. Dudley, Parkersburg, W.Va., 1909

John A. Salzer, LaCrosse, Wis., 1910

Peter Henderson, New York, N.Y., 1910, 1915

New England Nurseries, Bedford, Mass., 1910

Germain Seed Co., Los Angeles, Calif., 1911

J. B. Pilkington, Portland, Ore., 1912

Edward Gillett, Southwick, Mass., 1914

Glen St. Mary Nurseries, Glen St. Mary, Fla., 1914

Iowa Seed Co., Des Moines, Iowa, 1914

Champion Nurseries, Perry, Ohio, 1915

J. J. H. Gregory and Son, Marblehead, Mass., 1915, 1928

Union Seed and Fuel Co., Boise, Idaho, 1916

Comal Springs Nursery, New Braunfels, Tex., 1917

Ellwanger and Barry, Rochester, N.Y., 1917

Joseph Breck, Boston, Mass., 1917

Nebraska Seed Co., Omaha, Neb., 1918

Brand Nursery, Faribault, Minn., 1919

Ozark Seed and Plant Co., Nashville, Ark., 1919

Ferguson Seed Farms, Oklahoma, Okla., 1920

Arizona Seed and Floral Co., Phoenix, Ariz., 1921, 1925

Gurney Seed and Nursery Co., 1921, 1927

Barteldes Seed Co., Denver, Colo., 1922

Barteldes Seed Co., Lawrence, Kans., 1922

Harrison's Nurseries, Berlin, Md., 1922

State Nursery and Seed Co., Helena, Mont., 1923

Northwest Nursery Co., Valley City, N.Dak., c. 1924

William C. Duckham, Madison, N.J., 1924

Southwestern Seed and Nursery Co., Santa Fe, N.Mex., c. 1925

Tucker-Mosby Seed Co., Memphis, Tenn., 1925

Ernst Nurseries, Eaton, Ohio, 1926

Porter-Walton, Salt Lake City, Utah, 1926

Fiske Seed Co., Boston, Mass., 1927

Henry Field, Shenandoah, Iowa, 1927

Perfection Nurseries, Foley, Ala., 1927

F. W. Bolgiano and Co., Washington, D.C., 1928

Reuter's Seed Co., New Orleans, La., 1928

Whitten-Ackerman, Bridgman, Mich., 1928

Chapter 6. Landscapes for Modern Homes (1930–1960)

Aul, Henry B. 1944. Formal pools for the home garden. *The Home Garden* 4(4):33–34.

———. 1945a. Pergolas and arches. *The Home Garden* 5(2):70–73.

———. 1945b. Seats in the home garden. *The Home Garden* 5(2):32–35.

Bailey, Ralph. 1950a. What we need is more dooryard gardens. *The Home Garden* 15(2):15–16.

———. 1950b. How do you plan a dooryard garden? *The Home Garden* 15(4):37–39.

Barron, Leonard. 1935. *Gardening for the Small Place.* Garden City, N.Y.: Doubleday, Doran.

Bell, Louise Price. 1953. This garden path has style. *The Home Garden* 21(3):42–43.

Berry, Mrs. Charles F. 1944. Do you save rainwater? *The Home Garden* 4(2):38–39.

Carhart, Arthur H. 1935. *How to Plan the Home Landscape.* Garden City, N.Y.: Doubleday, Doran.

Church, Thomas D. 1939. 11 points on paving. *Sunset* 82(2):22–23.

———. 1983. *Gardens Are For People.* 3d ed. Berkeley: University of California Press.

Clarkson, Rosetta. 1939. *Magic Gardens.* New York: Macmillan.

Coffey, Clara Stimson. 1943. Introduction to small grounds planning. *The Home Garden* 2(2):38–40.

Cotton, Horace G. 1934. Build a barbecue for your Sunset garden. *Sunset* 72(5):14–15.

Dobyns, Winifred S. 1931. *California Gardens.* New York: Macmillan.

Editor. 1950. My favorite vegetable garden and how it works. *The Home Garden* 15(2):30–38.

Findlay, Hugh. 1934. *Garden Making and Keeping.* Garden City, N.Y.: Doubleday, Doran.

Free, Montague. 1951. How to build a perennial border. *The Home Garden* 18(5):56–61.

———. 1952. Permanent edges are made—not grown. *The Home Garden* 20(1):44–47.

Garrick, Marcia. 1944. Plan a wheel for a whirl with herbs. *The Home Garden* 4(6):36–39.

Gregory, Daniel P. 2008. *Cliff May and the Modern Ranch House.* New York: Rizzoli.

Griffith, John R. 1943. Flags without stone. *The Home Garden* 2(3):48–50.

Haislip, Martha P. 1953. How to furnish your outdoor living room. *The Home Garden.* 22(5):18–23.

Johnson, Leonard H. 1927. *Foundation Planting.* New York: A. T. De La Mare.

Johnston, W. R., and F. J. Johnston. 1945. Real vegetables on one man's roof-top. *The Home Garden* 6(2):87–89.

Kiler, E. Leslie. 1939. How to make a pavement for patio, walk, or terrace. *Sunset* 81(3):19.

Knight, Elsa L. 1934. What's new in porch and garden furniture. *Sunset* 72(5):12–13.

Matschat, Cecile H. 1934. Sky gardening in Manhattan. *Gardeners' Chronicle* 38(3):67–69.

Morris, Norman A. 1946. *Your Book of Garden Plans.* Culver City, Calif.: Murray and Gee.

Ortloff, H. Stuart. 1944. Face-lifting a foundation planting. *The Home Garden* 3(3):59–62.

Putz, Alfred. 1936. *Another Garden Notebook.* Garden City, N.Y.: Doubleday, Doran.

Raymore, Henry B. 1944a. Gates and entrances. *The Home Garden* 4(1):49–52.

———. 1944b. Walks and pavements. *The Home Garden* 4(2):49–52.

——. 1944c. Fences and fence-making. *The Home Garden* 4(3):70–72.

Robinson, Philip L. 1950. Planning the new place, part 2: play and service areas. *The Home Garden* 16(5):72–76.

Rockwell, F. F. 1943. Year round results from your victory garden. *The Home Garden* 1(1):11–16.

Stark Brothers Nursery. 1943. *Fruit Planting Guide for Your Victory Gardens*. Louisiana, Mo.: Stark Bros. Nurseries.

Streatfield, David. 1993. The arts and crafts garden in California. In *The Arts and Crafts Movement in California*, Kenneth R. Trapp, ed. New York: Abbeville.

——. 1994. *California Gardens: Creating a New Eden*. New York: Abbeville.

Sunset Magazine Editors. 1937a. Pots for patios. *Sunset* 78(4):33.

——. 1937b. Garden pools. *Sunset* 78(7):20–21.

——. 1938a. Back-yard ranching. *Sunset* 80(4):28.

——. 1938b. Roll-around patio furniture. *Sunset* 81(4):38.

——. 1939a. Adobe in the garden. *Sunset* 82(5):56.

——. 1939b. Come into the garden. *Sunset* 82(6):36–37.

Sunset Magazine Editors and Cliff May. 1946. *Sunset Western Ranch Houses*. San Francisco: Lane Pub. Co. Reprint 1999. Santa Monica: Hennessey+Ingalls.

Van Pelt Wilson, Helen. 1943. A one woman vegetable garden. *The Home Garden* 1(3):8–11.

Weingarten, David, and Lucia Howard. 2009. *Ranch Houses*. New York: Rizzoli.

Young, Paul R. 1943. Planning the very small vegetable garden. *The Home Garden* 1(1):72–75.

Plant lists

Allen's Nurseries, Geneva, Ohio, 1930

F. H. Horsford, Charlotte, Vt., 1931

Henry F. Michell, Philadelphia, Pa., 1931

Job P. Wyatt, Raleigh, N.C., 1931

Fremont Nursery, Fremont, Ohio, 1932

Fairbury Nurseries, Fairbury, Neb., 1933

Union Seed and Fuel Co., Boise, Idaho, 1933

California Nursery Co., Niles, Calif., 1934

Joseph Harris, Coldwater, N.Y., 1934

Maloney Bros. Nursery, Dansville, N.Y., 1934

D. Hill Nursery, East Dundee, Ill., 1935

Grand Junction Seed Co., Grand Junction, Colo., 1936

Allen, Sterling and Lothrop, Portland, Maine, 1937

Paul J. Howard, Los Angeles, Calif., 1937

George W. Park Seed Co., Greenwood, S.C., 1938

Bunting Nurseries, Selbyville, Del., 1939

Kiyono Nurseries, Crichton, Ala. 1939

Lamb Nurseries, Spokane, Wash., 1939

Oscar H. Will, Bismarck, N.Dak., 1939

W. E. Barrett, Providence, R.I., 1939

Wayside Gardens, Mentor, Ohio, 1941, 1960

Vaughan's Seed Store, Chicago, Ill., New York, N.Y., 1945

Peter Henderson, New York, N.Y., 1946

Chapter 7. Suburban Landscape to Green Revolution (1960–2000)

Carson, Rachel. 1962. *Silent Spring*. Boston: Houghton Mifflin.

Coulter, Steve, and Nancy Hall. 1983. Outdoor living. *Better Homes and Gardens* 61(6):43–53.

Creasy, Rosalind. 1982. *Edible Landscaping*. San Francisco: Sierra Club Books.

——. 1986. *Earthly Delights*. New York: Random House.

Damrosch, Barbara. 1982. *Theme Gardens*. New York: Workman.

Druse, Ken. 1989. *The Natural Garden*. New York: Clarkson N. Potter.

Editor. 1960a. Build yourself some summer comfort. *Better Homes and Gardens* 38(6):65–70.

——. 1960b. Outdoor living right at home. *Better Homes and Gardens* 38(7):42–47.

——. 1960c. We give this A-plus for planning. *Better Homes and Gardens* 38(8):50–53.

——. 1960d. Remodeling outdoors: the shape of shade to come. *House and Garden* 117(4):155–157.

——. 1960e. The playhouse grows up. *House and Garden* 117(6):113–117.

——. 1984. Outdoor living projects to spruce up your yard. *Better Homes and Gardens* 62(6):39–49.

Kiley, Dan, and Jane Amidon. 1999. *Dan Kiley*. New York: Bulfinch.

Kramer, Jack. 1972. *Garden Planning for the Small Property*. New York: Charles Scribner's Sons.

Lyons, Robert E. 1989. An annual meadow. *Fine Gardening* 7:22–26.

Oehme, Wolfgang, and James Van Sweden. 1990. *Bold Romantic Gardens*. New York: Acropolis Books. Reprint

Padilla, Victoria. 1961. *Southern California Gardens*. Berkeley: University of California Press.

Reader's Digest Editors. 1972. *Practical Guide to Home Landscaping*. Pleasantville, N.Y.: The Reader's Digest Assn.

Smith, Ken. 1985. *Home Landscaping in the Northeast and Midwest*. Tucson: HP Publishing.

Sunset Editors. 1965. *Landscaping for Modern Living*. Menlo Park, Calif.: Lane Pub. Co.

——. 1978a. *Landscaping and Garden Remodeling*. Menlo Park, Calif.: Lane Pub. Co.

——. 1978b. *Ideas for Small-Space Gardens*. Menlo Park, Calif.: Lane Pub. Co.

——. 1981. *Swimming Pools*. Menlo Park, Calif.: Lane Pub. Co.

——. 1986. *Spas, Hot Tubs, and Home Saunas*. Menlo Park, Calif.: Lane Pub. Co.

Wilson, Jim. 1992. *Landscaping with Wildflowers*. Boston: Houghton Mifflin.

GLOSSARY

adobe. Sun-dried brick made of clay and straw.

anachronistic object. One that is out of place in the chronological order in a historical sense.

arbor. A bower formed by trees, shrubs, or vines trained on a structure to create a leafy roof over a seating area or walkway.

architectural salvage. Materials reclaimed from the demolition of buildings and other structures.

aspect. A surface or slope that faces in a given direction.

asymmetry. A balance achieved more by feel than formula, it comes from placing objects of differing size at different distances to create the illusion of equal proportion.

base map. A plan drawing that includes all objects on the site pertinent to the design.

baseline measurement. Taking measurements along one line without moving the tape.

circulation. The patterns for movement through a site, either pedestrian or vehicular, such as driveways and paths.

concrete. An artificial, stone-like material used for various structural purposes, made by mixing cement and various aggregates (sand, pebbles, gravel, shale) with water and allowing them to harden.

concrete block. Uniform blocks made from concrete used for foundations or structures.

construction drawing. A drawing that shows the details and dimensions for building a hardscape.

cultivar. "Cultivated variety"; a plant that has been created or selected intentionally for specific characteristics and maintained through cultivation.

cultivated plant. A plant that is deliberately grown for a human purpose.

cutting. A piece, as a root, stem, or leaf, cut from a plant and used for propagation.

deadheading. To remove faded blooms, especially in flower gardens, often to help continued blooming.

dependencies. Any outbuilding or annex; for example, garden sheds or stables.

direct measurement. Measuring from one point to another.

edging plants. Low growing plants that are used along the front of the bed or border.

engineered wood. Man-made composite wood, made from various materials such as pvc, saw dust, and concrete.

erosion. The process by which the surface of the earth, or soil is worn away by water, wind, or other mechanical actions.

flora. A work systematically describing or depicting plants.

galvanizing. Coating metal (usually iron or steel) with zinc.

gazebo. A structure or pavilion with open or latticework sides used for outdoor entertaining or dining.

grade changes. Changes in the different slopes or levels of the ground (topography changes).

grading plan. A design drawing that shows the proposed changes in slope or topography.

graph paper. Paper printed with a regular grid used for plotting or drafting.

grotto. A cavern-like recess or structure.

hardscape. The constructed portions of a landscape, such as walls, walks, and patios.

heirloom plants. A plant that was grown in an earlier era and has been preserved and produced to be cultivated by modern gardeners.

herbaceous plant. One whose leaves and stems die down to the soil level at the end of the growing season.

herbaria. Systematically arranged collections of dried plants.

invasive plant. Non-indigenous, or "non-native" plant that adversely affects the habitats and bioregions it invades, economically, environmentally, and/or ecologically.

kitchen garden. A garden, usually near the house, used to raise vegetables, small fruits, and herbs for the table.

layout plan. A drawing that shows all the plants and dimensions of ground plane areas.

master plan. The design drawing that illustrates all materials, quantities, and specifications.

mulch. Protective cover placed over the soil to retain moisture, reduce erosion, provide nutrients, and suppress weed growth and seed germination.

noxious weed. An invasive plant species that has been designated by county, state or provincial, or national agricultural authorities as one that is injurious to agricultural and/or horticultural crops, natural habitats and/or ecosystems, and/or humans or livestock.

order. The overall framework of a design.

ornamental plants. Plants grown for decorative purposes in gardens and landscapes.

pergola. A garden feature forming a shaded walkway, passageway, or sitting area of vertical posts or pillars that usually support cross-beams and a sturdy open lattice, often upon which woody vines are trained.

period of significance. The time period one chooses to connect the landscape to the building. This period often is related to the architectural style of the house or the year or era in which it was built.

pH. The measurement of acidity or alkalinity in the soil that is a limiting factor as to which plants will grow in a given location.

planes of enclosure. The three planes used to create space in a landscape: ground, overhead, and vertical.

plant communities. A recognizable and complex assemblage of plant species which interact with each other as well as with the elements of their environment and is distinct from adjacent assemblages.

planting plan. A drawing that indicates the type, size, and quantity of plants and where they should be located.

pleasure ground. A landscape or garden area used for relaxation and recreation.

powder coating. A type of coating applied as a free-flowing, dry powder, mainly used for coating of metals.

prevailing winds. Those that blow predominantly from a single general direction over a particular point.

primary source. A historical document that was created at or near the time of the events studied, by a known person, for a known purpose.

property line. The line that determines a site's ownership boundaries.

provenance. The chronology of the ownership or location of an historical object.

rain barrel. A vessel used to collect and store rainwater runoff from rooftops that flows through gutters and downspouts.

raised bed. An area for growing plants that is above grade, and enclosed by timbers, boards, or other building material, allowing for ease of working and control of the soil environment.

regional character. The distinctive appearance and atmosphere of a given area due to its geographical and biological features.

rhythm. The design principle of creating motion or sequencing by the arrangement of objects in the landscape; includes the use of repetition, alternation, inversion, or gradation.

scale drawing. One that show the objects or elements of a landscape in true proportion to their original size.

secondary source. A document that discusses, interprets, analyzes, or summarizes information that originated elsewhere.

site analysis. Determining the problems and potentials created by the existing conditions of the site so the design can be tailored to fit those conditions.

site inventory. Identifying the important conditions of the site as it pertains to the design.

species. The basic unit used in classifying and describing living organisms.

stucco. A plaster used for moldings or to coat interior or exterior walls.

surveyor. A person occupied with surveying; the process of determining positions on the earth's surface.

symmetry. The perception that portions of the design are in equilibrium or balance with each other by arranging the design evenly around one or more axes.

thicket. A combination of deciduous trees with shrubs interspersed between them.

topiary. Trees or shrubs clipped into regular or fantastic shapes.

topography. The shape of the ground's surface, hills, valleys, plains, and slopes.

trellis. A structure or frame used to support climbing plants.

trelliswork. A pattern of wooden slats in trellis, fence, or other structure; also called lattice.

triangulation. Finding an unknown point's location by measuring from two known points.

unity. A oneness or harmony in design.

vernacular architecture. Building style that reflects the cultural and historical influences in a region. Construction materials are primarily those that are locally available.

woody plant. One which uses wood as its structural tissue and whose stems and larger roots are reinforced with wood produced adjacent to the vascular tissues; generally a tree, shrub, or vine, and typically perennial.

wrought iron. Literally, "worked iron." A form of iron, almost entirely free of carbon and having a fibrous structure (including a uniformly distributed slag content), which is readily forged and welded.

xeriscape. A landscape designed for little or no water use.

PHOTO CREDITS

INDEX

ABOUT THE AUTHORS

Moti Kopilovitch

Denise Wiles Adams is a highly respected historian of ornamental plants and American garden design. She has a Ph.D. in horticulture from The Ohio State University and is a prolific writer and lecturer on topics related to the history of American gardens. She is the author of *Restoring American Gardens: An Encyclopedia of Heirloom Ornamental Plants, 1640–1940*.

Jim Burchfield

Laura L. S. Burchfield taught residential design, plant selection, and landscape management at The Ohio State University. She has Master's degrees in both landscape architecture and horticulture from The Ohio State University and lectures and writes on many aspects of horticulture and landscape design. In addition she designs and installs residential landscapes for private clients.